The New
CIO Leader

The New CIO Leader

Setting the Agenda and Delivering Results

MARIANNE BROADBENT

ELLEN S. KITZIS

Gartner, Inc.

Harvard Business School Press

Boston, Massachusetts

Library of Congress Cataloging-in-Publication Data

Broadbent, Marianne.
     The new CIO leader: setting the agenda and delivering results / Marianne
Broadbent and Ellen S. Kitzis.
          p.   cm.
     ISBN 1-59139-577-1
     1. Chief information officers. 2. Information technology—Management.
3. Information resources management. I. Kitzis, Ellen S. II. Title.
HD30.2.B76 2004
658.4'038—dc22

                                                                     2004009972

For all the CIOs

we've worked with

over many years

Contents

Acknowledgments

For helping us get the research done . . .

First, we thank the hundreds of executives who have worked with us over many years—especially CIOs, their executive colleagues, and their teams. All these people have taken us into their confidence, sharing their achievements, their challenges, and their frustrations and worked with us by challenging our thinking and by implementing our suggestions—in essence, testing our ideas into reality. Many are named in the pages of this book, but many more are not named. We particularly thank Paul Coby (British Airways), Joe Locandro (Yallourn Energy), and Tom Sanzone (Citigroup Global Transaction Services) for working with us on extended case examples.

Second, *The New CIO Leader* draws on the work of many people, especially that of our Gartner colleagues as well as some business-school thought leaders and authors.

For just about every month since the late 1990s, Gartner Executive Programs (Gartner EXP, a membership-based organization of more than two thousand CIOs worldwide) has released a report prepared exclusively for its members. This work has been led by members of Gartner's CIO research team who work closely with program delivery teams from across the globe. This book has drawn on those reports, as well as the thinking and the case examples that went into them—or in some cases the examples that did not go into them! On the research side, we thank particularly Mark McDonald, Dave Aron, Dr. Marcus Blosch, Jeannette Kieruj, Patrick Meehan, Andrew Rowsell-Jones, Richard Hunter, Chuck Tucker, Roger Woolfe, and adjunct researcher Barbara McNurlin. On the program delivery side, we thank regional leaders Nick Kirkland (EMEA) and José Ruggero (AsiaPacific) and the many program team members who assisted us in working with CIOs they partner with and who alerted us to additional new CIO leaders.

In the area of managing by maxims, this book extends and updates work Marianne previously completed with our good friend and colleague Professor Peter Weill, from the Sloan School of Management at MIT. Peter Weill's groundbreaking work on IT governance at MIT in 2002 stimulated extensive research with Gartner EXP members.

We thank other thought and practice leaders who have variously coauthored EXP reports, provided substantial input at EXP member forums and symposia, or shared with us their perspective. These include Professor David Feeny (Said Business School, Oxford University), Peter Keen, Don Laurie, Professor John Henderson (Boston University), Bruce Rogow, Dr. Jeanne Ross (MIT Sloan School of Management), Dr. Jeff Sampler (previously London Business School, now Templeton College, University of Oxford), Dr. Mani Subramani (Carlson School of Management, University of Minnesota), and Professor Mike Vitale (AGSM, Sydney).

Among many Gartner research analysts and consultants, we particularly thank Audrey Apfel, Jackie Fenn, David Flint, Chris Ganly, Rob Gout, Mike Gerrard, Bob Hayward, Nick Jones, Andy Kyte, Al Lill, John Mahoney, Ken McGee, Simon Mingay, Diane Morello, Daryl Plummer, John Roberts, and Michael Smart.

For helping us give birth to the book . . .

Although the idea for this book was in our heads and hearts for some time, it was the experience of creating Gartner's first CIO

Academy in 2002 and then leading it many times that really illustrated the possibilities and need for this book. At the Academies, we saw that new CIO leaders were out there, that many wanted a guide on how to be a great CIO, and that we could help them. The hardworking Diana Cirillo deserves special mention as CIO Academy coordinator for extraordinary efforts in the Academy's birth.

On both a professional and a personal level, we especially thank Robin Kranich, Gartner's very gutsy Senior Vice President for Executive Programs, whose roles variously as a friend, colleague, boss, encourager, and advocate resulted in a very stimulating and rewarding work environment. Her complete support and enthusiasm for *The New CIO Leader* made our jobs much easier.

The work of a number of key professionals then nurtured the passage of the book. Heather Levy and Tim Ogden, Gartner Press's publisher and editor, respectively, worked with agent Susan Barry and Harvard Business School Press editor Jacque Murphy on the scope of the book. The very patient and focused Kent Lineback helped us find the right focus and tone. Kent worked with us on identifying our key messages among literally hundreds of thousands of words we already had available to us. Tim Ogden did an amazing job as editor for Gartner Press, constantly challenging us about what was really important. Then Jacque Murphy came into the picture, again poking and prodding the manuscript to make sure our thoughts and words flowed as well as they could. We believe that Jacque's keen feel for structure and flow has made it considerably easier to pick up our messages.

For helping us to get on with doing what we do . . .

Each of our lives required quite a bit of coordination—especially since this book was written while we were trying to just "get stuff done." To that, we owe a big debt to the duo of Tim Ogden and Kent Lineback, who worked with us to form a very harmonious and productive quartet. But other people helped hold things together or took on extra loads at critical times. For Marianne, this support came from members of the EXP research team, especially the calm, organized, and truly dedicated Jeannette Kieruj, who was then our team coordinator. For Ellen, this support came from Brendan Conway, Mark Deacon, Chris Goodhue, Ione deAlameida Coco, and Judy Perugini, who gave extra of themselves so that she could focus on the book, knowing that our EXP members and team would be well looked after.

Finally, we each want to thank our husbands and families and close friends for understanding and accepting the kinds of things we like to do. The opportunity to work with executives in many parts of the world means that you're away from home quite a bit, that your family becomes adept at self-help, that your calendar always has to be consulted, and that your husband has to answer the often-asked question, "So, where is she now?" We know that Robert Broadbent and Larry Stevens are pretty special people—at least everyone else tells us they are, and we have to agree. Thanks, guys, for always being willing to explain to the kids, the grandkids, or the cat "where she is now," even if sometimes you are not too sure. It is hugely appreciated.

Introduction:
The Crossroads

Two paths diverged in a wood...
and I took the one less traveled.

—ROBERT FROST

Chief information officers today stand at a crossroads. The role of each CIO is inevitably changing, because of two perspectives on information technology (IT). On the one hand, there is the lingering disaffection with IT from the Internet bust, the overexpenditure on technology capacity, the popular press's assertion that IT is now irrelevant in discussions of competitive advantage, and the hysteria about IT jobs moving overseas. On the other hand, IT is gaining renewed interest for several reasons. The global economy seems to be finally escaping the doldrums, and business executives are desperate for innovation. Additionally, the regulatory environment has put far more emphasis on the timeliness, completeness, and accuracy of corporate information. Finally, technology is playing a foundational, if not a central, role in virtually every product and service.

Standing still is not an option—every CIO will follow one of two paths based on these perspectives. The path influenced by the view that IT is irrelevant to competitive advantage leads to a role that might be called *chief technology mechanic,* a role that, while valuable, is far from being part of the executive team. The other path, influenced by the view that IT is at the heart of every significant business process and is crucial to innovation and enterprise success, leads to a role we call the *new CIO leader.* The new CIO leader bears all the prestige, respect, and responsibility of other senior executive positions (in fact, the position will be a not infrequent stepping-stone to COO and CEO positions).

As CIOs examine these paths, there is good news and bad news. The good news is that each CIO largely controls what path he or she will follow—becoming a new CIO leader is within the reach of every CIO who aspires to it. The bad news is that each CIO largely controls what path he or she will follow—the responsibility for the outcome rests on the individual's shoulders alone. Becoming a new CIO leader requires changes to the skills, approach, and priorities that CIOs have traditionally had. For the most part, these changes are evolutionary, not revolutionary; you will see no "everything is different now" statements here. Although these changes may lack the glamour of revolution, a CIO who does not make these changes will almost inevitably face extinction as an executive. To be clear, CIOs who consciously or unconsciously fail to make the shifts we discuss in this book and who become mere technology mechanics will not eliminate the role of new CIO leader in their organization— they simply won't have the job themselves. They will be working for someone who has embraced these changes.

If you think you are a new CIO leader, then the challenge for you is to continue to be one. If you're not changing and growing as your enterprise changes, then you're not keeping up. If you don't think like a constantly "re-new-ing" CIO, you may be on your way to becoming an ex-CIO. The demands on CIOs are changing that much and that fast.

This book is the culmination of years of research and hundreds of in-depth interactions we've had with CIOs and their executive colleagues. This research also includes Gartner's annual CIO survey, which captures the priorities and agenda of CIOs from organizations all around the world. In 2004, more than 950 CIOs took part. The largest survey of its kind, it examines the balance between business, strategic, technical, and management priorities. Statistical data on CIOs throughout the book are drawn from these annual surveys.

The New CIO Leader explains why CIOs are at this crossroads, what a new CIO leader is, and what it takes to be one. Our goal, our passion, is to help CIOs in these most interesting times as they look down the two paths. We firmly believe that those who embrace the challenge of these changes can become new CIO leaders and join their executive colleagues as irreplaceable parts of their enterprise's success. CIOs who want to take this challenge and succeed must understand exactly what is different now, how their role is changing, and the new skills, priorities, and actions they need to take to rise to the next level—to be new CIO leaders. That, in brief, is why this book exists.

It has been our privilege to work with hundreds of CIOs, their executive colleagues, and their information systems (IS) teams. We have participated with, learned from, listened to, conducted research for, and advised CIOs on every continent (excluding Antarctica!)— and led teams doing the same. Since the late-1990s, we have pursued these activities largely as part of our responsibilities working with the two-thousand-plus members of Gartner's CIO programs: Marianne led the global CIO investigative research team and provided on-site advice and counsel to CIOs and their colleagues on just about every continent; Ellen led the delivery of services to Gartner's CIO members throughout the Americas and helped develop those services globally. Our work with and for CIOs and executive teams has allowed us to explore the two paths facing CIOs and to study the approach and skills needed by new CIO leaders.

What are these changes in approach and priorities that lead to becoming a new CIO leader? Throughout the course of the book, we introduce ten critical points of focus that will distinguish new CIO leaders. These ten are not the only issues a CIO must pay attention to, but they are the ten that differentiate CIOs who will be enterprise leaders from those who won't. Of these ten points, two are the foundation that the rest build on. First, new CIO leaders must lead, not just manage. Second, they must know their enterprise inside and out, as thoroughly as, if not better than, their executive colleagues do.

The Crossroads Are Ahead

Our work has shown us that the crossroads are ahead for all CIOs. Of course, the speed at which the leaders approach these interchanges varies from organization to organization. Some CIOs have already taken the path to becoming new CIO leaders. You'll read about a great many of them in the following pages. Others won't see the pressing need to choose a path until it's too late, and the path is chosen for them.

This book is not another round of hype about new technology or new business processes. We're fully aware of the extent that IT, e-business, and the digital economy were hyped in the late 1990s. When that bubble burst, when Y2K came and went without much of a struggle, when all of commerce (indeed, all of life) failed to migrate immediately to the Internet, the reputation of CIOs and the perception of IT in general suffered greatly in many organizations. Some CIOs who had been moved up to report to the CEO found themselves reporting again to the chief financial officer (CFO). Other CIOs whose counsel had been sought on a variety of business issues discovered themselves relegated again to the back burner.

This book is about how CIO leadership is rapidly changing, independent of any particular new technology and, more importantly, independent of the current state of any enterprise. Through our research, we've found that enterprises at any given time tend to fall into one of three different categories—fighting for survival, maintaining competitiveness, and breaking away—and that this business context must be a significant influence on the CIO's priorities. We'll discuss these categories in much more detail throughout the book, but we think you'll easily recognize the categories and which one your enterprise fits into right now. We mention these categories here to point out that CIO's situations are different—and that they therefore need different priorities. Regardless of the situation, however, the need to become a new CIO leader doesn't change. Enterprises that are fighting for survival need a new CIO leader every bit as much as enterprises that are breaking away.

So, which aspects do change, based on your situation? We have already mentioned the two key priorities of new CIO leaders—leadership and thorough knowledge of their enterprise. The next priority, which is built on these two foundational points, varies by business context. CIOs whose enterprises are fighting for survival need to place the most emphasis on building a new IS organization. The CIO of an enterprise that is maintaining competitiveness needs to focus on IT governance. CIOs of breaking-away enterprises need to start with developing a compelling vision.

CIOs Come in Many Shapes and Sizes

Beyond their immediate situation, we know too that there are many different types of CIOs—those based in corporate headquarters, those who manage a team of regional CIOs, those running shared-services organizations, those in substantial divisions or business units, and those whose role is very much technology innovation rather than information and technology. In the government sector, on the other hand, many CIOs are focused on a policy role and are the purchaser rather than a provider. In many parts of the world, the term *chief information officer* is not used but the functions are there, nonetheless. The dozens of titles we come across include general manager, IT services; senior vice president, information technology; IT director; and assistant commissioner, information management. Again, though, the need to become a new CIO leader does not vary, whether you are the only CIO in your organization, a regional CIO, or a global CIO with a team of regional CIOs reporting to you. The cast of characters may be different, but new CIO leaders are needed just the same.

In this book, the term *chief information officer (CIO)* is used for the most senior executive responsible for identifying information and technology needs and then delivering services to meet those needs. While we're clarifying the term, we should also clarify the way we use *information technology (IT)* and *information systems (IS)*. In this book, IT refers to technology and IS refers to the organization responsible for managing IT and delivering IT services.

Who Should Read This Book and How They Should Read It

The New CIO Leader is aimed at IT executives who wish to become leaders facing the changing role of information technology and who are not content with the status quo, namely, a role as chief technology mechanic. At the same time, we expect that the book will be very useful to those working with CIOs or supervising them and who are looking to the CIO role in their enterprise to provide new leadership. In that sense, other "C"-level executives—CEOs, CFOs, and COOs—will find it useful to understand the scope of the new CIO role and the position's responsibilities, necessary skills, and reasonable expectations.

Additionally, many service providers—consultants, external service providers, and those developing various types of technologies for use in organizations—have CIOs as clients. This book will help illuminate how they might help make their clients successful.

But the primary focus of the book is CIOs who want to become leaders, who want to develop an agenda and deliver results that make an impact on their enterprise. The rest of the book assumes that you want to follow the path to becoming a new CIO leader.

What's Not in the Book

In *The New CIO Leader,* we spotlight the critical new points of focus for CIOs who want to become new CIO leaders. We begin with the personal challenge to grow and change as your enterprise and role changes, recognizing how quickly the world of both business and IT can shift. It is the level and nature of leadership demands on the CIO that most distinguish the new CIO—you need to lead, not by being the Lone Ranger, but by persuasion and with strong executive relationships. Subsequently, we address the two key domains of the CIO's role: demand-side leadership, in which you shape and manage informed expectations; and supply-side leadership, in which you deliver cost-effective services.

The book is by no means comprehensive—these days, the role of CIO can be so large it would take several volumes to do it justice. This is not a book about technology; nor is it a book about the day-in, day-out activities of a CIO. We focus only on those key elements that are now required of CIOs who want to be enterprise leaders. It doesn't cover all you need to know to be an effective CIO.

The New CIO Leader's Ten New Priorities

From research conducted with thousands of companies and CIOs, we have put together a picture of the new, more proactive CIO. Call it the new CIO leader's top ten. We've built the book around these ten issues.

1. *Lead, don't just manage.* Leadership and management are not the same; they are complementary. You need to both manage and lead. Leading is about change and influencing others to change. To do that, you need a personal vision and a point of view about how information and IT can make your enterprise more effective. True CIO leadership requires two

important abilities. First, you must lead with your business colleagues to set expectations and to identify what is valued by enterprise leaders (what we call the demand side and discuss in chapters 2 through 6). Second, you must lead your IS team to deliver on that—to provide cost-effective services (what we call the supply side and discuss in chapters 7 through 10).

2. *Understand the fundamentals of your environment.* You need to know your industry and your competitive environment and be able to engage key decision makers and stakeholders on their terms.

3. *Create a vision for how IT will build your organization's success.* As CIO, your enterprise knowledge then must be matched with the ability to envision how to better IT-enable your business or agency. This is why you are CIO and not some other executive position or a midlevel IS manager— you must have a vision for achieving your colleagues' business goals using technology.

4. *Shape and inform expectations for an IT-enabled enterprise.* This is the heart of your role as CIO, and using our years of research with CIOs and their executive colleagues, we provide some concrete suggestions on the best way to do this. You need to work with your colleagues to identify the key business needs, strategies, drivers, and so forth, and then articulate the IT guidelines (what we call maxims) necessary to address those needs.

5. *Create clear and appropriate IT governance.* Governance is really the secret to your success. Effective governance enables you to weave together business and IT strategies and to consistently build credibility and trust.

6. *Weave business and IT strategy together.* Your IT strategy is the content of key IT domains—IT maxims, infrastructure, architecture and application strategies, and investment priori-

tization—and their implementation over a defined period. IT strategy means developing and actively managing your IT portfolio to deliver success as measured by your colleagues.

7. *Build a new IS organization—one that is leaner and more focused than its more traditional predecessor.* Like the new CIO, the new IS organization must change some of the key ways it operates to achieve success. Three primary issues here are introducing process-based working, strategic sourcing of IT services, and putting IS on a sound financial footing.

8. *Develop and nurture a high-performing team in your IS organization.* Many of the competencies required of the IS team are different from those you might have recruited for previously. You need to know the competencies required for the new IS organization—one that relies much more on internal and external relationships—and to recruit and train for effectiveness.

9. *Manage the new enterprise and IT risks.* These IT-related risks are much more pervasive and potentially damaging than in the past. Think of issues of information security, data privacy, and cyber-terrorism and the need to ensure compliance with new regulatory structures. Business leaders have to be aware of these risks and need help managing them across the enterprise—and you as CIO will lead this process.

10. *Communicate IS performance in business-relevant language.* You must know and communicate how IT is contributing to shareholder value and the IT value indicators that are directly linked to business value measures. Today, how IT operates in your enterprise is crucial to the conduct of your business.

These are the most critical issues facing CIOs today. New CIOs must be prepared to take action on each of these items. This list does not include everything a CIO needs to do, but it does include the differentiators that will make a new CIO leader successful.

Some Caveats

Finally, before we continue, we want to note a few items about how you should read this book. First, no executive's job is sequential (first do this, then do that, then do this other thing). While the nature of writing a book forces a sequential flow, don't interpret this flow as an exact series of steps. Only rarely will you be able to finish any set of steps before you also have to work on some other topic. As you will note throughout, everything we discuss is circular; strategy influences organization, which influences delivery, which influences strategy.

Second, we present a number of models and diagrams in the course of the book. Many of them overlap each other. One of the major reasons for this variety is that no diagram or model will explain every situation or help every organization. We by no means intend that you the reader will use every model or diagram in your own organization; just choose the ones that seem to best fit your situation and your needs.

Third, please do not get hung up on terminology and vocabulary. As you probably know, there is no standard nomenclature for everything in technology (except for the rule that everything must have a TLA—a three letter acronym!). Wherever possible, we try to recognize different terminology while also specifying our preferred term. But don't read too much into the terms that we use, and don't feel bound to use them yourself!

Fourth, we have had to tread a fine line in the writing of this book, attempting to provide enough detail to be practical, while not turning this into *War and Peace*. We apologize in advance for any occasions you feel we are being too detailed or too superficial— we've done our best to not stray too far in either direction.

Finally, as you might want to benchmark yourself, we provide a self-assessment in appendix D. The questions are not intended to be comprehensive but are meant to serve as an easy-to-use guide to connect what we talk about to your present situation and help you "operationalize" what you read. The greatest use of the exercise will probably be found in filling out the assessment today and then again six months after you have read the book to see how things have changed.

With that said, please read on. Our passion is helping CIOs become the enterprise leaders they can, should, and need to be. We're certain that, through our years of research and work with CIOs, we can help you take that path if you're not there yet, and improve your performance if you are. The first issue that we need to discuss, and which underlies everything that will follow, is leadership.

1

Laying the Foundation:
Leadership

Two paths lie ahead of today's CIOs. One leads to becoming a trusted senior executive leader of the enterprise; the other leads to a technical management, "just keep the lights on and do it cheap" role. Why are CIOs at a crossroads at this particular point in time? What has changed to throw these two paths into such stark contrast at this moment?

The answer is a combination of factors. Certainly a big part of the answer is the growing dependence of all organizations on technology. Another significant issue is the explosion of globalization, which makes strategy and execution much more complex. Information technology enables global business and global sourcing. At the same time, the effective implementation of globalization is heavily dependent on good information and IT services.

The long-awaited emergence of the world economy from the recent doldrums and the drive for innovation to spur new growth is also part of the answer. Finally, we would also cite new regulatory environments around the world, especially the U.S. Sarbanes-Oxley Act, which places a fiduciary duty on CIOs, and privacy and security regulations in other jurisdictions. These additional regulations are changing the role of the CIO in relation to corporate strategy.

All of these are part of the reason CIOs now must either step up to a new level of enterprise leadership or take a big step back. So, while there is no specific break point between the old paradigm and the new paradigm of new CIO leader, CIOs must now choose what direction they will take.

Some CIOs are already taking the path to becoming new CIO leaders.[1] Take Bill Oates, worldwide CIO of Starwood Hotels and Resorts. Around 1997, technology in the hotel chains such as the Sheraton and Westin groups, which are part of Starwood, was limited largely to booking rooms and scheduling staff. But today, technology is integral to every major development and strategic decision in Starwood. "IT has had a huge impact on the hotel and resort business," explains Oates.

The big issues for Starwood are the level and timeliness of connectivity and Internet booking. "We've completed the installation of full Internet access and now are moving on wireless capabilities. We need to make decisions quickly in a very competitive environment," says Oates. "At the same time, the Internet and Internet booking has had a huge impact on the hotel industry. It has changed consumers' behavior and expectations. We [the IS organization] are deeply involved in driving people to our Web site, implementing global pricing, and now looking at how we help the business become a single source for travel and entertainment." As CIO, Oates is involved every day with nearly every key decision about how Starwood positions itself competitively.

Of course, many others have not begun to take the path. We still hear that "my CIO talks technobabble" and that, on average, CIOs still have a relatively short life span. But, in our research, this time span is lengthening and there is increasing understanding about the combination of business and technology acumen that a CIO needs to be really effective. The notion that *CIO* stands for "career is over" is giving way to the real job of CIO as chief integration officer and chief influencing officer. Or in the words of one of our CIO clients, from "career in obscurity" to "career in overdrive."

Corporate structural changes are largely recognizing the need for new CIO leaders. Though some CIOs are not in ideal reporting positions, the overall trend is toward a reporting relationship with the CEO or COO (chief operations officer) and membership in the CEO's team of senior executives who plot the course of the organization. According to our ongoing research, about 40 percent of all CIOs now report to the CEO. While the status of reporting directly to the CEO can be very useful for a new CIO leader, what is critical is that the CIO has a seat at the executive table where strategies are formed. Sitting at the executive table, where new CIO leaders can have the most influence and impact on enterprise performance, is more important than reporting to a particular person.

New CIO leaders will identify, ahead of their business colleagues, where the opportunities exist for their specific enterprise and will position themselves and the enterprise to move to the next level of performance. To do that, however, the CIO must take a real leading role as an enterprise executive, coaching and coaxing business colleagues about the potential business uses of particular technologies while also unlocking the information and business intelligence trapped inside business processes. For those CIOs who can master the skills and behaviors needed to lead effectively, it will be an exciting journey for them and their organizations. Exciting—and difficult, we should add. Chief information officers possess a unique perspective across the enterprise, and this gives them a unique ability to spot opportunities and solve problems.

But not all enterprises are the same. In fact, we've found that enterprises at any given time tend to fall into three categories. The number of enterprises and government agencies that fall into each of these categories varies from year to year. This variance is based not only on individual business performance but also on national and international business cycles. We call the three categories of enterprises *fighting for survival, maintaining competitiveness,* and *breaking away.*

Fighting-for-survival enterprises typically go through multiple layoffs and struggle to find ever newer ways to cut costs. As a result, they tend to cancel or scale back capital investments and any long-term projects, including IT development. Initiatives are dramatically tilted toward efficiency and cost savings.

Maintaining-competitiveness enterprises tend to mirror the economy. In tough times, they are cautious about any major new business projects as they wait to see what happens. Consequently, they make relatively small increases in budgets (including IS budgets) from year to year, focus on completing projects already started (rather than new projects), and enhance existing processes and systems. Initiatives are pulled between driving business effectiveness and supporting business efficiency measures. As the economy improves, the enterprises' take-up of new projects gradually increases.

Breaking-away enterprises tend to aggressively increase their business investments—and IT budgets—each year. They seek business innovation, including IT-enabled business innovation, to move ahead of the pack. Breaking-away enterprises are much more willing to invest in higher risk, long-term projects that offer possibilities for significant future competitive advantage.

The agenda and priorities for a CIO must change based on this business context; throughout the book, we'll often refer back to the specific priorities of CIOs in these different business contexts. However, the need for new CIO leaders does not change with business context. Enterprises that are fighting for survival need CIO leadership every bit as much as enterprises that are breaking away.

As obvious as it may seem, it bears stating explicitly that the primary factor that distinguishes the path of the new CIO leader from the path of chief technology mechanic is leadership. New CIO leaders must, above all, lead. And lead does not mean manage.

Every minimally successful CIO today should at the very least be a competent manager. Those who cannot manage shouldn't have been promoted into the job in the first place. But it is not management skill that will determine whether you become a key enterprise executive—it is leadership.

This chapter lays the foundation for all that is to follow. If you cannot lead, you cannot accomplish the other tasks a new CIO leader must take on. The good news is that leadership skills can be developed. Leadership isn't mystical or mysterious; it has nothing to do with immutable personality traits. Nor is it something for only the chosen few.

The first step in becoming an enterprise leader is to understand what leadership really is. And the fundamental aspect of leadership is credibility.

Executive Leadership Is Built on Credibility

Credibility is, quite simply, the coin of the realm for working at senior levels in any enterprise. New CIO leaders, like any other executive, need credibility as an executive asset. No major IT-enabled initiative can be launched and completed successfully without CIO credibility. The U.S. Federal Trade Commission's experience with the Do Not Call Registry shows what can happen when the CIO has credibility and is involved in every phase of a new strategy.

The FTC commissioner, Timothy Muris, decided in 2003 that the continual intrusion of telemarketers into the homes of U.S. citizens compromised their right to privacy. Protecting consumer privacy was part of his vision. Because of the credibility that Stephen Warren had established as a new CIO leader of the FTC, the commissioner invited Warren and his staff to be part of the team charged with creating a solution to the telemarketing problem that would allow consumers to limit the calls they received. Rather than just being brought in to implement a concept developed without his input, Warren was a member of the team from the outset. His credibility ensured his position on the team that mapped out a strategy to create a do-not-call list that all telemarketers would have to reference and honor. Warren's early participation was vital to the creation of a concept-to-implementation plan that delivered the new national registry in ninety days.

So You're Not the Only CIO in Your Enterprise

OUR EXPERIENCE working with CIOs has revealed that enterprises with more than $1 billion in revenues typically have multiple CIOs. So if you are a CIO at companies like J.P. Morgan, RJR Nabisco, Thomson Financial (it refers to its CIOs as chief technology officers), or State Street Bank and Trust Co., you will find lots of other individuals who seem to hold the same job title and description that you do. The reality is that you don't all have the same job description. You have distinctly different roles, depending on where you work in your enterprise.

The Corporate CIO

Very large enterprises tend to have one corporate CIO who holds the most senior IT position in the organization. The corporate CIO is the individual most likely to report to the CEO and have direct impact on IT at the strategic level of the enterprise. In many enterprises, this is the individual who communicates with the board and speaks for the organization relative to IT strategy and direction. Typically a very seasoned executive, the corporate CIO may have come up through the ranks, but is also very likely to have been brought into the position from the outside. On occasion, he or she may come from a business unit with the company. If you are the corporate CIO, you most likely have direct or dotted-line reports from divisional CIOs. You also probably chair the

---

The response to the registry was far greater than expected. More than 28 million people (twice the planned volume) registered in the first seventeen days. Of those registering, 88 percent used the Internet. The unexpected volume of calls did not require more operations staff, nor did service levels at the registry deteriorate. The system was hailed in the national media as a great success, an example of government's getting things done.

The registry project illustrates what a new CIO leader can accomplish by weaving together business strategy and IT capability.[2] The

IT committee for the enterprise. One of your key imperatives is to identify and leverage potential synergies across the enterprise.

Regional or Divisional CIOs

Enterprises may have many divisional CIOs; we have worked with some extremely large enterprises that have as many as fifty to seventy-five CIOs distributed at both the regional and the divisional level. The CIOs in these positions may have one or two key roles. They may be responsible for leading on both the demand and the supply side and may manage significant IT budgets in their own right. In large enterprises, these divisions can be billion-dollar groups. In some cases, the divisional CIOs may be more focused on leading demand-side activities, portfolio setting, and sourcing products and services only for that division. If you are in this role, you often face several key issues. You must obtain sufficient visibility for your goals, justify your budget or resources, and convince CIOs or business leaders in other parts of the enterprise to work jointly on IT-enabled opportunities.

In sum, there may be more than one type of CIO in an enterprise. However, the choice of becoming a leader or a technology mechanic remains the same. To reduce complexity, the rest of the book speaks primarily to the corporate CIO. Nevertheless, the agenda we prescribe is equally applicable to regional and divisional CIOs. The cast of characters may change (business unit or regional business head instead of CEO, and regional CFO—chief financial officer—instead of corporate CFO), but the need to lead business colleagues and the IS organization you oversee is the same.

IS organization was at the core of the FTC's mission and among the highest priorities of senior leadership. The CIO contributed to decisions affecting how the registry would work, its feasibility, and its estimated implementation and operating costs. The CIO and IS understood the legal and business requirements for the registry, how it needed to work, and the information it needed to manage. Through the CIO's involvement, the IS organization was able to make the infrastructure upgrades to handle the anticipated increase in transaction volumes from the Web and the FTC's consumer complaint call center. This involvement also enabled IS to look for a vendor partner early in the process.

The result: a system fully functioning above planned scale within ninety days of authorization and appropriation of funding. The Do Not Call Registry demonstrated that electronic channels can handle citizen transactions at a national level.

We find that many CIOs are somewhat confused about where credibility comes from. They believe that their knowledge, experience, and tenure create credibility. Others focus on how they've met IS milestones for projects. Credibility, however, comes from one place only: delivering results *that your enterprise leadership cares about.* We can't overemphasize this observation, which too many CIOs overlook. The only success metrics that matter are those of your executive colleagues. Even if you deliver projects on time and under budget, if they don't help your executive colleagues meet their business goals, your credibility suffers.

Let's take a deeper look at the CIO credibility cycle. In fact, credibility is the result of an ongoing process that feeds on itself (figure 1-1).

The CIO who is literally new in his or her position is given initial credibility. Based on that credibility, the new CIO receives resources

FIGURE 1-1

The CIO Credibility Cycle

Delivering outcomes important to executive colleagues builds credibility, which improves your ability to successfully deliver other projects.

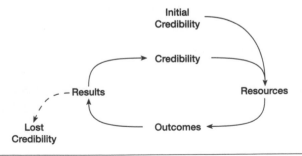

and permission to undertake various IT initiatives. Those initiatives have outcomes and results, which, depending on what they are and whether they benefit the enterprise—in the eyes of the enterprise leaders—either enhance or diminish the CIO's credibility. The whole process becomes either a virtuous cycle or a downward spiral. Every success—again, in the eyes of the leaders—builds more credibility. Every failure or nonsuccess chips away at the CIO's credibility.

An example of a virtuous cycle that built credibility can be seen in Philadelphia's city government. Dianah Neff, CIO for the city of Philadelphia, helped implement data warehousing and interdepartmental information systems, now deployed in six departments and several outside agencies. The city was very keen to improve information sharing and efficiency, but decision making had become very complex, particularly for external agencies trying to deal with multiple municipalities around the city. The solution Neff developed generated new relationships with other departments, social service agencies, and constituent groups. Because of their standing in the community, these groups could get the mayor's attention. Their support for the CIO and the role IS played in the solution created a source of credibility outside normal channels. That credibility, based on results, gave Neff greater access to the informal network of municipal and related executives.

It may seem that CIO credibility, or its loss, comes entirely from successes or failures, and in the long run, that's true. But the results of complex IT projects may not be crystal clear, or they may vary with the different parties involved. The objectives and drivers of long-term projects may change over the life of the project. As a result, the development of CIO credibility is sometimes not as purely results-based and straightforward as it seems.

The fluid nature of business projects makes the development of credibility more complex. Credibility requires building strong personal relationships—being politically smart, in other words—with executive colleagues. It requires clearly integrating IT objectives with enterprise objectives. It means anticipating business needs to deploy a predictable stream of technology-enabled business solutions.

To a large extent, leadership is built on the complex task of building and maintaining credibility. Credibility is truly the most basic asset needed by members of any enterprise leadership team. And this asset is just one aspect of how leadership and management differ.

Leadership and Management Aren't the Same

How does a CIO lead? First, you must recognize that leadership is not management, and understanding the difference is critical. We've found CIOs to be generally strong on management, but often less strong as leaders. It's their leadership skills that they need to strengthen. As mentioned earlier, such skills can be developed in anyone willing to work at obtaining them.

Leadership is about change and influencing others to change. It's focused on doing things differently. Because it's about change, leadership requires vision, strategy, inspiration, and passion. On the other hand, management is about execution and control. It's focused on getting things done and doing things better. It's about planning, organizing, control, and analysis. If leadership is seeing the potential for a transcontinental railroad and lining up the resources to build it, management is getting the trains to run on time.

Joe Locandro, a new CIO leader we work with, says management is about answering the question "What did you do today?" But "leadership, on the other hand, brings people forward on a journey by focusing on outcomes and directions. It says, 'Come along with me.'"

Though distinct, leadership and management are complementary. Both are crucial to the work of any enterprise. "Each has its own function and characteristic activities and both are necessary for success," according to John Kotter, retired Harvard Business School professor and author.[3]

Leadership has little to do with charisma, the almost magical ability of some people to attract others to their cause. Charisma can be helpful, and it can hurt, as we've seen in recent years, when charismatic leaders led their organizations astray. Top-performing leaders have steely determination and a compelling sense of where the group they lead should go, but often they're also quiet and unobtrusive, according to Jim Collins in *Good to Great*.[4] They don't depend on force of personality to influence others.

According to Ron Heifetz, a professor at Harvard's Kennedy School of Government and author of *Leadership Without Easy Answers,* leaders are those who foster *adaptive change* in any group of people.[5] Adaptive change, says Heifetz, is the kind of deep change that requires people to alter their habits and comfortable ways of acting, even the way they think and feel. It's hard. Adaptive change makes people uncomfortable because it asks them to leave the familiar and go someplace new. So people often resist, and that resistance can take many forms.

Management can be about change, too, but it's what Heifetz calls *technical change,* which doesn't require such fundamental shifts as does adaptive change. People can make technical change with their existing knowledge and skills, because it involves improvement, doing something better or faster, rather than doing something new and different. People may resist technical change, too, but generally it's not the kind of deep resistance that adaptive change can elicit.

The Elements of Leadership

Because of the intimate connection between leadership and change, effective leaders seem to share a number of characteristics.

Vision

First, effective CIO leaders have a vision, a clear and compelling point of view, for how IT can take their enterprise to the next level. Paul Coby, CIO of British Airways, expresses his vision this way: "It's about putting the customer in control and having customer and staff use the same systems. It's about transparency. It's about customer enablement and employee enablement—using the same processes and systems. We are driving transactions to self-service and simplifying business. We are driving simplification and automation."[6]

Much, obviously, depends on what the vision is. Any old vision won't work. It must fully align with the goals and vision of the enterprise as a whole. To get executive colleagues to follow, CIOs must push, cajole, hassle, threaten, promise, and plead in equal measure. If a CIO's vision doesn't resonate with fellow executives, if it doesn't help them achieve their own goals and solve their problems, it's not appropriate and they won't accept it.

Vision is far from the only characteristic of effective leaders, but it's probably the most distinctive. Without it, there is no leadership. What is your vision for your organization and the role information and IT can play in its success?

Communication

Having a vision isn't enough. CIOs must communicate their vision to fellow executives whose buy-in is needed for approval and implementation. But to do that, CIOs must first articulate their vision clearly and compellingly. Like a Hollywood producer, they need a pitch, a way to express the vision that grabs the attention of others and excites them.

Effective communicators express themselves in the language and values of their audience. Do they prefer numbers? Graphics? Words? Pictures? Do they want it short and to the point? Or do they prefer longer, more detailed explanations?

For the most part, we've found that effective CIO communicators keep their message simple and aren't reluctant to repeat key points. Above all, the vision they communicate always contains a strong and positive "What's in it for me?" message addressed to the audience.

Effective communication isn't just the CIO's talking and presenting. It encompasses all means and forms of spreading the message—any way that works. It can require everything from explaining and coaching to pushing, prodding, educating, and stimulating. For example, British Airways and other organizations use IT fairs with booths and exhibitors from inside and outside the organization to explain the business potential of new technologies. At the Australian Bureau of Statistics, posters are one means of communicating the future technology of the firm. The posters purposely minimize techno-babble, so that all staff members can understand them easily. At Met Life, CIO Steven Sheinheit has developed a brochure for internal users that clearly communicates the IS organization's service delivery strategy.

The higher the CIOs rise in an organization, the more time they spend on communicating their vision to fellow executives. We know CIOs at large, IT-savvy enterprises who spend 20 percent or more of their time simply explaining, often again and again, the potential they see in technology for the enterprise. Every year, we conduct an extensive survey of CIOs around the world. This research clearly shows that the more CIOs communicate their vision, the more effective they are at getting buy-in and endorsement from the executive leadership team. If the time you spend informing and convincing others of your vision frustrates you, or you begrudge the need to do so much of it, you should probably rethink your concept of your job.

Relationship building

Communicating is part of a larger context—building relationships—that's critical for CIO leadership. Just as CIOs spend more time communicating as their role increases in importance, they also spend much more time building and maintaining relationships with executive colleagues.

If you have a strong technology background, a key aspect of becoming an IS leader is recognizing that your principal focus must change as you move up through the ranks. On the way up, priorities are 90 percent functional and 10 percent relationships. The higher you rise, the more this mix changes. In the CIO position, it is more like 10 percent functional and 90 percent relationships (which require solid communication).

The required people skills for this relational approach can be learned, and the payoff from developing them can be huge. The skills are not easy to develop, but it's possible. Accumulating evidence suggests that they're directly and crucially linked to performance. As you think about these skills, ask yourself how well you practice them. Don't neglect to consider as well how others might assess you. Researchers have found, unfortunately, that the higher they looked in organizations, the wider the gap they found between leaders' self-assessments and others' opinions of the leaders.

Some CIOs balk at this aspect of what the new CIO role requires, because they see it as becoming involved in organizational politics. Certainly, the CIO does need to become involved in politics, because that's how organizations work. Corporate politics are complex, because they involve human relationships. But you can conduct yourself with honesty and integrity and still be effective in a political context.

Effective CIOs need to know when to take a stand and when to be political. *Political* here means "knowing the context, knowing your environment, and knowing when to concede a point to win support for some longer-term position." One CIO describes this approach as "building political capital." But, he warns, "you can't have an infinite supply of political capital, and memories can be short." Perhaps it's not so much that you need to become political yourself as you need to learn how to act wisely and shrewdly in a political environment. You can't avoid politics, so be smart about the role of politics.

The relationships you build are with other people—with a wide variety of IT stakeholders—so the relationships need to be both professional and personal. *Personal* doesn't mean you become involved in others' personal lives, but that you treat them as people with desires and fears and all the other feelings that human beings have, just like you. Loyalty, honesty, and integrity still count for much in most organizations we know—indeed, probably more than they used to.

Here the notion of emotional intelligence popularized by Daniel Goleman is crucial. According to Goleman, author of *Emotional Intelligence* and *Primal Leadership,* emotional intelligence accounts for 90 percent of what distinguishes truly skilled leaders from those less able.[7]

Goleman has identified four basic dimensions of emotional intelligence:

Self-awareness: the ability to recognize our own feelings. Many of us are raised to pay little attention to what's going on inside.

Self-management: the ability to manage our feelings and emotional life. All of us have ups and downs, but the emotionally mature person can recognize feelings and avoid being captured and controlled by them.

Social awareness: the ability to recognize the feelings of others. The key skill here is empathy, the ability to see the world through someone else's eyes, to feel what he or she is feeling, to put ourselves in the other person's shoes. As someone described it, sympathy is feeling *for* someone else, while empathy is feeling *with* someone else. Empathy is virtually the foundation of everything else in human relations.

Social skill: the ability to act on and accommodate effectively the feelings of others.

These four skills—emotional intelligence—are fundamental to leading through influence. You must develop your emotional intelligence, particularly social awareness or empathy, if you are going to be a new CIO leader. Goleman says the ability to recognize the feelings of others and to empathize with them is fundamental to any relationship. Empathy enables you to see the world through someone else's eyes. It doesn't mean you necessarily agree with the person, but you're able to put yourself in his or her shoes. It's the lifeblood of all relationships, professional and personal. No empathy, no relationship. And no relationship, no ability to persuade or communicate your vision as a leader.

Leading Through Influence

All of these elements of effective leadership are important for anyone, but they are doubly important for the CIO leader. Why? Because CIO leaders must operate away from their base of formal power much of the time. They usually have no formal organizational power with their executive peers. They must rely on persuasion and relationships to influence others. This is what one financial services CIO we know calls leading from the back. Being able to succeed from this position is the ultimate test of leadership vision, communication, and relationships.

In our description of adaptive change versus technical change, we explained that leadership is about adaptive change, which requires people to undergo some major alteration in set ways of behaving or thinking or even feeling. Adaptive change is often painful and always carries with it a degree of uncertainty and perceived risk. People resist adaptive change, often angrily.

What they resist is not simply the change itself but the messenger of change, or the leader. According to Ron Heifetz, who has studied how people approach adaptive versus technical change, this resistance can take personal forms—the leader calling for difficult change may be marginalized, belittled, ostracized, and even pushed out.[8] These are extreme responses, but they're not unusual and any leader should be prepared for them.

It's no wonder, then, that leadership calls for a number of personal skills and qualities. Courage and resilience are only two of them. Persistence. Ego strength (a strong ego as opposed to a big ego). Decisiveness. Motivation. Personal energy. Emotional intelligence. All these, based on our experience with many CIOs, deserve to be on the list.

If you are to lead through influence, though, we also need to talk about personality type and leadership style. One of the key elements of emotional intelligence is self-awareness. You have to know how you naturally act, communicate, learn, and react to stress (i.e., you must know your personality) so that your natural reactions don't control you and get in the way of your effectiveness as a new CIO leader. You also must develop leadership styles that are appropriate to leading through influence.

Understand your and your colleagues' different personality types

It's a cliché, but still worth stressing, that each of us is different. We're different in how we face the world and other people, in how we deal with difficulties, and in how we solve problems. It's a matter not only of courtesy but common sense that we should try to communicate with others in terms most comfortable for them, in ways that match how they prefer to deal with the world. This attitude is central to working with your business colleagues—you must understand both how they personally get work done and how they like to interact and work.

For example, some people constantly need to rise above the fray and look at the whole picture—they're big-picture people, the ones who always step back in meetings and say, "Where are we? What are we trying to do?" Other people, however, prefer to focus on what's in front of them. They wrestle and wrestle with problems until they're solved. They're the ones always seeking more data, doing more analysis. If these two people work together and don't understand the differences in their preferences, they're guaranteed to drive each other crazy—how much does this sound like your interactions with the CEO or other business leaders? Aren't you better off understanding your colleagues' different preferences and accommodating them? It's one form of empathy.

To make this kind of accommodation, you must know first your own preferences (so they don't control you) and then be aware of the preferences of those with whom you interact to appropriately accommodate and influence them. To give you a real sense of how this approach can help, we've included in appendix A a short assessment of personality type, one of the best-known and best-documented systems of identifying personality preferences (or types). The short test was created by consulting psychologist Richard Grant, a Myers-Briggs Type Indicator certified practitioner who has led sessions at Gartner CIO forums. The appendix contains an abbreviated but applicable set of questions that you can use to assess your own preferences. Once you know your own preferences, you can think about how your executive colleagues behave and interact differently. If you better understand their personality types, you can plan your interactions with them for maximum impact.

Practice different leadership styles for the situation

Everyone is familiar by now with the notion of leadership styles. Like the individual preferences we just discussed, your leadership style is your preferred way of acting in a leaderlike way.

All of us are capable of acting in many ways. The shyest among us will jump up in a burning theater and yell, "Fire!" Still, there are ways we prefer to act as leaders, and when the chips are down, we're all the more likely to revert to our preferred ways. Those ways constitute our leadership style.

The following list shows a continuum of six leadership styles, from commanding to democratic (with some overlap between them). For each leadership style, we present a verbal expression that typifies the way the leader manages his or her group:[9]

Commanding: "Follow me because I say so!"

Pacesetting: "Follow me—do what I do."

Visionary: "Follow me because I see the future!"

Affiliative: "Follow me because we're in this together."

Coaching: "Try doing it this way."

Democratic: "What do you think?"

These styles are based on survey work by Hay/McBer (a consulting company) involving close to four thousand executives around the world, plus earlier work on situational leadership.[10]

At the autocratic end of the continuum is the commanding (alternatively known as the coercive) style, which demands immediate compliance, "or else." At the opposite end is the democratic style, which forges consensus through participation. Near the middle is the visionary style, which mobilizes people toward a vision.

Whatever you may think of the different styles, they all have their time and place. You may normally dislike the leader who leads by command, but in a crisis, most groups desperately want a commander (though, ideally, one who at least listens to different opinions). There is no perfect style that works in all situations and with all people. That's why you need the ability to use many styles, not just the one you normally prefer. For instance, when you are leading with your business colleagues, the commanding style is unlikely to work (imagine saying "Because I say so!" to the CFO or CEO!). There are three particular leadership styles that you need to practice and perfect to lead through influence: visionary, affiliative, and democratic. As we'll discuss shortly, a key task of the new CIO leader is to develop and communicate a vision for the role technology can play in enterprise success. The CIO needs visionary leadership to share that vision effectively with business colleagues. Considering our earlier discussion of the role of the new CIO leader, the advantages of affiliative and democratic leadership styles are probably obvious.

As a new CIO leader, you must understand the range of leadership styles, know when each is appropriate, and be able to use each when needed. Effective leaders employ a variety of styles, depending on the situation and the individuals involved.

CIO Leadership Takes Two Forms

We've painted a picture of leadership that is both crucial and difficult. We've said the new CIO leader's most distinctive trait is that he

FIGURE 1-2

The Demand and Supply Sides of the New CIO Leader Role Build On and Continually Reinforce Each Other

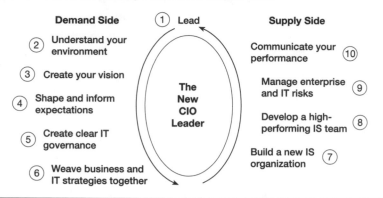

or she leads. This leadership involves a number of acquired skills and behaviors. For the most part, CIO leadership is not dependent on whether your enterprise is fighting for survival, maintaining competitiveness, or breaking away. While the components or the elements of your leadership—your vision, your communication, and your relationships—must be sensitive to your environment (more on that in chapter 2), the importance of leading does not wax or wane with the situation. It is every bit as important that the CIO of a fighting-for-survival enterprise leads as it is that the CIO of a breaking-away enterprise leads.

We've divided our analysis of CIO leadership into the two natural components of the CIO's job: demand-side leadership and supply-side leadership. We separate the two because the CIO operates from a different base in each (figure 1-2).

On the demand side, CIOs must lead as peers, colleagues, and even subordinates. This situation is truly leadership by persuasion and relationship. On the supply side, the CIO does have the formal authority that comes from the position held in the organization. As any experienced leader and manager can attest, such authority often counts for less than theory says it should. Still, it counts for something and does set the CIO, as formal head of the IS organization, apart from the CIO as a member of the enterprise's executive team.

In each of those realms, we will present a detailed picture of what's required of a new CIO leader. We base our observations on our extensive ongoing research and work with thousands of CIOs around the world.

PART ONE

Demand-Side Leadership

This part of the book focuses on the need for the new CIO leader to lead the enterprise in determining the demand for information and IT. To meet this need, CIOs need to determine the "why" of IT and set both reasonable and ambitious expectations—helping business colleagues see what is actually possible today as well as what is unimaginable today, but will be possible tomorrow. We call this process leading with your business colleagues, *because the kind of leadership exercised here will be that of a team member working among peers. It's a different kind of leadership than leading from a base of formal power.*

Five of the new areas of focus (chapters 2 through 6) for the new CIO leader fall on the demand side of the equation—which, when combined with taking a leadership approach, means that 60 percent of your new areas of focus are on the business side, not in your IS group. This is an essential characteristic of the new CIO leader.

We cover these five areas of focus in part 1. First, you must understand the fundamentals of your business: You can't lead with your business colleagues if you don't understand their goals. Second, create your vision: Enterprises will look to the new CIO leader to provide a vision of how technology can dramatically improve the business. Third, shape and inform the expectations for IT: Succeeding in the eyes of your business colleagues (the measure that matters most to a new CIO leader) requires you to lead your business colleagues to set appropriate expectations for what IT can do. Fourth, create appropriate IT governance: Your IT decisions need to be grounded in business reality, and your business colleagues must trust the way these decisions are made. Finally, weave business and IT strategies together: Beyond alignment, you need to ensure that your IT strategy flows clearly and directly from business strategy.

2

Understand the Fundamentals of Your Environment

A key element of leadership is vision. One of the distinguishing characteristics of new CIO leaders is their clear and compelling vision for how information and technology can dramatically improve business performance in ways that matter to other executives. Developing this vision requires technical knowledge, but also an even deeper knowledge of your business, because your vision must outline how your enterprise will gain competitive advantage by bridging business and technology. Therefore, you must know your enterprise as well as, if not better than, you know technology.

If your vision isn't deeply rooted in the fundamentals of your environment, it is worthless. And you can't lead with a worthless vision. If that isn't a compelling enough reason to become a student of your organization, here's another. Knowing the business is the only way you can gain the trust and acceptance of your executive colleagues. If you don't understand what they do and how their businesses work, you'll have no credibility with them. As we said earlier, credibility is the foundation of all you do. Fortunately, as CIO you possess a special view of your organization. You have the vantage point and responsibility to look across the whole enterprise. You're in a position to spot new opportunities and new solutions to business problems. These are solutions that may be missed by fellow executives, whose points of view are more limited. Perhaps the only other executive in your enterprise who shares this unique viewpoint is the CEO. Other executives, often because of the nature of their responsibilities, tend to focus on specific business areas. Few of these people are in a position to grasp how all the pieces of the enterprise's jigsaw puzzle fit together. Knowing the business allows you to recognize what is and isn't critical to business performance—what will make a difference and what doesn't matter.

Certainly, whether your enterprise is fighting for survival, maintaining competitiveness, or breaking away makes a difference here. Many CIOs have an instinctive understanding of which of these three categories their enterprise falls into. Knowing your enterprise means going beyond this instinctive understanding to a deep knowledge of why you are in the category.

In this chapter, we'll look at all the elements of what it means to understand the fundamentals of your enterprise and its environment. This understanding means, first, knowing the enterprise itself. Then it means engaging the key decision makers in the enterprise and coming to understand them as individuals.[1]

Know Your Enterprise

We've divided what you need to know about your enterprise into some logical groups: (1) the industry and competitive environment within which your enterprise operates, (2) the business (or operational) fundamentals of your enterprise, (3) the key people within your enterprise, and (4) the trends likely to impact your industry and your organization.

Know your industry and competitive environment

Effective CIOs know the rhythm and tempo of the industries they're in. Every industry has a natural beat and speed at which things get done. You've probably been made keenly aware of this if you have changed industries and realized that you felt like a fish out of water. There's sometimes variation between individual businesses, or even units within an enterprise, but more often than not, certain cycles and seasonalities will characterize entire lines of business.

For example, one CIO at a Gartner meeting described working in a brewing company. This brewer and most of its competitors worked around a monthly business rhythm. It was standard industry practice to bill customers monthly. There was also an annual element in the cycle, as the industry progressively ramped up production for the hotter months of the year.

Retailers have an entirely different cycle. Tracking daily sales numbers is critical, because that's how people in the industry tend to look at the business. Overlaid on this is a weekly business cycle that juggles discounts—for example, selling on Monday those perishables that didn't sell over the weekend. And overlaid on this again is a third cycle of Christmas and summer peaks and fall and spring collections. Traditional direct (or catalog) retailers in the United States, on the other hand, work toward the big seasons of early fall, Christmas, and the winter period following the New Year.

As CIO you must be sensitive to the ebb and flow of the industry and business you're in and shape your schedule to that of your business colleagues. When talking with other executives, it's important to know where in the cycle they are and how far ahead they're looking. Certainly, it would be difficult to introduce major change or seek input when your colleagues are focusing on hot spots in the cycle.

Besides looking at the ebb and flow of industry cycles, companies must deal with an investment climate that can shift dramatically with industry and business performance. Over time, the opportunities for aggressive or risky investments might be curtailed or expanded based on what's going on in the industry and the world. The downturn in many countries following the e-business boom and bust illustrated this type of overall reduction in business investment. Where the CIO is acutely aware of market and industry conditions, he or she can work with colleagues to proactively shift priorities and resources—and be seen in the process as someone who truly understands the business.

There are also industry matters that can have a large impact on your business. Your colleagues are certainly watching legal and regulatory issues, new products introduced by competitors, the entry of new competitors, the success or failure of a major competitor, a change in industry pricing, changes in the price of important raw materials, and the list can go on and on. Like any other significant executive, you must be aware of all these changes and other events.

How can you make sure you're plugged in and aligned with your colleagues? Read the major trade magazines that your colleagues read. Use the industry alert services that they do. Attend one of the major industry trade shows and conferences. Join a colleague at an industry event, and you'll get an even better sense of how key issues might affect your business. Network with other CIOs in your industry. Meet important customers and vendors (especially those that supply others in the industry, too) so that you understand how your business looks from their perspectives. The staff you've hired from outside your firm and analysts' reports are also excellent sources of insight.

It's especially important that you understand the competitive context within which your company must operate. Rapidly developing technology, new markets, fierce competition, and higher customer expectations can turn a whole industry inside out within a few years. The worldwide telecommunications industry is just one recent example. Industry changes inevitably wash through individual enterprises and force them to change, too. Dramatic change can occur not only in markets served and products offered, but also in the way enterprises operate internally—for example, in the synergies between business units, divisions, and product groups.

You can no more remain oblivious to such external events and conditions than the colleagues you work with can. Explaining away your failure to consider the competitive context because of lack of time or thinking that it's really someone else's job is not an option. If you're not aware of what's going on, you won't be accepted as a member of the executive team, no matter what your title or whom you report to.

Know the business (or operational) fundamentals of your enterprise

There are several key steps you can take to know the business fundamentals, or in the case of government organizations, the operational fundamentals, of your enterprise. The following sections describe how you can take these steps.

Understand your company's business model

Nothing will drive your colleagues crazier—or damage your credibility more—than failure to understand the basic economic model of your company. An economic model is nothing more than a concise description of how your company makes money. What does it sell, and to whom? How is that product or service made and delivered, and at what cost? How does the company acquire and keep customers? How, in the long run, does the company (or each individual business unit) manage to bring in more money than it spends?

For example, here's a common economic model: A company invests in acquiring new customers, on whom it loses money the first year or two but on whom it eventually makes money over the customers' lifetimes with the company. For a model like this, the lifetime value of a customer is critical to know, and the company needs to track carefully all the metrics associated with that long-term relationship. Business information is crucial, both to keeping the model working well and to improving it.

Government organizations have operating models rather than business models. What is the organization's mission? How is it completed? What are the metrics of success?

If you don't understand your organization's model and how it works, you and your IS organization can hardly envision ways technology might improve it.

Keep on top of the latest enterprise numbers

You also need to know and track the metrics that your stakeholders also track. Stakeholders track enterprise-level measures of business performance, such as revenue, revenue growth, earnings, earnings per share, and return on assets (or some other ratio—do you know which one your company emphasizes?). We were surprised recently in a meeting with senior CIOs in a financial services company because they couldn't tell us which business performance metric was most important to the company—return on assets, revenue growth, margin contribution, or some other measure. On the other hand, we knew that the CIO of a major manufacturing company was in good shape when he told us he had been asked at a recent executive team meeting to report on a business unit's performance in the absence of the business unit leader.

Board members and senior executives tend to focus on such top-level value measures because investors use them to rate corporate success, and so these measures influence share price. If your company has several business units, each will have a set of key financial performance indicators. You should know these indicators as well, because your colleagues who run those units will know them.

Many companies track key indicators beyond financial measures, and you should also track these if your enterprise uses them. The Balanced Scorecard, for example, has become a widely used framework of financial and nonfinancial metrics.[2] As a rule of thumb, keep track of the key performance indicators, financial and otherwise, that your colleagues track. Since IS probably wrote the programs that generate these key enterprise indicators, you are in a unique position to understand how they're generated and what they mean.

Understand the strategic intent of the enterprise

Strategic intent refers to long-term, enterprisewide targets and embraces the long-term vision for the enterprise as a whole. It usually remains fairly stable over time.[3]

Here are a few examples of strategic intent statements, often called mission statements:

- To be the preferred financial partner for the region's best-performing companies as they move to operate in global markets

- To be the most customer-intimate globally operating telecommunications company for medium to large worldwide multinational companies

- To be the world's leading provider of entertainment and information

- To be an integrated financial services provider, offering a one-stop shop to high-value customers

- To create books for businesspeople who want to make a difference, not just a living

If these statements don't include explicit reference to the competitive advantage that allows your company to survive and thrive, you need to dig deeper. Make sure you understand what your enterprise believes will make it competitively different.

One useful approach to competitive advantage has been outlined by Michael Treacy and Fred Wiersma in *The Discipline of Market Leaders.*[4] They say three so-called value disciplines encapsulate the major ways enterprises differentiate themselves:

Operational excellence: emphasizes efficiency and reliability (e.g., supply-chain optimization)

Customer intimacy: emphasizes customer service and responsiveness and is based on deep customer or client knowledge, segmentation, very specific targeting (increasingly the focus of public sector agencies), or some combination of these factors

Product/service leadership and innovation: focuses on pursuing innovative products and services, such as being first to market, with rapid R&D to commercialization processes

Which of these strategic approaches has your company chosen as its competitive focal point? Or is the enterprise shifting from one competitive model to another?

You need to understand your enterprise's key strategies because the success or failure of many initiatives, including IT-enabled business initiatives, will be measured against them. A successful initiative moves the enterprise toward its strategic intent; an unsuccessful initiative moves the enterprise nowhere, or away from the intent.

Be familiar with the firm's strategic endeavors

Strategic endeavors are important initiatives launched to carry out the enterprise's strategic intent. They typically have a one- to three-year time horizon and are concerned with major or fundamental changes in business models and industry structures, with the ways customers or suppliers or both interact with your business, and even possibly with what business you're in.

You need to know about strategic endeavors for all the reasons we've already covered, not the least of which is because the endeavors are likely to have a strong IT component and involve your IS organization. If you and your IS team don't understand each endeavor in total—how it relates to the enterprise, its overall corporate strategy, and its economic model—you'll overlook ways that IT could better serve the company.

Understand the culture and dynamics of your enterprise

Every organization differs in the values it espouses (its culture—"how we do work around here") and in the working relationships among business units. These features are partly driven by similarities among business units and are partly a matter of management philosophy, which often comes from the legacy of a company's past. Business units may share many customers, competencies, and processes and may even sell similar products. These overlaps present opportunities for synergy, but whether these opportunities become reality will depend on the enterprise's management philosophy.

For example, at Valeo, a large European automotive supplier, the business units are given a great deal of autonomy so they can make decisions quickly. Each unit is responsible for its own operations, sales, and profits and for such functions as finance, human resources, and IS. Indeed, a division can design, produce, and sell a product all on its own.

Because autonomy is such an important management value at Valeo, the guiding principle is to keep local decisions in the divisions. Valeo's CIO divides IT activities into infrastructure and business applications, with the corporate IS group responsible for infrastructure, and the business units responsible for applications. A division can decide to outsource its data center, as long as the outsourcer complies with certain overall IT standards. The corporate group can have input, but at the divisional level, the CIO focuses on topics that deal with either the communication infrastructure (to foster sharing) or final purchasing decisions (to receive volume discounts).

In another organization with a different philosophy, the CIO and IS organization might act in very different ways. In every instance, though, the CIO must understand the philosophy and culture of the enterprise and shape an IS approach accordingly.

Understand the enterprise's basic business outlook

The elements we've just discussed are all fundamentals of your enterprise and how it operates. You also need to understand how well these fundamentals are working in the present. In other words, understand the enterprise's basic business outlook. In our research among nearly two thousand organizations, we have identified three basic business outlooks that can profoundly change the way you and other executives act. We've discussed these earlier, but we'll review them here and then discuss the effects they can have on the CIO's challenges and behavior.

> *Fighting for survival:* This outlook is characterized by multiyear deep budget cuts in business and IT, cancellation of new initiatives, multiple layoffs, and a continuing search for ways to further reduce business and IT costs.

> *Maintaining competitiveness:* In difficult times, this outlook is characterized by fairly flat budgets from year to year and the

completion of existing programs and systems, but there is caution about starting major new business initiatives, especially IT-enabled ones. As economic conditions improve, these enterprises begin to invest in more new and large projects.

Breaking away: Enterprises that are breaking away show significant increases in business and IT budgets and take aggressive steps to move ahead of competitors.

Where does your company fit? The answer is often obvious, but not always. There are gray areas between categories, and you'll sometimes need to look for subtle clues, since few enterprises will announce publicly which category they're in. Sometimes the category also varies within enterprises; one business unit may be losing market share while another is opening up new markets.

In the fighting-for-survival environment, you'll obviously be looking for ways to cut IT costs and to use IT to reduce business expenses. You'll be trying to find the right balance between cutting back and avoiding excessive risk by too severe a reduction in capabilities. If your firm is maintaining competitiveness, you'll focus on implementing proven systems and processes, while positioning yourself and IS for possible growth. And in the breaking-away mode, you'll be actively looking for ways to use IT to spur innovation, without under-delivering on day-to-day IT needs.

Over time, organizations move from one category to another, but it's important to know at any given moment which description fits your enterprise, because your job and what you do—your priorities and your focus—will differ in each category. Most important, you should act in ways consistent with the basic business outlook of your enterprise. Imagine the response if you followed or recommended a breaking-away IT strategy when your enterprise is fighting for survival. Even some lesser error—for example, remaining in a maintaining-competitiveness mode when your enterprise has moved on to the initial stages of breaking away—may still do much harm to your credibility and make you appear out of sync with the business.

Know the trends likely to impact your industry and your enterprise

Once you know the fundamentals of your enterprise and where it currently stands, you need to start looking at what major trends are likely to impact your organization. You need to be able to spot the clues of change now to anticipate important developments. There are six key areas to watch:

Economic environment and line of business: Cycles and investment climates shift and change, but usually not without some foreshadowing signs.

Technology: Where is technology going? How might it affect your enterprise, your work, and your services, and what technologies are competitors reviewing or testing?

Competition: Surprises can spring from competitors, near-competitors, or new players—but less often for those who regularly keep track of the both their immediate industry and the wider economic environments.

Enterprise: If you're systematically tracking your enterprise's key performance indicators, you'll have a strong sense of where it's going and you can get ready—or even proactively help guide the firm to a better direction.

Politics: The power and influence of key people can wax and wane. You'll be better off, though, if you keep track of who sets enterprise agendas and why.

Culture: Real cultural changes usually occur slowly, but keeping your antennae up can alert you to subtle shifts in the unspoken ways organizations do work.

Much of this trend-watching only requires that you stay informed in all the ways we've described already, but equally important, you must keep alert for changes. Your goal is to detect change as it happens so that you don't have to go into fire drill mode later.

All these recommendations can be summarized in one statement: *Become a serious student of your business and the world in which it operates.*

Two reasons make following this recommendation urgent. Knowing your enterprise is crucial if you are to develop a vision of the enterprise enabled by IT. And you need to be knowledgeable—and appear that way—if you want your executive colleagues to take you seriously.

Good reasons, both.

Engage Key Decision Makers and Stakeholders

Knowing your enterprise is an important part of building and maintaining credibility and the very necessary underpinning to your vision. To flesh out that vision and understand how and when to implement parts of it, you must engage key decision makers and other stakeholders.

Managing the growing number and diversity of IS stakeholders presents a complex, demanding leadership challenge for CIOs. As boundaries stretch to include more parties and as different types of stakeholders fall within IS's bounds, the stakeholders' motivations and desired outcomes diverge. The potential for logjams on decisions and for political gridlock abounds.

An IS stakeholder is any group or individual who can affect or is affected by the achievement of IS's decisions and operations. Today, these stakeholders include corporate and business units, the board of directors, business partners, IS staff, service providers, external customers, and external agencies. Their interests range from long-term priorities to daily operations, and they often hold divergent views about what you and your IS organization should do. Without proper management, stakeholders may block your initiatives or simply become passive participants who do not contribute to the initiatives' success.

It's easy to see the stakeholder who wields positional (in the corporate hierarchy), financial, or relationship (influences decisions made by others) power. But less noticeable stakeholders, who have urgent or legitimate needs, often require just as much attention. Stakeholder management deals with how to achieve an outcome in the face of supporters and opponents. The outcome you seek as CIO might be as operational as retaining the right to supply IS services to a business unit. Or it might be as fundamental as integrating the supply chain, globalizing customer management, or setting IT strategy. To achieve success as a new CIO leader, you must identify all your stakeholders, determine which need close attention, and then decide which approach works best for each.

Know who your stakeholders are

IS stakeholders grow constantly in number and diversity. Initially, they came from the core business. In yesterday's simplified world, IS stakeholders were directly involved in the enterprise's activities—mainly employees, but also some suppliers and perhaps distributors. For core-business stakeholders, internal organizational mechanisms were usually enough to handle most contentious IS situations.

As enterprises extended their boundaries through alliances, joint ventures, partnering, and focusing on members of their value chain, the number of IS stakeholders increased as well. They can now include vendors, outsourcers, customers, suppliers, regulators, interest groups, and even competitors and strategic alliance partners. We can now find IS stakeholders everywhere in the business ecosystem (figure 2-1).

Not long ago, Sacramento County, California; the city of Sacramento; SMUD (Sacramento Municipal Utility District, the area's electric and gas utility); and the Sacramento area county governments formed a geographic information systems cooperative. The goal was to create a single database that all the participants could use by combining the information each member possessed about parcels of land. The county had tax data on parcels, SMUD had utility

FIGURE 2-1

IS Stakeholders and the Business Ecosystem

There is a wide variety of IS stakeholders, which can come from anywhere in the entire business ecosystem.

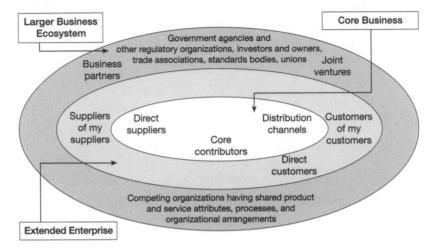

Source: Adapted from J. F. Moore, *The Death of Competition: Leadership and Strategy in the Age of Business Ecosystems* (New York: HarperCollins, 1997).

information, the city had water information, and so on. By combining the data and correcting the errors, the group hoped to reduce the cost of gathering and maintaining this information.

It took the group two years of talking to develop the trust required to agree on the operating principles and rules of the road for implementation. The first project was a master address database, which was first used by city police. Such cooperative projects, designed to reduce costs and serve constituents better, meant that Sally Nagy's job as the city of Sacramento's CIO had expanded outside city limits to encompass working with the county and the region. This expansion in the scope of her IS world was never recognized formally or officially, but it was real nonetheless. As Nagy's example shows, to engage key decision makers, you must first recognize this kind of expansion and identify *all* your stakeholders in a more and more complex world.

Segment your stakeholders

The next step is to segment your stakeholders so that they can be managed effectively. There are usually too many stakeholders for a CIO to manage all equally. A new CIO leader needs to divide them into meaningful groups. One common, and unfortunately wrong, practice is to segment stakeholders by how demanding they are. Demand is not necessarily the best determinant of priority, even though demanding stakeholders would like you to think so.

Some CIOs we've worked with have found a far more useful approach: Distinguish stakeholders by their *pull* and their *stance* in relation to IS issues. Pull has to do with the amount of influence stakeholders have on an IS issue, and stance concerns whether they support or oppose an IS issue.

The pull of stakeholders, in fact, has three attributes: power, urgency, and legitimacy. Think of them as P, U, and L (PUL):[5]

- *Power* (clout): How much political, financial, or other clout does a stakeholder have to affect a decision? The more power, the more pull.

- *Urgency* (immediacy of a claim): What's the true time pressure of a stakeholder's claim? Immediacy can increase pull.

- *Legitimacy* (right to make a claim): How much moral, legal, contractual, or other right does a stakeholder have in a decision? The more legitimate the stakeholder's right to be heard, the greater the pull.

Most managers focus only on the power element of PUL. Power provides lots of pull, but urgency and legitimacy also matter because they can increase a stakeholder's influence. To segment stakeholders effectively, determine the pull of each, using *all three* attributes. A stakeholder's pull ranges from low to high, with each attribute—power, urgency, or legitimacy—adding to the whole.

For example, stakeholders with only a legitimate claim have the least pull. But don't underestimate those with only one attribute, like

FIGURE 2-2

Stakeholder Quadrants

Mapping the pull and stance of stakeholders sorts stakeholders into four types. Use this quadrant to categorize and track the importance of different stakeholders.

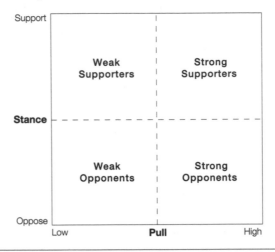

legitimacy. Add urgency, whether real or apparent, and their pull increases. Add a powerful spokesperson or alliance, and their influence increases still further. Individuals with a legitimate cause can gain power very quickly via networking. Don't be taken by surprise.

Stakeholder stance is the amount of a stakeholder's support for, or opposition to, an IS issue. Discovering the stance of a person or group might seem a daunting task at first. But talking directly to the stakeholders or to people who have previously dealt with them—like IS staff members or even outside vendors—can help you ferret out their current position and underlying motivation.

As figure 2-2 shows, clustering stakeholders around pull and stance will yield four stakeholder groups: strong and weak supporters, and strong and weak opponents.

Manage stakeholder stance

To some readers, this entire discussion may sound like political maneuvering, something you'd prefer to avoid. Many CIOs we know think of politics as cutting deals, scoring points, putting one over, manipulating, and being otherwise devious. Politics, they think, is based on who you know, not what you know, and they don't think the world should work that way.

But what they call politics a new CIO leader knows actually concerns human relationships in an organizational setting. Organizational politics is about collaboration, influence, and relationships. It's about understanding your organization and how it works: who gets to make decisions, who has what agendas, and where the bases of power reside, as well as issues of culture and style. You can treat politics as psychological game-playing—and we agree that many people treat it that way—or you can conduct yourself with integrity. But new CIO leaders do have to do politics. It's up to you how you do it.

Keep this in mind: The purpose of all this is to convert as many stakeholders as possible into influential supporters. Supporters of what? Of you personally? No. Supporters of the power of information and IT, and specifically a vision for how IT can vastly empower your enterprise, which will work to everyone's benefit. If it's just about you, then we agree—it's just politics. If it's about an IT vision for your firm, then it's about being organizationally street smart.

Let's look at the four stakeholder segments around pull and stance:

- *Strong opponents:* High pull, opposing stance. These stakeholders are the most dangerous and the most likely to prevent you from achieving your objectives.

- *Strong supporters:* High pull, supporting stance. This group is your power base.

- *Weak supporters:* Low pull, supporting stance. This group supports you but has little influence at present.

- *Weak opponents:* Low pull, opposing stance. This group could prevent you from achieving your objectives, but lacks the influence to do so—at the moment.

Having segmented your stakeholders into these groups, look at the members of each group. At any given moment in every organization, there are issues and struggles within and between groups and units. Be aware of this reality, and add it to the knowledge of your enterprise that you need to maintain, as previously discussed. These issues are rarely written down or discussed formally, but they profoundly influence the positions and actions groups take. The only way to find out people's opinions and positions is to network with them. Ask questions to understand their thinking and how they arrived at it. You can't guess; you need to know.

As Karen Evans, CIO at the U.S. Department of Energy, says, "Networking is essential to helping the people in your chain of command. The informal network is where executives learn and debate alternatives. If you wait for formal channels, then you'll miss the boat."

With the political understanding gained from the kind of analysis we've just outlined, you'll be ready to prioritize and deal with each of the different stakeholder segments. Here are some priorities we recommend as you work with each of the groups.

Priority 1: Convert influential opponents to the cause

Focus first on influential opponents because they are most likely to prevent you from achieving your objectives. Exploit existing relationships. Use your "bank of political capital," as one CIO put it, plus any other bargaining chips you have, in return for these stakeholders' support. Sometimes, just engaging with opponents and hearing their arguments can be sufficient to reduce their opposition. They may become more sympathetic to your position (or you to theirs). Better yet, they could become supporters, especially if there is something in it for them. Small changes to accommodate them can yield large rewards.

Priority 2: Restrict influential opponents you can't convert

If all your sincere efforts fail and you cannot convert some influential opponents, your last resort is to limit their influence. Use the decision-making process to counterbalance their pull. Work with senior management to define an alternative direction. If you can, use your IT council and other processes to lessen the impact of their opposition. This may require preliminary meetings with supporters so that they understand the need for their strong participation.

Priority 3: Retain your influential supporters

Once you've determined how to address your influential opponents, deal with your influential supporters. Your goal is to maintain their support and protect their influence.

The most effective way to handle supporters is to work with individual stakeholders or groups directly, rather than keeping in touch only through group meetings or councils. Informal networking, requests for their suggestions, and the inclusion of their concerns all strengthen ties with these crucial allies. Be sure these stakeholders continue to play a major role (or at least an influential one) in the decision-making process; otherwise, they may lose their pull. In fact, it might be wise to increase their role or visibility as much as possible, to increase their pull. Use of senior management, governance, and committees can also encourage this group to remain steadfast in their support.

Priority 4: Recognize your weak supporters

When considering your weak supporters, recognize their importance, and work to boost their pull. Bring them in with your influential supporters to strengthen their position and yours. Use decision councils and other processes to replace the weaker pull of individual stakeholders with the much stronger pull of an influential group. We've seen the position of weak supporters on investment councils bolstered by the commitment of other supporters.

Priority 5: Keep track of your weak opponents

They might not seem to warrant much of your attention, but you ignore your weak opponents at your peril, because they may not remain weak. They can gain influence by forming coalitions with strong opponents or by finding ways to increase the urgency or legitimacy of their claims.

Choose the right management tactics

As you work with various stakeholder groups, keep in mind the tool kit of management tactics and techniques available to you. Different techniques can considerably change the dynamics of managing the pull of your IS stakeholders.

- *Senior management intervention:* Substituting the stance and pull of some vocal stakeholders with that of senior management can shift the balance to a small, influential group of supporters, particularly if they are recognized as credible leaders in their own right.

- *Governance:* Understand the power of thoughtful and transparent governance (detailed in chapter 5). Clarity about who has decision rights and who's accountable can sometimes result in rethinking who should be involved in the decision-making processes.

- *IT councils or IT boards:* Using top-level IT councils or boards as part of the governance process can help make the positions of individual stakeholders more transparent to others. Unable to remain silent (or unable to simply undermine your efforts), opponents will have to articulate and defend their position openly.

- *Relationships:* Use existing relationships directly to change the stance of opposing stakeholders. Trade on your bank of goodwill. You can use relationships with stakeholders to influence their stance or to give them your own power. Or use your relationships with influential stakeholders to get them to increase the influence of your weak supporters.

- *Negotiation:* Negotiation involves modifying a stakeholder's stance, often by making mutually beneficial trade-offs. Remember, negotiations are often about viewpoints and perspectives, rather than specific issues. It's good to understand opposing perspectives. If you can accommodate them, you will gain supporters and probably improve your solution as well.

- *Engagement:* By engaging stakeholders in dialogue, you can better understand their stance and pull. Relationship, negotiation, and engagement all aim at changing (or embracing) the stance of an individual, whereas senior management, governance, and steering committees change the power or pull of individuals. Engagement is by far the most appropriate first technique to use. It might appear to be the most passive, but it's a door opener for further steps, such as negotiation and relationships. Indeed, if you don't engage, you can't form a relationship or negotiate. Engagement also preserves a relationship, even if you and the other person or group disagree on a particular issue.

The CIO of Food Services Corporation (a pseudonym) has this to say about the trade-off between engagement, which can take time, and the need for quick decision making: "Our corporate culture is to reach consensus on a decision by consulting and involving all of a decision's principle stakeholders. This process can seem protracted at times. But execution is quick. The alternative—fast decisions and poor implementation—is worse."

Getting things done by ignoring or disengaging with stakeholders can damage your credibility, regardless of other outcomes. Work hard to get what you need, but do it in a way that builds bridges rather than burns them.

Understand how to influence different types of people

As you work with key decision makers, it's critical to work with them one-on-one as individuals. Getting the attention of any senior executive is difficult, yet having that attention is important to gaining influence and trust for IT initiatives. But attention is not one-way only, from the executive to you. It works both ways—if you want attention, you must first give attention. Joanne Stubbs, former

Asia Pacific CIO of GMAC Financial Services, speaks to the importance understanding different types of stakeholders: "I have a variety of different approaches to deal with my different stakeholder groups. The choice of approach depends on the personality of the people. Counseling and personal negotiation, a history of delivering service, and a good escalation procedure all play a part. But the most effective way of dealing with stakeholders is through good relations. Relationship management is critical." In our experience, smart CIOs build strong one-on-one relationships with all their executive colleagues and other stakeholders, in order to build a base of trust and human connection.

One way to start is to recruit an internal mentor—if possible, a senior business executive who knows the individual executives involved. This mentor or coach can provide another lens for you to understand the personal situation of your colleagues.

Here are some suggestions for connecting with key business decision makers:

- Understand the problems they face, and look for opportunities to support them and to exercise your business judgment.

- Find out what they read and watch, and seek out those they talk to.

- Know what their bonus rests on, and communicate to them that you see it as part of your mission to help them achieve that.

- Volunteer for assignments that will demonstrate to them your deep business perspective.

- Conduct frequent peer reviews, and solicit their feedback and insights.

- Keep your message to them simple, and focus on "How can I help you be successful?"

- Look for ways—traveling together on a business trip, for example—to spend "soak time" with them. To the extent they're comfortable, talk about experiences, family, and things in common.

- Equip and coach them to be confident, IT-linked road warriors.

- Make them heroes at home. Install a high-bandwidth network at their home—a wireless network might spur their imagination concerning mobile deployment.

Keep in mind that if you want a good relationship with colleagues, you must keep them informed as well—no information, no support. This is simply because failure to keep them informed often leads to opposition through what we call the *logic of resistance*, which occurs when an issue comes before an executive who has not been briefed. When that happens, the executive's first reaction is to view the issue as unimportant: After all, he or she thinks, "If it were important, I would know about it." Executives won't place their credibility at risk by supporting something they don't know about— or don't believe is important. This deadly combination of ignorance and apparent inconsequence will leave them only one course of action: resistance.

Deal with key decision makers in terms of who they are and what they want. Remember that relationships are a key part of leading through influence and are built on accommodation. So learn your colleagues' preferences, and deal with others in the terms they, not you, prefer. It's a matter not of politics, but of leadership.

Dealing with the CEO and CFO

Although you must deal with many stakeholders as a new CIO leader, clearly you must prioritize the development of a relationship with two senior executives: the CEO and the CFO. To do so, of course, you need to give some preliminary thought to how both of these executives think, what they care about, how they like to receive information, and how you can best form a positive relationship.

The CEO

For years, Gartner research has tracked the reporting relationships between CIOs and CEOs. After five years of global tracking, it's clear that many more CIOs now report to the CEO than to other executives, but the percentage seems to have leveled off recently at a little less than 40 percent.

The CEO–CIO relationship is plainly not always a marriage made in heaven. In fact, the research shows that CEO–CIO relationships tend to exist at four different levels: *adversarial, transactional, aspiring,* and *trusted ally.* These relationships usually correlate with different levels of CIO influence at the executive level and different levels of value generated from IT for the enterprise.

In *adversarial* relationships, the CIO isn't delivering at acceptable service levels—his or her interactions with the CEO are largely about the CEO probing problems. In the *transactional* relationship, which is the most common, the CIO is a service provider to the organization, like other functional leaders—such as the head of human resources. Interactions are about confirming how the CIO's organization will deliver on the business's strategy. The *aspiring* CIO has nailed the delivery of services and proactively engages the CEO (and other corporate officers) on business issues. Finally, in the *trusted ally* relationship, the CIO's interactions with the CEO include the co-creation of strategy. This involvement with enterprise strategy is your aim as a new CIO leader.

CIOs can be relatively successful in all relationships except adversarial. To move to more influential relationships, you need to understand first where you currently stand. How would you characterize your relationship with your CEO? One of the most common issues we found was failure of the CIO to actively engage the CEO in a regular, meaningful discussion. Do you know how your CEO views you?

Very few CIOs make the leap from adversarial to trusted ally in one step. Becoming a new CIO leader in the eyes of the CEO takes time; you need to plan on moving from step to step, not trying to make the change all at once. CIOs who skip steps are likely to fall off the ladder or get burned.

Here are some suggestions on how to enhance your relationship with the chief executive of your enterprise. These suggestions were developed by our colleague Ken McGee, a Gartner Fellow. You'll find they correlate well with all we've just discussed.

1. What are the CEO's top-of-mind issues?

   • Identify the CEO's specific top priorities.

   • Identify the CEO's specific programs to meet these top priorities.

   • Establish guiding principles for new IT initiatives.

2. How should the CEO judge your success?

   • Propose new metrics on how you should be measured.

   • Determine the CEO's view of threats to your initiatives.

   • Ask "the question": How will you measure my success?

3. As the CIO, what new ideas can you bring to the executive table?

   • Be prepared to present three specific answers.

   • Constantly refresh your answers.

The CFO

Since the late 1990s, the CFO has become a more strategic player for the CIO, regardless of the reporting relationship that might currently exist. Why now? Because, as the role of the CIO has changed, so too has the role of the CFO.

Traditionally, as the financial control officer of the enterprise, CFOs have focused on managing earnings and costs. More recently, though, CFOs have extended their focus to drive more aggressive financial management strategies for the enterprise. These typically include managing risk and investments, creating and communicating

CIOs and the Board of Directors

A S THE CIO, you want to be viewed as a credible member of the leadership team. There are various way you assess your credibility. Until recently, the ultimate measure of credibility was reporting directly to the CEO and becoming part of the executive committee. Today, some CIOs have a new measure—whether they are regulars at board meetings (in European terms, we mean the external board comprising largely nonexecutive directors). Increasingly, CIOs are participants in board meetings as key members of the executive team. As a matter of routine at meetings, they may present their vision and the progress of investments and IT-enabled initiatives as part of reporting on the development and execution of business strategy.

At present, relatively few CIOs are board members of *Fortune* 500 companies (their own company's board or that of another company). Experts estimate that CIOs are on less than 5 percent of GLOBAL *Fortune* 500 boards.[6] There is a trend away from the inclusion of more than one or two executives as full board members on their own organization's boards. These positions are typically held by the CEO and president or CEO and CFO, depending on the company structure. At the same time, though, CIOs are becoming members of boards of other enterprises. Some very visible brand-name companies, such as Wal-Mart, Gap, the Times-Mirror, Best Buy, and Sybase, all have current or former CIOs on their boards of directors. Michael Fleisher, former CEO

value, balancing short- and long-term objectives, and enforcing financial and legal controls (inspired by the Sarbanes-Oxley Act and other regulations), as well as managing for enterprise agility.

CFOs now work more closely with the enterprise business units and the COO to optimize efficiency and effectiveness. This is what drives the new, closer relationship between the CFO and the CIO. They now come together around the enterprise's IT strategy. Unfortunately for some CIOs, this new interest by the CFO has made the relationship confrontational.

Although many CFOs have worked hard to become a better partner to operations and IT, most are still relative newcomers to at Gartner, recruited Maynard Webb, currently chief operations officer (COO) of eBay Inc., and previously president of eBay Technologies and CIO of Gateway, Inc., because he wanted the board to think about technology as both a strategic weapon and a key asset of the business. Fleisher argues: "I advise other CEOs all the time that they should have a CIO on their board. If your board is not having a discussion at every board meeting which touches on technology, then you are probably not having the right discussions."[7]

Vince Caracio, president of the Harvard Group, an organization that specializes in working with boards of directors, believes that CIOs are the least prepared, but at the same time the most untapped, resource for board positions: "Regardless of a company's core competency, every company today should have a trained and experienced CIO as a director." He clearly sees a gap between need and available talent. CIOs who make great board members are those who, in their own enterprise, can think in business terms; act on a profit-and-loss statement; utilize the benefits of scale, particularly with mergers and acquisitions; and drive transformational change.[8] In other words, they are new CIO leaders.

If you are to be invited to present to the board regularly, or even become a member of the board at your own organization or another, the messages are the same. As Caracio says, you have to be credible—and credibility lies in a deep knowledge of the business and its key players. We'll discuss communicating with the board much more in chapter 10.

technology. Think of where your CFO fits in to the two ends of the spectrum—what we describe as Type 1 and Type 2 CFOs.

Type 1 CFOs lack an understanding or an appreciation of the truly IT-enabled enterprise. They drive every IT investment to the lowest-cost approach and fail to see the ability of technology to create business value. Other CFOs of this type simply manage investment by setting IT costs as a percentage of revenue and ignore opportunities to break away or lead in their industry through IT-enabled innovations. If you find yourself reporting to a Type 1 CFO, the result can often limit the impact that you or the IS organization can have on the business. Therefore, the CFO should be the first executive you engage. If you can build a relationship with, and change the stance of, a Type 1 CFO, you'll know you're well on your way to becoming a new CIO leader.

If both you and the Type 1 CFO report to the CEO, you may win 50 percent of the disagreements. Unfortunately, however, wins in this situation usually make both parties look bad from the top seat. A good governance model that includes clear decision rights regarding investment is your best vehicle for ensuring that every opportunity enjoys a full and fair assessment (see chapter 5 for more on this topic).

Happily, many CFOs have turned out to be the CIO leader's best executive ally. Type 2 CFOs are one of the few executive team members who have a truly enterprisewide view of the business. They can help drive initiatives that cross business unit boundaries and support projects that a single business unit may not put at the top of its priority list. As influential users of IT, Type 2 CFOs may often be early adopters of new systems or solutions and can be advocates with less supportive business unit leaders.

Don't take even these supportive CFOs for granted, however. While they see value in IT generally, many were also burned with the excessive hype and returns projections bandied about during the Internet bubble. Though IT advocates on the whole, they're more skeptical now than they were several years ago.

Whatever kind of CFO you must work with, understand how to communicate and cooperate with this key person. Most CFOs are metrics- and detail-oriented. They require evidence or proof. Case studies, proven-practice examples, industry trends, and other statistics are the types of information you'll need to support your position.

One CIO we spoke with succinctly expresses how many CFOs feel about IS organizations today: "CFOs feel they have to go more than halfway to work with IS, because they work harder to understand IS's objectives than IS tries to understand theirs."

So what do CFOs want from IT? Based on our conversations with CIOs and CFOs who work together effectively, here's a starter list:

- A single, integrated strategy portfolio across all IT and non-IT investments

- Clear IT and business alignment

- Financial metrics showing costs that IS has avoided or reduced and what revenues IS will attract

- Realistic business cases, rigorous execution of approved projects, and early warning signs of situations going bad

- Solid, ongoing program management, measurement, and reporting, including formal audits that show how you and the IS organization are learning from your mistakes

- Effective management of resources and assets, and elimination of waste and duplication of effort

At the end of the day, CFOs want the same things that new CIO leaders want—technology that adds value to the enterprise. This is your foundation for building a mutually supportive relationship with this key stakeholder.

As we have discussed in chapter 1, leadership is the underpinning of all that you do as a new CIO leader. Here, we've laid out the specific information you need to know to have credibility and build relationships with your executive colleagues. Only when you know your enterprise—the fundamentals of your business—will you be credible in your conversations with your executive colleagues. And only when you're credible will you build the strong relationships necessary to lead. Now we can turn to your vision as CIO for building your organization's success with information and IT. It is this credibility and these relationships that will enable you to make your vision a reality.

3

Create Your Vision

This is the time to become a new CIO leader, despite all the day-to-day problems and short-term issues that beset CIOs, because IT truly is changing how business and work gets done and how people and organizations interact. This is a time of great opportunity.

Now that you've built a foundation based on enterprise knowledge and you understand and have relationships with key stakeholders, you can take the next step toward being a CIO leader by developing a vision of how technology can improve, even revolutionize, your enterprise. To do so, you need to take the knowledge you've acquired and begin envisioning what your enterprise could be like if it were using technology and information in the best possible way. What new growth opportunities would exist? What relationships (customer and supplier) would be strengthened? Whose productivity could be doubled, or even quintupled? What costs could be cut?

There are innumerable answers to these questions, depending on your enterprise (we don't know your enterprise like you do now; hardly anyone should!). So we will leave the specific answers to those questions to you. However, we will highlight two broad, interrelated trends that your vision for a truly IT-enabled enterprise should encompass, no matter what industry, geography, or enterprise context you lead in: the network era and the Real-Time Enterprise. Then we'll discuss other inputs and a process you can use to create your vision.[1]

The Network Era

As technological developments accelerate, their biggest overall effect for years to come will be the creation of an increasingly connected world, what we call the network era. Dot-com euphoria might be dead, but Internet-enabled business networks continue to thrive and change how just about every business operates. Analysts at Gartner predict that by 2007, more than 60 percent of the European Union and U.S. population fifteen to fifty years old will carry or wear a wireless computing and communications device at least six hours a day.

But as big as that shift will be, the real watershed is elsewhere, and only a short way off. Just think about the number of devices that you carry with you today and that weren't even part of our lexicon a few years ago. Soon there will be more devices than people connected to networks. That eventuality will herald the real network era, a world densely populated with alert, aware, always-on machines that continuously monitor their surroundings for particular activities and transmit information about what they have seen and heard to other machines for follow-on action. The power of the network era will lie in its ability to connect processes, products, and services on demand, creating entirely new sources of value.

As N. Venkatraman of Boston University sees it, the network era is being driven by three laws. The effect of each law is extensive on its own. Taken together, their effect is multiplied many times.

- Moore's law says the power of a chip doubles every year and a half.

- Gilder's law says communications bandwidth doubles every six months.

- Metcalfe's law says the value of a network rises with the square of the number of users.

Pioneering network applications are already transforming processes, products, and services in many enterprises, such as manufacturing, agriculture, consumer photography, and health care.

SKF, a Swedish manufacturer of equipment for the paper industry, is a network-era pioneer. It is using technology—specifically, network-era technology—to move from selling undifferentiated products (roller bearings) to selling highly differentiated services (machine and factory uptime guarantees). "The idea that you can add value through networks has been one of the drivers behind the SKF Group going through a major change," says group IT strategist Stig Johansson. By exploiting the laws of the network era, SKF is now well on its way to new growth and success.

To make this transition, SKF has combined its engineering know-how with new network technologies. From experiences in the aircraft and automobile industries, SKF developed an electronic ABS (brake) sensor that could be built into automotive wheel bearing units. SKF then applied the process-monitoring technology developed for the auto industry to a host of other rotating machines, including those in paper mills.

By adding local computer processing power (affordable because of Moore's law), SKF was able to create an accurate picture of machine wear and tear and therefore could predict maintenance requirements. The company added wireless connections so that the data could be monitored remotely. Then, by responding speedily to early electronic warnings of equipment failure, SKF boosted both productivity and safety. That service opened the door to SKF's sale of uptime rather than machine components. Taken in aggregate, these evolutionary steps have meant major changes at SKF, which has acquired several electronics companies and now routinely forms partnerships with some of its strongest competitors to secure engineering and manufacturing capacity.

Another example of a company using the technological advances of the network era is Health Maintenance Corporation (a pseudonym), one of America's largest not-for-profit health-care organizations, which offers preventive, diagnostic, hospital, medical, and pharmaceutical services to eight million members. The company is working on the problem of an aging population in which more people live with chronic conditions, such as hypertension and diabetes, that require constant monitoring and treatment. At some point, current medical systems will be overwhelmed by the sheer number of such patients—baby boomers who are living longer because of advances in the treatment of their conditions. Health Maintenance Corporation is working with a consortium of health-care and technology companies to address this future bottleneck. The consortium is focusing on using technologies for in-home remote biometric monitoring, which could enable patients to manage themselves.

In the network era, products will migrate to services, as in the example of SKF, and both products and services will become embedded in new processes. The value-adding effect of mutual reinforcement will open up whole new revenue opportunities.

These developments will also create new dangers, especially for those companies caught unaware of significant shifts in technologies, which create shifts in customers and markets. We're all familiar with what's happened to the music industry with the emergence of Napster and subsequent file-sharing services. For this industry, the network era represents a huge discontinuity that is forcing tectonic shifts. A very similar struggle for the movie business is now upon us as bandwidth grows enough to accommodate high-quality video files easily. Imagine for a moment being a competitor of a company like SKF, continuing to try to sell based on price per bearing when the market has shifted to guarantees of mill uptime.

What impact will the networked future have on your enterprise? How can you exploit the power of the network? How can your enterprise capture technology-enabled network-era opportunities before your competitors? There's opportunity here for you as a new CIO leader to seize the initiative, but there's danger, too. You need to play a leadership role in steering your enterprise away from the missed-opportunity trap. Don't let your industry be transformed while your back is turned. Your answers to the preceding questions should be a large part of your vision for IT-enabling your business.

The Real-Time Enterprise

The second key area in which technology is rapidly transforming the way businesses operate is the availability of real-time information.[2] We are less than 150 years removed from the first human beings who were able to have real-time information about events occurring beyond earshot (with the invention of the telegraph). In the last century and a half, we have come to take for granted the ability to see events as they happen on the opposite side of the world. Today, however, businesses rarely take much advantage of the ability to detect events as they happen.

There are a number of reasons for this oversight. Among them are management biases toward reacting to events rather than detecting events, the assumption that there is too much data available now to make sense of any of it, and the belief that the truly significant data can't be obtained in real time. The reality is that if your enterprise is using technology at even an average level, then you can enable your business colleagues to receive the data they need in real time to avert business surprises and to seize new opportunities before competitors do. In fact, drawing on his extensive research, Gartner Fellow Ken McGee has shown that before virtually every negative surprise or business opportunity, "there is always warning"—meaning that data revealing coming events was available well in advance.

Real-Time Enterprises (RTEs) are those that recognize the value of real-time information for providing this warning. Specifically, in Gartner's definition, an RTE "engages in real-time opportunity detection in all its most important business processes by monitoring, capturing, analyzing, and reporting all the events that are critical to the success of the company the moment those events occur.

Additionally, an RTE further improves its performance by redesigning all the processes needed to respond more efficiently and effectively when required."[3]

This definition may seem a little pie-in-the-sky, but there are numerous companies moving in this direction and reaping considerable benefit. A residential construction company in Phoenix, Arizona, is providing real-time information on subcontractor work to job overseers, allowing improved scheduling. As a result, the company has cut the time to complete houses by 15 percent and boosted margins 20 percent. Wet Seal, a fashion retailer, has installed local processing power and networking (there's the network era again!) in point-of-sale systems that allow real-time inventory and personnel tracking. As a result, corporate management collects the vast majority of variable cost and revenue daily—giving senior management dramatic insight into financial results. General Motors has dramatically improved quality and productivity by installing real-time quality and productivity monitoring (via computer monitors) on factory floors. With assembly-line personnel able to see up-to-the-minute information on how they are performing against productivity and quality goals, they are able to make needed adjustments on the fly. In each of these cases, a CIO leader has played a vital role in defining the vision for how technology can get the right real-time information to the right managers to deliver substantial value.

But how do you develop the right vision, an informed vision that colleagues will find compelling, especially when technology has lost much of its seductive power? Of course, your vision also needs to be grounded in your knowledge of your enterprise, its current stance, and its key players. If you're in a fighting-for-survival enterprise, you should be looking for ways that the network-era enterprise and RTE can save money, cut overhead costs, and produce near-immediate return on investment (and, yes, that is possible!). If you're in a maintaining-competitiveness enterprise, you should be keeping a sharp eye out for competitors' efforts in these areas. Additionally, your vision should include ways to build such technology advances into existing projects with minimal disruption. Finally, if you're in breaking-away mode, you should be looking at network-era and RTE technologies for ways of changing the game, as SKF has by introducing dramatic new innovations to its products and services. In fact, while having a vision cannot be neglected, in any enterprise situation, having such a vision is an absolute requirement for CIO leaders in breaking-away enterprises and should be one of your top priorities.

As you can see, to take all this into account, you need systematic rather than just an opportunistic approach. Let's take a look at some tools and approaches for ensuring that your vision includes what it should, and not what it shouldn't.

Avoid the Technology Hype Cycle

The belief that IT is an unbridled source of competitive advantage has given way to a more mature business view of IT's role in the enterprise. This is no short-term shift, because most organizations have an established technology base that reduces the opportunity for cashing in on breakthrough technologies. There is also reduced appetite for taking on too much technical and business risk associated with untested technologies—few companies want to be "bleeding edge" implementers. Nevertheless, time scales for looking at emerging technologies have shrunk from three to five years to eighteen to twenty-four months.

Consequently, now more than ever, new CIO leaders must demonstrate the relevance of any technology—especially emerging technologies—to business needs. Explicitly linking business demand to technology opportunities in your vision will demonstrate value, gain management attention, and secure resources for innovation and investment.

One way to avoid making mistakes in choosing the wrong technologies or in overcommitting on time frame or impact is to understand what Gartner calls *the technology Hype Cycle* (figure 3-1). The history of the media's and IS groups' overenthusiastic response to

FIGURE 3-1

The Gartner Hype Cycle for Emerging Technologies

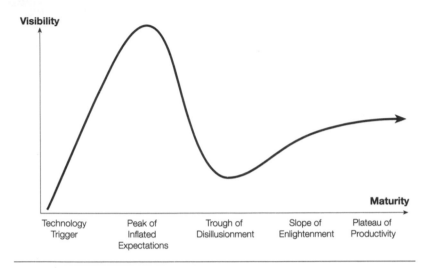

Technology	Peak of	Trough of	Slope of	Plateau of
Trigger	Inflated	Disillusionment	Enlightenment	Productivity
	Expectations			

technology hype is a major reason that so many of your business colleagues are technology skeptics.

The Hype Cycle is a graphic representation of the life cycle of any specific technology. Even if the graph didn't have labels, you'd recognize the parts that we will describe.

The *Technology Trigger* is a breakthrough, a product launch, or another event that generates significant press and interest.

The *Peak of Inflated Expectations* is a frenzy of publicity-generated overenthusiasm and unrealistic expectations. There may be some successful applications, but typically there are more failures.

Technologies enter the *Trough of Disillusionment* because they fail to meet overinflated expectations and quickly become unfashionable. Consequently, the press usually abandons the topic and the technology.

Though the press may have stopped covering the technology, some businesses continue through the *Slope of Enlightenment* and experiment to understand the technology's benefits and practical applications.

A technology reaches the *Plateau of Productivity* as its benefits become widely demonstrated and accepted. The technology becomes increasingly stable and evolves to second and third generations. The final height of the plateau varies according to whether the technology is broadly applicable or benefits only a niche market.

Perception of a technology through the Hype Cycle is largely driven by press coverage and market behaviors, not the efficacy of the technology. Understanding the cycle will help you understand where the "pack" is on a particular technology, but it won't help you make specific decisions on how to address your business needs—unless your vision calls for using only risk-free, market-proven, commodity-like technologies.

Here's our point: The new CIO leader's approach to technology planning of any kind—whether for developing an overall vision for your enterprise or to review a specific technology for a specific application—cannot begin with the technology itself. Trying to ride the Hype Cycle will get you nowhere. Your approach must move from technology discovery to *business value definition*.

By placing greater emphasis on the fundamental business needs of your enterprise, you can create a compelling vision for making your organization technology-enabled. This stress on fundamentals is particularly important in enterprises that find change difficult. Taking this approach will foster innovation, build executive understanding, and help executives invest with a clear vision of the opportunities, the trade-offs, and the results. This is where we come back to the need to know your enterprise fundamentals.

A Systematic Approach to Building Your Vision

Recall that the fundamentals contain three basic components: the basic economic model of the firm, the strategic intent of the firm, and the strategic endeavors of the firm and its individual business units. As mentioned, to develop your vision, you need to ask questions around these three basic elements. For example, how can we:

- increase the number of customers, our revenue, or both?

- create new sales channels and products?

- retain or regain pricing power (i.e., the ability to set our own prices rather than follow the market)?

- reduce sales cycle time and costs?

- establish our brand as the market leader?

- reduce production and distribution costs?

- reduce order cycle time?

- increase forecast accuracy?

- reduce overhead—administrative costs and so on?

Don't forget to ask as well if your product or service can be improved to answer such questions positively *for your customers*. Improving your customers' capital requirements, cycle times, and needs for resources represents ways your firm can strengthen its value proposition.

We intend the preceding list of questions to be a guide, not exhaustive. It's only to suggest the kinds of questions pertinent for every business at any time, because they deal with persistent business needs. (In the next section, we explain how to capture and articulate the answers to these questions in a disciplined way.) The questions are meant to uncover better ways of reaching the goals and of keeping the model in good running order, through technology.

Asking such questions can lead, for example, to interesting new products or better ways to attract customers. That was the experience of the Walt Disney Company.

Disney works hard to understand its customers and their tastes, wants, and needs. That work generated an opportunity when Disney spotted a new trend: People were using Disney resorts as a common meeting place for multiple family groups, such as family reunions or vacations involving multiple families. This insight led the company to create two new offerings: Magical Gatherings for families and a few friends and Grand Gatherings for larger groups. These offerings involved the following requirements:

- Enabling remote vacation planning and coordination of multiple groups

- Providing greater planning control of the vacation experience and events, for all involved, rather than having customers purchase standard package plans

- Coordinating multiple reservations and parties into a single portfolio

- Providing greater access to such unique Disney events as custom dining experiences, golf reservations, and workshops

- Managing multiple sources of requests for Disney resources from large groups.

Enabling these gatherings with technology required bringing capabilities across business units into a single customer-driven view, accessible from a vacation-planning portal. Planning a small group event can be a complex task, and Disney backs the portal planning tools with access to a Disney vacation planner who helps the event leader take advantage of all the offerings for a given location.

The lesson of the Disney story couldn't be simpler: The technologies that matter to your organization are those that address its fundamental strategic goals and persistent business needs. Those technologies move your enterprise closer to achieving its goals, replace capital, reduce cycle time, trim resources required, or accomplish some combination of these four results.

Such technologies should fill out your vision for IT-enabling your firm. Looking at potential technologies through the lens of goals and persistent business needs is exactly the right way to develop your vision. That's why it's so important to start by knowing your enterprise. Otherwise, you can't know what these persistent needs are. Focusing on goals and needs also provides a common context for the business and the IS organization. Your business colleagues form expectations of technology in terms of these needs and goals, which thus become the implicit criteria for IS success.

It's safer to make long-term investments in the satisfaction of persistent needs because they're unlikely to change in the short run. And because they're wrapped around the fundamentals of the enterprise, their solution is likely to have significant, long-term benefits.

Here's a simple, straightforward process, a matrix, for assessing which potential technologies might be most useful to your enterprise—for deciding, in other words, which technologies will be part of your IT vision:

1. Create a matrix (table 3-1). On the left side, list the strategic intent and strategic endeavors you have identified for your enterprise, and the key questions relating to your firm's economic model and persistent business needs. We've summarized these into some key but standard categories—customers, capital, resources, and cycle time. Revise these or expand on them as appropriate for your business.

2. Along the top of the matrix list the technology candidates—those technologies you think might help your firm achieve its goals or meet its basic needs.

3. Fill out the matrix with concise descriptions of how each technology will address each goal or need, being as specific as possible. Include time frames.

Your understanding of your enterprise's strategic goals and persistent needs will let you cut through the technology hype. You'll be able to focus on the exact purpose, business intent, and expectations for the emerging technology. The first pass through the matrix

TABLE 3-1

Persistent Business Needs Matrix

	Radio-Frequency Identification	Web Services	Wireless
Description	Automated data collection (ADC) technology that enables equipment to read and write to identification tags without contact or line of sight	Application interfaces accessible via Internet standards used for lightweight integration across devices, systems, and locations	Technology supporting point-to-point and point-to-multipoint device networked communications without a physical connection to the network
Impact on Customers	Enhances customer interactions and customer service by enabling inventory assessment without manual intervention; increases revenue by increasing stock availability	Increases the availability of data and application services to customers in a flexible manner	Extends company ability to reach customers at their point and place of need
Impact on Capital	Reduces capital requirements as asset tracking and logistics improvements increase utilization and reduce the amount of inventory required to service customers	Reduces capital demands for technology by increasing reuse and broader use of existing systems and information	Improves capital asset flexibility as assets can be reallocated without requiring a change to the physical or technical infrastructure
Impact on Resources	Reduces efforts to manage inventory and assets and reduces required inventory levels to serve customers	Increases reuse and application of existing systems and business rules, reducing the need for additional applications	Decreases resource requirements as field service and other assets can be dynamically rescheduled and reallocated; increases need for support and management
Impact on Cycle Time	Reduces time and effort to track and trace inventory and other assets; improves replenishment, maintenance, and support cycle times	Accelerates the introduction of new products and services by shortening application development and deployment time	Accelerates cycle time as it decreases the delays between data/decision capture and business response

should readily identify those technologies that offer real promise and those that seem attractive but don't fit your enterprise well.

Do as many passes as necessary to produce a matrix of those technologies you believe should be incorporated into your vision. Include concrete descriptions of how each will address what matters most to your enterprise and its leaders—the basic goals and needs of the firm. Once you're happy with the matrix, it will become the foundation of your vision for IT-enabling your organization.

At this point, when you might think you've finished the vision, there's only one potential problem. You've been doing this on your own. Although you need to do some solid thinking about your vision on your own, the outcome should not be the result of a solitary exercise. Don't go off, develop your IT vision alone, and engrave it in stone. (And, by the way, developing a vision entirely within the IS organization isn't much better.)

When we said new CIO leaders need to develop a vision for IT-enabling their enterprise, we meant the CIO must *lead* that development. You must start with a vision in your own mind, with passion in your heart for enabling your business to succeed using IT. But now you need to take the next leadership step: working with your business colleagues to evolve your vision and theirs into a cohesive vision for the whole enterprise. And of course, you'll have to create the tactical plan for achieving your joint goals. How to do so is the subject of the next three chapters.

4

Shape and Inform Expectations for an IT-Enabled Enterprise

All we've discussed previously leads to this, the unique role of the new CIO leader: bridging the gap between business and technology. To do so, you must have credibility with your executive colleagues, you must be able to lead through influence, you must have a deep understanding of your enterprise, and you must have a vision built on this understanding.[1] But how do you bring all these pieces together to build the bridge that the new world requires?

The first essential step is for you to work with your colleagues on articulating an agreed-upon set of business guiding principles, what we call maxims. These principles or maxims succinctly state what is most important to the enterprise. From business maxims, you can then develop IT maxims. IT maxims are statements that express how your enterprise needs to design and deploy IT across the organization to meet business goals and support the business maxims. These two steps are the building blocks for the bridge between business and IT strategy; they enable you to create shared expectations about the role of IT in your enterprise and are the first steps to making your vision a reality.[2]

Management by Maxims Weaves Together
Business and IT Strategies

Many CIOs find it difficult to identify the IT implications of their firm's business strategy. Broad statements of corporate strategic intent, mission statements, and value propositions are valuable starting points, but often are not enough. You need more, but usually you won't find what you need in documents, because real strategy isn't written down. It's in the heads and hearts of those responsible for implementing it. That's why you have to be part of the process to understand fully what's going on.

What complicates the situation even more is that organizations tend to work on multiple strategic initiatives simultaneously across different organizational boundaries. The synergies across these boundaries are often unclear, which leads to confusion over roles and responsibilities, what knowledge is required to leverage the synergies, and the impact on the product portfolio.

It's not a happy situation for your business colleagues either. The decision-making process around IT initiatives and investments is often convoluted, and the range of possibilities unclear or presented in technical terms. When they authorize expenditure for a large IT-enabled business initiative, managers may still not be sure what they have consented to or what capabilities will be delivered to support their business.

Management by maxims is a process for dealing with this issue.[3] It draws on the strategic context of the enterprise to tease out key business maxims or business principles, and then works on what these mean for IT investments (we'll use the term *maxims* from here on out). This process begins to create a very needed "trail of evidence" that weaves together business and technology strategies. We developed the management by maxims process after tracking how and why some large enterprises obtained better value from their IT dollar. Successful enterprises, it turned out, had a process for surfacing a few critical maxims for which the information and IT implications could then be articulated. Importantly, business and IT executives did this together. Marianne and one of her colleagues, Peter Weill, gave that process its generic name: *management by maxims.*

Maxims are a series of short statements expressing the shared future focus of the business in actionable business terms. A maxim translates aspects of strategic context—strategic intent, business strategies, mission statements, customer value propositions—into terms that can be easily communicated and understood across the organization. Maxims build on each other, starting with the business strategy and culminating with IT maxims, which are necessary to support and implement the business strategy.

The process for integrating business and IT goals is diagrammed in figure 4-1. Business strategies are converted to business maxims, which lead to IT maxims and finally to IT strategies. All this takes place in the context of business and IT governance—how your enterprise makes business and IT-related decisions and allocates responsibilities. Governance—an important subject—will be discussed in chapter 5. For now, we'll focus on the maxims process itself.

In using the term *maxim,* we refer to its classic meaning: statements that specify a practical course of conduct. Business maxims express the shared focus of the business in actionable terms.

The difference between a maxim and a strategy is that a strategy represents how an organization is going to compete in its chosen market. Maxims, on the other hand, represent a shared understanding

FIGURE 4-1

Flow of Business Strategies to IT Maxims

IT strategies flow from enterprise strategic intent via maxims. Each step in the process of integrating business and IT goals flows out of the prior step.

Strategic Intent	Strategic Endeavors	Business Maxims	IT Maxims	IT Governance	IT Strategies

of what needs to happen if the organization is to successfully execute the strategies. Maxims can focus the attention of all employees on key messages and do much to foster common understanding.

Articulate Your Business Maxims

The maxims process is designed to bring together key business and IT executives, first to articulate business maxims and then to identify the implications for what IT capabilities are required for the implementation of strategic initiatives. Usually at the heart of the maxims process is a one-day structured executive workshop. These workshops are often not comfortable experiences for those involved—the encounters tend to foster heated debate about what really matters to the enterprise strategically. In fact, many executives may find the process threatening. Therefore, we strongly recommend engaging external—and neutral—professional facilitators to assist in this process.

Business maxims express several aspects of a business outlook:

- The firm's competitive stance in a clear, actionable way (or, in the not-for-profit sector, the mission and positioning of services)

- The extent to which the enterprise seeks to coordinate business units and to leverage synergies (e.g., autonomy of business units, cross-selling, and sharing of resources)

- The type of capabilities necessary to achieve the strategy (e.g., management of talented people, management of organic growth)

These business maxims dictate the needed type of management of information and IT, which is later articulated as IT maxims. A business maxim for an insurance firm with three business units might be "All sales employees are decision makers about taking new policies and cross-selling." This maxim implies that the firm's IT services need to give all employees (regardless of location) access to the data and systems required to make decisions about insurance policies. This maxim would be one of five or six that, together, strongly and concisely state the firm's business requirements.

Changes in a firm's competitive environment require the firm to reshape its business maxims, because maxims express where a firm is going rather than where it has been. For example, the Royal Automobile Club of Victoria (RACV) is a membership-based provider of vehicle insurance and roadside and other services in Victoria, Australia. RACV has a membership base for roadside service covering more than 60 percent of Victorian drivers, and home and motor insurance covering about 40 percent of the Victoria market. The provider faced little competition until the equivalent organization in a neighboring state extended its base into Victoria, resulting in intense competition in the general insurance area. RACV then needed to develop a strong focus on membership acquisition and customer needs, together with innovative products and services. The revised business maxims articulated in this situation recognized the critical importance of cross-selling and increased the urgency of developing shared customer databases and transaction-processing systems across all the business units in the enterprise.[4]

The maxims process can be used for organizational groups of all sizes, such as business units, departments, and work groups. (Business maxims are also extremely useful for developing other types of maxims, such as human resource or finance maxims.) In the next section, we'll discuss how to turn business maxims into IT maxims.

Using business maxims overcomes three common problems. First, many enterprises have no strategic statements with the required qualities of sharpness and comprehensiveness; maxims provide the refinement and insight needed to bring IT implications to the forefront. Second, some firms have an excess of strategies, which are insufficiently focused and for which the implications are obscure or cannot be readily put into practice; maxims help narrow these down to an actionable few. Third, because business and IT executives often do not collaborate on strategies, the *process* of business and IT executives working together on maxims is at least as important as the maxims they create.

Six categories of business maxims

Although the language of business maxims can be as varied as the people producing them, the maxims can be grouped into six categories. The first three relate back to the notion of value disciplines covered previously. Here are some examples of business maxims in each category. (Appendix B includes more questions about your enterprise strategy and approach to synergy to help you get started creating business maxims.)

1. *Cost focus:* drawing on the value discipline of operational excellence

   - Price products and services at lowest cost

   - Drive economies of scale through shared best practices

2. *Value differentiation as perceived by customers:* drawing on the value discipline of customer intimacy

   - Meet client expectations for quality at reasonable cost

   - Make the customer's product selection as easy as possible

   - Provide all information needed to service any client from any service point

3. *Flexibility and agility:* drawing on the value discipline of product and service innovation

   - Grow in cross-selling capabilities

   - Develop new products and services rapidly

   - Create capacity to manufacture in any location for a particular order

4. *Growth:* how the base of the business will expand

- Expand aggressively into underdeveloped and emerging markets

- Carefully grow internationally to meet the needs of customers that are expanding their businesses

- Target growth through specific product and customer niches

5. *Human resources:* where people policies fit in

   - Create an environment that maximizes intellectual productivity

   - Maintain a high level of professional and technical expertise

   - Identify and facilitate the movement of talented people

6. *Management orientation:* different aspects of business governance and decision making

   - Maximize independence in local operations with a minimum of mandates

   - Make management decisions close to the line

   - Create a management culture of information sharing (to maintain or generate new business)

It's possible to develop a long list of maxims for your enterprise, but we've found that five or six is the most that can be communicated by top management and absorbed by operational managers. Keep in mind that if you don't limit your maxims to the most critical ones, you will probably find that you can't fund and deliver all the business and IT capabilities they imply; some part of the enterprise, often the wrong part, will go lacking. So you and your colleagues must prioritize to ensure that you work with the top six maxims—the six that capture the most important messages for the future.

Limiting the number of maxims is a valuable strategic exercise that will test your focus. Having a large number of maxims indicates fuzzy thinking or overambitious planning and will reduce the chances of successful implementation.

The Implications of Value Disciplines on IT

YOUR ENTERPRISE'S strategic intent has implications for how you want to compete or position your products and services. A helpful way to think about competitive positioning is the notion of three value disciplines, discussed in chapter 2 (operational excellence, customer intimacy, and product leadership). Successful organizations, according to Michael Treacy and Fred Wiersma, usually lead at pursuing one of these basic approaches. Different value disciplines also lead to different types of IT portfolios, often with tailored infrastructure capabilities.

Operational excellence requires transactional systems that are fast, robust, and cost-effective, with strong emphasis on systems that streamline transactions and reduce costs.

Customer intimacy requires greater attention to the storage, analysis, and availability of more extensive information on customers than is necessary simply to complete business transactions. More comprehensive customer databases are required, in both structured form and electronic form as images of letters, notes, perhaps phone conversations, and other documents. Powerful analytic tools will be needed to extract information to manage customer relationships more proactively. It takes significant focus on integrating all the different points of customer contact to present a consistent face to the customer.

It is vital for you to have begun developing your vision for the IT-enabled enterprise before you enter into these discussions with your colleagues. By exploring the answers to these questions, you can bring your enterprise and technology knowledge together to help your colleagues see the potential gains—and you can clearly act as an enterprise leader. Your ability to translate the possibilities of technology into the language of strategic intent may very well change your colleagues' answers to these questions. If you're going to lead your business colleagues, now is the time to do it.

We hope you'll review with your business colleagues your thoughts on which five or six maxims are correct for your enterprise (and your answers to the questions in appendix B). An integral part of

Businesses that compete predominantly on product leadership put more energy into managing the flows of ideas, including the interrelationships between many different parts of the organization, such as R&D, engineering, IT, and marketing. Here, systems (or applications) to support the management of ideas are concerned with context and communication, rather than the content of the data, as in transactional systems. Product leadership often involves more emphasis on support for high-performance teams that might be physically dispersed.

In multibusiness firms, different value disciplines can coexist across the different businesses. This pattern has obvious implications for the nature of synergies in the firm and, in turn, for the extent and depth of firmwide IT initiatives and infrastructure investments. When you are creating firmwide maxims in a company with diverse businesses you need to clearly specify how important synergy is to the future of the business. For example, if one business unit competes on being the lowest cost provider and another on having deep knowledge of individual customers, the two units' management and business processes will be very different. Their information and technology needs will consequently also be very different. It's much harder to achieve synergies across the enterprise in situations like this than when business units compete on the same basis. Therefore, maxims must clarify the level of firmwide synergy implied by the enterprise strategy.

the management by maxims process is asking executives to identify the most critical maxims for the future business individually, and then sharing the results. Often one of the most revealing findings is the wide range of responses among the heads of different business units and even among corporate executives. Achieving clarity and agreement on the answers to these questions is essential to understanding the freedom business units have to make their own decisions and the freedom you have to work across the enterprise.

Now we turn to using business maxims to create IT maxims. IT maxims are what new CIO leaders need to guide the enterprise's expectations regarding the nature and use of technology in the enterprise.

Identify, Communicate, and Validate Your Enterprise's IT Maxims

The second step in shaping and informing the expectations of your business colleagues is to develop IT maxims from the business maxims you've identified. Just about every business decision today has an information and technology implication. And business and IT executives should together identify what these are, at least at a top level. That is the purpose of IT maxims.

IT maxims illuminate the information and technology implications of business maxims

IT maxims are statements that express how your enterprise needs to design and deploy IT across the enterprise to connect, share, and structure information. These maxims result from considering the information and technology implications of your firm's strategic context, business maxims, and persistent business needs.

Here's an example of an IT maxim from a global telecommunications company:

> Customer information must be kept in a consistent form and be accessible to both the customer and the staff any time and anywhere the customer interacts with the firm.

This statement might sound simple enough, but it has profound implications for how customer information is gathered, processed, stored, and made accessible.

IT maxims express fundamental long-term goals and needs for IT and identify the ways your organization needs to accomplish the following tasks:

- Lead or follow in the deployment of IT in its industry (e.g., the role of IT and the required level of investment relative to competitors)

- Process transactions

- Connect and share data sources, information, and systems across different parts of the firm

- Connect and share data sources, information, and systems across the *extended* enterprise, including customers, suppliers, regulators, strategic alliance partners, and so forth

- Maintain common IT architectures, including policies and standards, across the enterprise

- Access, use, and standardize different types of data (such as financial, product, and customer data)

- Identify appropriate measures for assessing the business value of IT

IT maxims need to be concise, compelling, concrete, easily communicated, and readily understood as statements that people throughout the entire organization can use as guidelines for making decisions and taking action. When done well, the maxims bring statements of goals, strategies, and long-term intent a step closer to the tangible world of operations. In short, IT maxims serve as a basis for IT strategizing and planning.

From experience working with many companies, Marianne and Peter Weill found five major areas or categories of IT maxims:

1. *The role of IT:* expectations for IT investments in the enterprise

2. *Information and data:* how information is gathered, stored, accessed, and used

3. *IT architecture and standards:* the level of enforcement of IT architectural guidelines and the standards that flow from these

4. *Communications:* the extent of communication capabilities and services

5. *IT assets:* the nature of hardware and software resources available and how they are made available

Because a major purpose of IT maxims is to explain the IT implications of business strategy and business maxims, IT maxims are best expressed as explanatory sentences. They need to communicate the *why* as well as the *what* of the maxim. Because one business maxim can have more than one IT implication, there are usually many more IT maxims than business maxims.

Real-world examples of translating business maxims into IT maxims

Let's look at how some real-world companies have laid the foundation for their IT strategies through business and IT maxims. ResearchCo (a pseudonym) is a multibusiness international applied research and manufacturing firm. One of ResearchCo's business maxims was "Enable agile business units that leverage appropriate synergies." From this business maxim, ResearchCo developed the following as one of its IT maxims:

> Selected enterprise-wide relevant data must be in a consistent form that facilitates aggregation worldwide. These data are to enable global management of customers and suppliers, provide knowledge of suppliers who are also customers, and globally manage materials and general finance.

Some key words in this maxim are *selected* and *aggregation*. ResearchCo had in the past been a set of autonomous businesses. There was no global understanding of large customers or vendors. As a consequence, large customers sometimes felt ill treated, and ResearchCo missed many volume discounts with large suppliers.

The business maxim responded to the vision of ResearchCo's new CEO, who sought the right balance between requiring cohesiveness and synergy across the enterprise versus granting the local autonomy needed to deal with specific markets. He describes the balance he wanted this way: "Each business has its own strategic needs that must be served while sharing information at an enterprisewide level. Differences among business units that contribute meaningfully to business results are appropriate; differences that don't are not. IT, in the context of our business redesign, is the single most valuable tool to allow us to become more effective in the marketplace." The CEO was able to identify which data needed common systems to be managed across the firm and which did not. As a consequence, ResearchCo took a selective approach to agreed-upon architecture and standards.

Other ResearchCo IT maxims reflected this stance:

- We will adopt an agreed-upon IT architecture for those parts of the IT infrastructure that support shared services, including standards needed to manage knowledge for enterprise decision support.

- We will enforce some standards for hardware and software selection to streamline resource requirements and reduce incompatibilities and costs.

- Provided they meet certain data requirements and selected standards, business units can determine the most appropriate applications for their businesses.

Coors Brewing Company, on the other hand, has a business maxim that emphasizes creating "cross-business synergies." At Coors, this emphasis has led to IT maxims that dictate strong adherence to architectures and standards across all business units, including maximizing synergies across the IS organizations themselves.

Another organization we worked with took a position at the opposite end of the scale, with this business maxim: "We will have a minimum of corporate mandates." This maxim implied no investment in firmwide IT infrastructure or shared services. The organization willingly gave up possible business and IT synergies. In fact, it had only one IT maxim: "IT expertise and technological solutions are shared on an informal basis." Once a year, the leaders of the IS organizations in each of business units came together voluntarily to see if there were experiences they could and should share. This was entirely consistent with the way the business operated. We should note that while this organization had only one enterprisewide IT maxim, CIOs of each individual business unit had business and IT maxims for their own units. The enterprisewide IT maxim, however, dictated that these maxims did not have to agree with one another.

Some examples of IT maxims

Here are some generic examples of IT maxims taken from Weill and Broadbent's study of various organizations.[5] The maxims fall into one of the five aforementioned categories (obviously not all of the example maxims would apply to the same firm).

Role of IT

- We use IT to reduce costs through eliminating duplication of effort.

- IT expenditures must improve customer service levels.

- IT is a service provider focused on satisfying end-user requirements.

Information and data

- When data is first captured, its potential usefulness beyond the area immediately responsible for its capture must be considered. [Note, by the way, what this means for IT personnel's engagement with the business.]

- Business processes and systems must ensure that financial and sales data are captured and maintained together.

- Mobile users must have ready access to the same data they have at the desktop.

IT architecture and standards

- We have a recommended IT architecture, covering hardware, software, and connectivity requirements only.

- We require data standardization for financial and sales data only.

- We will maintain short lists of supported products and preferred vendors in each technology category. Users may purchase other products, but IT will not support them.

Communications

- Our corporate network must provide access to a wide range of applications essential to the delivery of consistent customer service.

- Our corporate network must be capable of carrying high-bandwidth applications such as imaging and videoconferencing.

- We require maximum penetration in the use of real-time Electronic Data Interchange and related technologies to streamline business processes essential to our supply chain.

IT assets

- We will have one set of systems only. These will be the same for customers and employees, including those at the call center.

- We will have common systems across business units that can cross-sell.

- We will always buy rather than build, and when we buy, we implement with minimum customization.

- We will minimize capital investments in IT by leasing or out-sourcing capital assets whenever possible.

The number of IT maxims will vary firm by firm, depending on the breadth and depth of business maxims. IT maxims tend to be longer statements than business maxims, because they address implementation issues. As noted earlier, one business maxim usually leads to several IT maxims. There is often overlap among the IT maxims generated from several business maxims. You will thus need to work on the wording of each maxim to achieve a concise and comprehensive set of statements. Resist the temptation to create a longer list of IT maxims than is absolutely necessary.

You may find it helpful to see a few sample business maxims and the sample IT maxims developed from them. To be concise, we present only one IT maxim (with one exception) for each business maxim, but as we noted, each business maxim usually yields more than one IT maxim.

Business maxims	Related IT maxims
• Service the client from any service point.	• Customer service representatives must have access to a complete file of each customer's relationship with the firm.
• Drive economies of scale through shared best practice.	• We enforce standards of hardware and software selection to reduce costs and streamline resource requirements.
	• We centrally coordinate purchasing of IT from major vendors to minimize costs and ensure consistency.
• Be able to detect and respond to subtle shifts in the marketplace.	• Centrally coordinated information flow should allow all parts of the firm to more easily and quickly spot trends and use these to the firm's advantage.
• We have a management culture of information sharing to generate new business.	• The usefulness of data must be recognized beyond the area immediately responsible for its capture so that it is not lost.
• Be able to develop resources for new products quickly and judiciously.	• New systems must provide a foundation on which new products and services can be added without major modifications.

Remember the great advantage of developing IT maxims: When you finish defining your IT maxims, you should be able to link them all the way back to your enterprise's business strategies, long-term goals, and persistent business needs. This in turn radically improves your ability to inform and engage your business colleagues about IT issues and their impact on the business. Your IT maxims, combined with your vision for the IT enablement of your enterprise, allow you to lead your colleagues and shape informed expectations for the role of IT in your enterprise. They are how you connect business reality to business possibility via technology.

The ability to make such a connection is something most IS organizations find extremely difficult to do. It's the reason we stress developing business maxims first, and then turning them into IT maxims in short order. In describing IT maxims, however, we've probably made them sound overly easy to develop. It is easy, conceptually. But we understand this is like most other areas of business practice: The concepts are simple and straightforward—but often difficult to put into practical use.

Maxim Development: A Procedural Approach

Since IT is your domain, you may be tempted to produce IT maxims yourself or entirely within the IS organization. We understand this impulse, but strongly advise against it. There are significant and long-lasting benefits to involving your business colleagues in the *entire* process.

In the previous section on business maxims, we began to describe some of our experience working on maxims with various enterprises around the world. Let's now outline the entire business and IT maxim development process so that you understand how it all works together.

As we described, the process centers around a day-long workshop involving you, corporate, business unit executives, and selected other IT executives. Participants are interviewed and surveyed prior to the workshop, primarily around their business strategies and execution challenges, their perception of how the enterprise and its businesses compete, and the enterprise needs for synergy versus autonomy.

The first hour of the workshop is spent sharing the tabulated results from those discussions, including the enterprise's strategic context, major strategic initiatives, potential synergies between business units, and the degree to which the firm wants to capitalize on those synergies. Essentially, this discussion is about the participants' responses *in aggregate* to questions asked and answered before the workshop, and how and why those responses varied. The focus is on gaining greater consensus about these responses and working through the reasons for the variations.

The second part of the workshop is devoted to the development of five or six business maxims. In our experience with this process, the group will quickly agree on the first three maxims and then spend considerable effort reaching agreement on the next two or three.

Discussion of the business maxims is usually intense and uncovers plenty of substantial issues (which is why the use of an external facilitator or two is strongly advised). These issues often have been lurking just below the surface in regular executive meetings and now can be openly discussed. An important part of the process is continually explaining why some differences around issues need to be resolved. The participants need to reach resolution to make judicious and well-informed IT decisions.

Again, an open discussion of all these issues contributes to the mutual education of business and IT executives. Initiating this kind of discussion can also help enormously to build your relationships and credibility.

Now the group is ready to tackle IT maxims. Usually we do this by subdividing the group into work groups of three or four participants. We ask each group to begin by developing IT maxims for the category addressing the role of IT in the enterprise. Each group then takes the responsibility for completing maxims in one or two of the other IT maxim categories (information and data, IT architecture and standards, communications, and IT assets). If you follow this process, make sure that each work group contains a diverse mix of participants, including at least one member with a strong IT background.

When the small groups have finished their work, they present the IT maxims they've developed. You're likely to find that much of the whole group discussion focuses on responses to questions in the first category (which every subgroup answered) about expectations for IT investment in the enterprise. Maxims for other areas are also discussed in turn. They are refined, checked for internal consistency and enterprise specificity, and then mapped against the business maxims previously identified. As happened with business maxims, this discussion will probably uncover barriers to the achievement of the IT maxims. Again, the participants need to discuss and agree on a path for resolution of these barriers. The IT maxims will still need some refinement after the workshop. The task of refining the maxims is usually done by a smaller working group, and reviewed later.

At this point, we can take the workshop discussion one further step, especially if the purpose is to identify why future investment will be needed across the whole enterprise as opposed to limiting it to specific businesses.

Use IT Maxims to Identify Infrastructure and Shared-Services Strategies

Discussion around how each business unit competes and the desire (or lack thereof) for greater synergies will inevitably flow into a consideration of how "thick" or "thin" shared services should be across the enterprise. This consideration is underpinned by the enterprise's IT infrastructure investment: To what extent does the enterprise have access to critical IT infrastructure capability? IT infrastructure plays a critical role in every organization, consuming about 60 percent of the IT budget in typical enterprises.[6] As a result, we ask the workshop participants to consider any implications of the enterprise maxims for the firm's IT and infrastructure services.

The focus and language of the IT maxims—from restrictive to expansive—provide a clear guide to the enterprise's infrastructure view: Should infrastructure or shared IT services be seen as extensive or minimal across the enterprise, and what does that mean for levels of enterprisewide IT investment and the level of executive commitment needed? Executives are sometimes surprised that these sorts of decisions are truly theirs to make. When business maxims stress synergy and all the business units compete in a similar way, or share the same group of customers, there is generally a higher level of enterprisewide investment and a greater range of enterprisewide services.[7] But to make the right investments and then obtain value from the services requires much coordination and cooperation across the enterprise. Otherwise, you will have an enabling set of services that fail to return good business value.

At this stage, you can do an illustrative gap analysis in two or three key areas to obtain a rough idea of the extent of shared services required to achieve the business and IT maxims. The base for this is a set of seventy services grouped into ten clusters of capabilities. (See appendix C for a list of these shared services.[8])

Your IS team needs to have done some preliminary work by checking which IT services you already have in place. With that knowledge and with the IT maxims you just developed, you can lead a discussion of which new services will be needed. We suggest focusing here on just two or three service clusters. This will be a "quick and dirty" exercise, but it will highlight for your business colleagues how achieving their business goals depends on having specific IT capabilities. The session is bound to reveal gaps between current IT services and those required at some point in the future.

It's also not unusual for this discussion to reveal the need for a higher level or different pattern of infrastructure investment. If the business executives balk at such change, then you need to point out that the business maxims are probably not achievable. It is time for a reality check. On quite a few occasions, we have explained to the business executives around the table that they won't succeed in their strategies if they don't make the requisite IT investments. As a result, we have sometimes reworked the business maxims to suit a constrained budget. There is no point in creating expectations for IT services that cannot be met, as you well know. This is the time to make that gap explicit. It will be easier to persuade business executives to support higher funding or lowered business expectations while the issues are so clearly laid out. For this reason, don't back off in this discussion thinking you can return to it later.

Finally, the last step in this day-long roundtable discussion is a wrap-up review of how all the enterprise-specific components fit together. These elements include strategies, strategic initiatives, business maxims, IT maxims, and infrastructure requirements, along with the various barriers identified and recorded throughout the day.

These roundtable discussions never fail to generate an agenda of IT strategies and priorities and some sense of the IT investments that the firm's strategic goals and plans will require. The great advantage of the approach is that any outcomes, like an agenda, will receive far more attention and support throughout the enterprise, because they've been developed jointly by IT leaders and business leaders. Your role in the process will also be a powerful illustration of the need and benefit of having a new CIO leader in the executive suite.

How to Reverse Engineer Business and IT Maxims

While the process we've just described works extremely well, it works best if you can bring the right players to the table at the same time. As many CIOs well know, this may be impossible (especially if you are still in the process of building or rebuilding credibility).

John Petrey is executive vice president and CIO of Banknorth, the largest independent bank in New England.[9] When he took the position, he found that the history of the IS organization meant he would be unable to put together an early discussion of IT maxims.

He found the IS leadership team at Banknorth struggling with three challenges. First, IT wasn't pulling its weight in the ongoing operations of the bank. It had problems delivering both daily services and new applications. Consequently—problem number two—managers of the bank's business units didn't value the IS organization.

The units often made IT decisions without involving IS. And third, Banknorth's most senior corporate executives were almost completely disengaged from IT or the work of the IS group.

While fixing the operational problems—daily service delivery and applications development—Petrey also began working on deeper underlying issues within IS, such as poor alignment with the business, limited business acumen within IS, and opaque IS processes. As he worked on these problems, it became clear there was no long-term vision or strategy for IT in the company.

Determining an IT strategy quickly became a priority, but creating one soon proved to be more challenging than Petrey had first thought it would be. The major obstacle was a lack of business strategy documentation at a sufficiently detailed level for the IT implications to be clear.

"I found plenty of what I would call 'artifacts' of strategy, such as e-mails, memos, public statements by executives, and personal conversations," recalls Petrey, "but it was hard to get a handle on business direction that had the sort of detail I needed. I didn't want to develop a set of IT [maxims] in a vacuum. To work, they had to be based on the business directions, and at a reasonably granular level."

Because the enterprise strategy was only evident in what he called artifacts, Petrey had to work backward. He and his IS team reverse engineered a set of business strategies and maxims from the strategic artifacts. From those, they constructed a straw man or what-if set of IT maxims. The team then set about discussing the derived business strategy and the consequent IT maxims with Banknorth executives. From those discussions came a set of formally validated and accepted IT maxims. Now Petrey and his staff have much greater input to the tough decisions around their IT strategy—decisions around investing time, money, and energy to IT-enable the business over the next two or three years.

At this stage, you should have a clear grasp of your enterprise's priorities, your vision for the IT enablement of your enterprise, and, as you finish the maxims process, some solid IT maxims. These maxims will help you build an action plan for IT-related investments and IS leadership and are clearly tied to the enterprise goals. You may be tempted to take your new list of maxims as soon as you have it and start implementing a strategy right away. While maxims do form the basis for your IT strategy, there is another crucial step to turning maxims into sustainable strategies: IT governance. That's where we turn our attention next.

5

Create Clear and Appropriate IT Governance

The focus and priorities of the new CIO leader that we've described so far are all "setting the stage" priorities. To review, so far we've covered how a new CIO leader needs to accomplish the following steps:

- Lead, not just manage

- Know the fundamentals of his or her enterprise—its strategic intents and goals, its persistent business needs, and its key decision makers

- Create a vision for the enterprise as IT-enabled, avoiding hype, but creating a compelling vision for the impact of technology, especially the network era and the Real-Time Enterprise

- Shape expectations for the use and usefulness of IT by using maxims—concise, compelling, and clear statements of direction and guidelines expressing what the enterprise must focus on to accomplish its goals

Leadership, vision, and maxims all set the stage for getting things done. Now we begin to look at the processes that enable you to accomplish the new CIO leader's task of enabling the enterprise to enjoy the benefits of technology. The first step is developing and implementing good IT governance.[1] This is still the demand side of CIO leadership, for governance determines whose demands are met. Beyond that, good governance gets those who demand IT services deeply involved in decision making.

Governance concerns something very basic and important: how IT decisions are made, who gets to make them, and who's accountable for what. IT governance is not synonymous with IT management. Governance concerns input and decision rights to drive desirable behaviors, whereas IT management is making and implementing specific IT decisions.[2]

While perhaps not sounding like the most exciting topic, effective IT governance is absolutely crucial for a new CIO leader. In fact, you might think of good IT governance as your secret weapon for success. Many CIOs think initially that governance will make their lives more complex. They soon understand the opposite is true: Done right, it will make their life much simpler.

New CIO leaders cut through the increasing complexity of technology and organizations by using IT governance to bring together top-level business and IT executives for better decision making. Governance is what takes maxims from words to reality, what ties together and *keeps together* IT strategies and business strategies. Good governance enables faster, better decision making. It provides a clear line of sight for converting IT maxims into strategic actions. Governance is especially critical for CIOs who are in maintaining-competitiveness environments and who must constantly work to balance initiatives that address efficiency and those that address effectiveness.

Why You Need Strong Systems of IT Governance

Why is good IT governance so important? For many reasons, good IT governance helps the enterprise make better and faster IT-related decisions.

1. *Good IT governance builds trust.* It's impossible to sustain trust in your leadership as CIO if your colleagues across the enterprise don't understand and support how IT-related decisions are made. When IT governance is done right, it makes IT-related decisions and accountabilities transparent and therefore trustworthy.

2. *Good IT governance means better delivery.* Ultimately your credibility will depend on delivering business value from IT. When IT governance works properly, it will ensure that only IT projects in support of business goals and likely to achieve success (as defined by your business colleagues) will be undertaken and assigned resources. Therefore, IT projects are more likely to receive ongoing support from business leaders, and completed projects will more often be seen as important business successes—all of which will build your and your IS organization's credibility.

3. *Good IT governance synchronizes IT strategy with business strategy.* A difficult aspect of modern business life is that business strategy and IT strategy, almost by necessity, move at different rhythms and in different cycles. As recently as the early 1990s, business strategy was developed by an extensive planning process that resulted in a documented three- to five-year plan. In that environment, IT projects that lasted one, two, or even three years could be undertaken with reasonable expectations. As business cycles have sped up, however, there are virtually no static three-year plans left. More and more, planning and execution happen simultaneously. Business strategies, driven by rapid changes in the business context, change more frequently. That's where the need for strong systems of governance come in. Real ability to integrate business and IT can exist only when clear and robust systems of IT governance exist. Nothing can reduce action to a crawl as quickly as uncertainty about who decides what and who's responsible for what. With good IT

governance, the enterprise is more effective at synchronizing IT strategy with business context.

4. *Good IT governance encourages desirable behaviors in the use of IT.* Ultimately, IT governance creates the environment, the foundation, for desirable behaviors in the use of IT— behaviors such as cost lowering, customer data sharing, or the stimulation of innovation. The encouragement of these activities is important because you cannot be everywhere in your organization, personally influencing and checking every IT-related decision. Think of good governance as an extension of yourself, of your vision for the enterprise, and of your agenda for supporting business growth throughout the enterprise. Good governance helps ensure that actions taken by individuals and groups throughout the enterprise will be consistent with the goals of the enterprise, whether or not you or other members of your staff are present.

IT governance is difficult because of constant change—in the environment, in your industry, in personnel, in technology, in everything—that affects how you and your executive colleagues think about the future and the direction your enterprise should take. But IT governance is something every new CIO leader needs to get right, and you cannot leave it unsettled or unclear.

Over the course of this chapter, we'll discuss various forms of governance. There's more than one way to do it, and the right form will depend on your enterprise and how it prefers to work. Let's begin with a few characteristics of effective IT governance and how your IT governance works now.

Six Markers of Effective IT Governance

There is much folklore and many platitudes about good governance. To determine what truly separates the good from the mediocre and bad in IT governance, we worked with more than 250 organizations in a study with the MIT Sloan Center for Information Systems Research. From that study, we found that enterprises with effective IT governance, that is, where such governance positively influenced business goals, shared six common markers.[3]

Clearly differentiated business strategies

Given all that we've discussed so far, it shouldn't be surprising that the first marker of good IT governance concerns business strategy rather than IT. We asked each enterprise we studied to rate the importance of the three value disciplines—operational excellence, customer intimacy, product or service leadership and innovation (chapter 2)—on their future business strategy and operations. On average, those enterprises that thought everything was important scored low on effective IT governance. Higher IT governance performance went hand in hand with clear and well-differentiated business strategies. A focused business strategy makes it easier to concentrate on desirable behaviors in all management processes, including IT governance.

Clear business objectives for IT investments

Enterprises that focused on specific objectives for their IT investments—such as improving product quality, reducing time to market, or improving employee collaboration—also showed more effective IT governance. By putting their energies into fewer, more important areas, the businesses had a better chance of delivering good results. Good governance ensured that business objectives were clear and well understood.

High-level executive participation in IT governance

Perhaps this is obvious, but we can't emphasize it enough. CEO involvement had the greatest positive correlation of all factors studied, followed by the COO, business unit leaders, and business unit CIOs. Involvement of corporate CIOs and CFOs had lower impact, but still had a significant positive correlation with IT governance performance. An easy and effective way to gauge executive involvement, we found, was executive understanding of how IT governance worked. CIOs in our research indicated that, on average, 39 percent of their business executives could accurately describe their enterprise's IT governance arrangements. The higher the percentage, though, the higher the enterprise's governance performance.

Stable IT governance, with few changes from year to year

Stability in governance processes proved to be important. Too many changes made it hard for business executives to understand how IT governance operated. If they didn't understand it, it simply wouldn't work as well (see previous marker). The top third of governance performers made only one change per year, whereas the bottom third made three changes, on average. The trade-off was clear. More changes generally led to lower performance (though changes are unavoidable when enterprise strategy changed).

Well-functioning, formal exception processes

Enterprises with effective IT governance had established ways of dealing with exceptions and disagreements. Take the example of an investment bank we worked with. A business unit wanted to introduce a new product that required software that didn't meet the agreed-upon architectural guidelines for products. The first proposal was knocked back by the investment committee because of the nonstandard software. But there was an exceptions process in place, which the unit then pursued. The initiative was ultimately approved on the grounds that it was innovative and provided potentially new revenue sources. The software was monitored carefully, and eventually it became part of the bank's approved products.

In the words of Peter Weill at MIT, "Exception processes are how organizations learn."[4] If you don't have procedures for handling exceptions, you might find you're missing great opportunities. But the exception processes that work are known and transparent to all participants. Enterprises with such processes were viewed as visible and fair; this in turn led to fewer nonsanctioned IT decisions or investments. You can look at this from the inverse perspective: If you have much nonsanctioned IT activity in the enterprise, your IT governance is probably not effective or appropriate for your organization. (Don't confuse this problem with rigid, dictatorial enforcement of IT governance, which won't work, either.)

Formal methods of communication

Effective IT governance employs formal communication methods and mechanisms, which serve to reinforce the relationships between CIOs and executive colleagues. These formal methods also help strengthen many of the other markers of good governance, such as stability, executive participation, and exception processes.

Upon examining this list of markers, you may wonder which are causes and which are effects. It's impossible to answer definitively; all we can say is that we know these markers go hand in hand with good governance. Just as credibility and results operate in a virtuous or destructive cycle, these markers and good IT governance either reinforce or undermine each other. Good governance makes it easier to have executive involvement, and executive involvement both strengthens the process and helps ensure better outcomes, which in turn improve executive involvement.

The Three Major Elements of IT Governance

We suspect that the preceding list has revealed at least one area in which your IT governance can be improved. The first step toward improvement is to create an accurate picture of your current governance. Creating that picture requires defining some terms.

Three major elements make up any IT governance system, and we use specific terms to describe them:

1. *Domains:* the various IT areas in which decisions need to be made

2. *Styles:* who makes decisions and who has input in each of the IT domains

3. *Mechanisms:* techniques and organizational devices used to implement governance styles. A committee is an example of a much-used mechanism.

Let's look at each of these components in more detail.

Domains

Domains are the major intersections between business and technology and represent where decisions must be made. There are five domains.

IT maxims: We discussed maxims in chapter 4. Because the business environment changes constantly, your business maxims will change too, in turn requiring changes in your IT maxims. An important piece of IT governance is recognizing that the maxims you've created must change and determining who will change them and how these people will do it.

IT architecture: What technical guidelines and standards will be used in your enterprise? IT architecture defines the technical choices that guide the enterprise in satisfying business needs.

IT infrastructure strategies: How will the extent and nature of shared services be decided? IT infrastructure strategies describe whether, why, and how the enterprise will build and sustain a tailored set of shared and reliable services to meet business goals. For example, implementing customer profiling requires the development and management of certain standard applications across business units.

Business application needs: What applications are needed? These are business applications that must be acquired or built to meet business requirements, including those for business units or divisions.

IT investment and prioritization: Prioritization is important for IT investments. It addresses questions such as how much and where to invest, how to justify and approve IT-enabled business initiatives, and how to ensure their accountability.

Governance styles

IT governance styles define who has input into decisions and who gets to make decisions—specifically which levels and parts of the organization are involved. Different governance styles invoke different combinations of business and IT executives at different organizational levels. A different governance style may be used for each of the five IT domains. For convenience, we used a naming convention for the different domains based on the key participants.

In a *business monarchy,* only business executives have the decision rights. At the United Nations Children's Fund (UNICEF), for example, the so-called C-level executives (CEO, CFO, COO, and CIO) have the decision rights for four domains: IT maxims, IT infrastructure strategies, IT architecture, and IT investment and prioritization.

In an *IT monarchy,* IT leadership holds the decision rights. At one U.K. bank we studied, the Information Management Leadership Group holds the decision rights for three domains: IT infrastructure strategies, IT architecture, and business application needs.

In a *feudal* style, business unit leaders, or their delegates, possess the decision rights, and authority is local. This style is found in enterprises with relatively autonomous business units and is often used to provide local responsiveness.

In the *federal* style, governance rights are shared by C-level executives and at least one other business group. At one international automobile manufacturer that was part of our study decision rights in two IT domains—IT maxims and IT investment and prioritization—

are held jointly by its Global (Internal) Board (which parallels the executive committee of a North American corporation) and business division leaders.

In a *duopoly*, the rights are shared by IT executives and just one other business group (as opposed to multiple levels of business executives), such as C-level executives or business unit leaders. A duopoly is the governance style for all domains at a large financial services group in South Africa we studied. The organization's IT governance style seeks to balance pressures for both synergy and autonomy.

The sixth style, *anarchy*, exists where individual process owners or end users have the decision rights. Ad hoc decisions are made to satisfy local needs.

Governance mechanisms

Mechanisms, the literal ways and means of implementing styles, can be formal, such as a standing committee, or informal, such as discussions with colleagues. Each governance style has many mechanisms that can bear out this style, as the following possibilities show. (We have omitted anarchy as it is not a commonly used style in large enterprises.)

Business monarchy

- Executive committee (e.g., CEO and direct reports; CIO is included if he or she is a direct report)

- Operating committee (often a subgroup of executives such as the CEO, CFO, and COO working together)

- Investment council

- CEO decree or fiat

IT monarchy

- IT leadership council (usually comprising IT executives from both corporate and business units)

- IT executive (CIO and direct reports)
- CIO decree or fiat

Feudal

- Business project council *or* division leaders forum (presidents of each of the businesses)
- Business process owners
- One-on-one meetings of CIO and business president

Federal

- Business investment council (comprising corporate and business unit executives)
- Business application forum
- IT policy board (comprising corporate, business unit, and IT executives)

Duopoly

- Business–IT relationship managers
- Information steering group (comprising corporate business and IT executives)
- Project council (comprising senior business and IT executives)
- Enterprise architecture council (where business executives are included)

These mechanisms can be specific to one IT domain or span multiple domains. In theory there are as many governance mechanisms as human ingenuity can devise, but the most common include these mechanisms:

Executive committee: Typically this mechanism makes major, enterprisewide decisions, including IT-related decisions, at the

C level. This approach encourages a holistic view, but unless there is top-level IT input via the CIO, the decisions might not be well informed about IT issues.

IT leadership committee: This group typically includes the most senior IT executives across the enterprise. This mechanism is particularly important in large, multibusiness enterprises, where responsibilities for infrastructure services are shared.

Process teams: The teams are composed of members from many parts of the enterprise. Including IT members on these teams will help insure that IT is used to best advantage when business processes are reengineered.

Business–IT relationship managers: These executives act as intermediaries between the business and the IS organization and play a critical daily two-way role. They help bridge any communication gaps between IT and business units.

IT councils: These groups generally include both business and IT executives and focus on several levels of IT policies and investments, often in more detail than considerations at the executive committee level.

Architecture committees: Members of these committees define architectural guidelines and often involve both business and IT management.

Service-level agreements, chargeback arrangements, tracking of IT projects and resources consumed, and tracking the business value of IT are other mechanisms often used for various purposes in many enterprises.

Develop a Matrix to See What Your IT Governance Looks Like Today

Now that we've defined the three elements of governance, you can create a matrix to depict how your IT governance is working today.

Corporate Boards Are Now an Important Part of IT Governance

Enterprises—both commercial companies and not-for-profit organizations—are controlled by systems of governance, that is, by arrangements about what decisions get made, who makes them, and who is accountable. At the top level, boards are responsible for corporate governance. That is, they ensure that strategic direction is defined and monitored, that the CEO is effective, and that necessary controls and accountabilities are in place. The executive team, led by the CEO, is responsible for shaping and implementing informed strategies, encouraging desirable behaviors, and managing key assets for sound performance.

From a board perspective, the significance of information and technology as assets has risen dramatically since the late 1990s. With the increasing importance of IT and the prevalence of IT-influenced risk, boards must now address their IT issues swiftly and with expertise. Just as boards monitor financial risk, so too do they need to monitor information and technology asset risks.

Some boards are now creating an IT committee in the same way they already have audit and risk committees. In the words of one nonexecutive director, "the role of the IT committee is not delving into the technology. It is to focus attention on major areas of initiative and risk and being able to 'walk through' the whole process with executive management."

Clearly, if your organization's board has formed an IT committee, this mechanism needs to be taken into account and included in your governance plans.

This matrix will provide several benefits. It will clarify how the many pieces of IT governance fit together. It will also give you a clearer picture of the current situation in your enterprise. Finally, a matrix can serve as an effective way to begin discussions with your business colleagues and your IT team about governance.

To create a matrix of your IT governance systems, list across the top of the matrix the five IT domains (see table 5-1, which we've filled in for DBS, a multinational Asian bank). On the vertical axis,

TABLE 5-1

IT Governance Arrangements Matrix for DBS, a Multinational Bank

		DOMAIN								
	IT Maxims		IT Infrastructure Strategies		IT Architecture		Business Application Needs		IT Investment and Prioritization	
STYLE	Input	Decision	Input	Decision	Input	Decision	Input	Decision	Input	Decision
Business Monarchy		Corp Office CIO						Corp Office CIO		Proj Council Corp Office
IT Monarchy			CIO IT Leaders	CIO IT Leaders		Arch Office CIO				
Feudal										
Federal					Biz Leaders IT Leaders		Biz Leaders Biz Proc Own			
Duopoly	Biz Leaders IT Leaders								Biz Leaders IT Leaders BT Managers	

GOVERNANCE MECHANISMS:

Arch Office, office of architecture
Corp Office, corporate office (includes CEO, CIO, and three business heads)

Biz Leaders, business leaders
IT Leaders, IT leadership group

BT Managers, business technology relationship managers
Biz Proc Own, business process owners

CIO, CIO office and staff
Proj Council, regional project councils

list the IT governance styles (again, we have omitted "anarchy" as it is not a commonly used style in large enterprises). Then fill in the matrix by identifying, in the appropriate cells, who has the input and decision rights and what mechanisms they use to exercise those rights for each domain. You should have one cell filled in for each column—indicating the style for each of the domains by inserting the name of the key mechanism used for that style. Transparency in IT governance matters. It's hard to know who is responsible for what—with considerable impact on decision speed—if there is no clear picture of your governance systems laid out for all to see.

DBS, which has been growing rapidly through acquisition, actively uses IT governance to bring about change and help drive growth. The changes involve shifting to a greater focus on customers and increasing synergies across business units without abandoning local accountability.

To achieve these strategic goals, DBS business executives, including the CIO, have agreed on a set of IT maxims, which they carry through in their decisions about both business applications and IT investments and priorities. Every initiative is assessed against an agreed-upon set of financial and nonfinancial criteria. Within IT, a group of business–IT relationship managers who report to the CIO work at the intersections between the IS organization and the rest of the enterprise. The IT leadership group has the decision rights for IT infrastructure strategies and IT architecture.

As you can see in the matrix (table 5-1), DBS uses different styles for different purposes, with at least eight mechanisms or decision makers. The style used depends on the IT domain and the nature of related business governance.

Assess the Needed Changes in Governance

Once you've created the matrix and have a clear picture of how your governance functions today, you can begin to evaluate the changes needed to more effectively link your IT governance to your business strategy. Keep in mind that you will need to plan carefully and stage the implementation of any changes—you can't change all of your governance at once, or you'll bring everything to a standstill and create widespread confusion.

The first point to consider when redesigning your IT governance is, again, the enterprise context. It's important to know your enterprise and define your business maxims before you attempt to redesign IT governance. You are most likely to find that the maxims process will reveal a need to improve your governance and will highlight who should be involved.

Consider your business orientation

Enterprises vary in their *business governance*—that is, how business decisions are made and implemented. Business governance creates the context for IT governance. For example, if your enterprise strategy leads the organization to be highly centralized, this has obvious implications for IT decision rights and accountabilities. On the other hand, if your enterprise has a strong history of autonomous business units, this would have equally strong implications. As we noted, an IT governance system that creates and attempts to enforce strict, enterprisewide standards in an autonomous business unit enterprise will only be self-defeating.

Three business orientations—synergistic, agile, and autonomous—shape different business governance arrangements (table 5-2). While your organization probably has some attributes of all three, one will (or should) predominate. The business maxims you developed with your executive colleagues should reveal which of the three orientations predominates in your enterprise and in each business unit. If you can't tell which orientation tends to prevail, engage your business colleagues again; otherwise, you will struggle with your IT governance.

These business orientations create the context for IT governance—take a quick look at your matrix, and you may immediately see some disparities between your current IT governance and your enter-

TABLE 5-2

Business Orientations and Governance Arrangements

Enterprise Characteristics	BUSINESS ORIENTATION		
	Synergistic Enterprises	Agile Enterprises	Autonomous Enterprises
Business Processes	Standardized and integrated across business units	Modular, adaptable, and easily combined	More distinct and independent
Coordination and Skills	Specified synergies mandated, duplication removed	Firmwide, front-line responsiveness	Local innovation and competitive strengths
Management Systems for Coordination	Business units focus on both unit and firmwide strategy	Business units adapt to local conditions within firmwide organizing logic	Enterprise financial and risk management mandates only
Information and Information System	Substantial integrated firmwide infrastructure, shared services	Modular capabilities centrally coordinated and architected	Thin layer firmwide, each business unit infrastructure tailored

Source: ©2003 MIT Sloan Center for Information Systems Research (Weill). Peter Weill and Jeanne Ross, *IT Governance: How Top Performers Manage IT Decision Rights for Superior Results* (Boston: Harvard Business School Press, 2004).

Synergistic enterprise details drawn from Jeanne Ross et al., "Aligning IT Architecture with Organizational Realities," *MIT Sloan CISR Research Briefing* 3, no. 1A (March 2003). Agile enterprises details drawn from Nancy B. Duncan, "Capturing Flexibility in Information Technology Infrastructure: A Study of Resource Characteristics and Their Measure," *Journal of Management Information Systems* 12, no. 1 (fall 1995): 37–57, and V. Sambamurthy and Robert W. Zmud, "The Organizing Logic of IT Activities in the Digital Era: A Prognosis of Practice and a Call for Research," *Information Systems Research* 11, no 2: 105–114. Information and information systems details, and autonomous enterprise details, drawn from Timothy R. Kayworth, Debabroto Chatterjee, and V. Sambamurthy, "Theoretical Justification of IT Infrastructure Investments," *Information Resource Management Journal* 14, no. 3 (July–Sept. 2001): 5–14, and Peter Weill, Mani Subramani, and Marianne Broadbent, "Building IT Infrastructure for Strategic Ability," *Sloan Management Review* 44, no. 1 (fall 2002): 57–66.

prise's business orientation. Don't be discouraged if you do find many differences. That's a situation we see often. You may even be comforted to understand finally why you've struggled to get some specific initiatives off the ground. While some aspects of IT governance are common among the three orientations, each orientation will dictate a different emphasis within the IT governance that supports it.

Shape new governance efforts to fit business orientation

Many IT mechanisms are necessary in every orientation (table 5-3). For example, councils or committees may appear in all three orientations. What will differ among the councils or committees will be their membership, the way the groups are used, where they

TABLE 5-3

Key IT Governance Styles and Mechanisms

Governance Attributes	BUSINESS ORIENTATION		
	Synergistic Enterprises	Agile Enterprises	Autonomous Enterprises
Decision-Making Styles	• Tight corporate coupling between business and IT executives	• Business and IT leaders combine for specific purposes	• IT works with individual business units and process owners
	• Top-down man-dated technology decision making	• Enterprisewide arrangements emphasize coordination and learning	• Emphasis on local business decision making
Focus of Key Mechanisms	• Well-developed business and decision processes	• Extensive use of IT maxims	• CIOs work through one-on-one negotiation
	• Executive-level committees	• Business ownership of IT projects	• Standards achieved through socializa-tion and peer pressure
	• High-level, centrally reporting business–IT relationship managers	• Planned IT–business educa-tion experiences	• Business–IT ser-vice arrangements are in place
		• Transparency and communication	
Case Examples	• ADVO, direct-mail advertiser	• Duke Energy International	• Valeo, European automotive supplier

© 2003 Gartner, Inc. and MIT Sloan Center for Information Systems Research (Weill).

are located in the enterprise, and the extent and nature of their responsibilities.

Synergistic enterprises are enterprises that face strong pressures for firmwide integration from their marketplaces, and/or those which want to leverage similarities across their business units. Synergistic enterprises need clear decision processes, executive input, and high-level business–IT relationship managers. In striving for business unit synergy, these enterprises take an enterprisewide approach as much as possible. They increase integration, leverage similarities, and implement common processes across business boundaries. They also mandate standards, especially for IT infrastructure components, such as desktops, e-mail, IT security, enterprise resource planning, and other enterprisewide applications.

We found in top-performing synergistic organizations that some governance styles worked better than others. For IT maxims and IT investment and priority decisions, it was critical to have top-level, enterprisewide business involvement in both input and decision making. For IT infrastructure and IT architecture decisions, top-down technology mandates were generally made by IT monarchies, but with high-level business input.

ADVO, the U.S. direct mail advertiser, illustrates the tight coupling necessary between business and IT decision making in a synergistic firm. Its top two IT governance mechanisms—an IT steering committee and an IT prioritization team—are mainly composed of business members. The IT steering committee, with eight business functional heads, makes IT capital spending decisions and monitors progress monthly on large projects. The IT prioritization team governs the expense side of IT. Each business function is represented on the team, which meets every two weeks with IT's applications maintenance director. Each function brings its top three maintenance service requests to the meeting, and from that total list, the team approves the top ten items, based on established criteria.

Agile enterprises aim to make decisions and take action faster than their competitors. Their nimbleness comes from paying close attention to their markets, generally at a local level, and their enter-prisewide structures emphasize the coordination—rather than the complete integration—of processes and other activities. These enter-prises should emphasize maxims, education about IT capabilities for business executives and professionals, and communication about how different parts of the enterprise are using IT effectively. For example, IT executives at Duke Energy International (DEI) use IT maxims to inform and guide faster IT-related decision making in their sprawling company. Their maxims explain when there is a need to coordinate and when there isn't. In DEI's experience, good maxims shorten decision processes and lead to better relationships because the ground rules are very clear.

Agile enterprises also tend to foster strong business ownership of IT projects. At DEI, the corporate investment process is the same for all investments, including IT. Business leaders define the busi-ness case and are responsible for delivering results.

Autonomous enterprises provide little central guidance; gover-nance must depend on one-on-one negotiation and peer socializa-tion by the CIO and his or her team. The goal of an autonomous enterprise is to un-tether units so that they can compete most effec-tively in their local markets. IT governance must reflect this autonomous decision making with a focus on the front lines, not the corporate center.

Standards—where they exist—are achieved through socializa-tion and peer pressure. The CIO of Valeo, a European auto parts company we worked with, describes the power of peer pressure: "When you have a hundred plants that have implemented a stan-dard on time, it's hard for the others to convince anyone they can't do the same." Business unit performance metrics are published reg-ularly, and none of the units wants to score at the bottom. This peer pressure encourages the units to implement IT and other functional standards as fast as they can.

Often, corporate IS groups in autonomous firms act as internal service providers for IT infrastructure, leaving the applications to the business units. Service-level agreements, benchmarking, and chargeback arrangements tend to be more important in this context and are often similar to those of external service providers.

Sometimes, autonomous enterprises use mandates to achieve greater synergies in specific areas. Groups such as finance, human resources, and IT are expected to provide common infrastructures, which can present a challenge in an autonomous enterprise unless the groups are given more central control than usual.

What Works and What Doesn't

Obviously, IT governance is not one-size-fits-all. That being said, during the course of our research, we have reached some general conclusions about what works well and what doesn't in most enterprises, all else being equal.

IT-only and business-unit-only decision rights usually don't work well

When the IT leadership team owns the decisions rights for IT maxims—that is, IT by itself gets to define all IT maxims—we tended to see ineffective governance. IT maxims usually need to be validated by business executives. We found a similar result for the decision rights around business applications needs. Where they were owned by business units only, we often found ineffective IT governance. Increasingly, enterprises are making major decisions about business applications at the corporate level by the executive committee (with input from the CIO, if he or she is not already a member of that group). The purpose is to foster better investment decisions by taking into account the broad interests of the whole enterprise.

Autonomous enterprises provide the only exception to the rule that IT-only and business-unit-only decision rights usually don't work well. Autonomous ventures lack enterprisewide business drivers.

Here we found some effective approaches where executives had given the decision rights for IT maxims to the IS organization, and for business application decisions to the business unit leaders. But this seemed to be the only instance in which IT or business monarchies worked well.

Decision making that tightly couples business and technology executives does work well

Top IT governance performers usually bring together senior business and technology executives for joint decision making in two of the IT domains: IT maxims and major IT investment and prioritization. From CIOs in such companies we often hear things like, "There is no such thing as an IT project here. They're all business change projects." At DBS, for example, business unit heads have authority for all tactical investments. One of three regional project councils reviews and approves investments between $1 million and $5 million, or any regional initiative. This is the same mechanism used for all investments, whether they concern IT-related initiatives, new banking products, human resources, or properties. The corporate office handles any investment over US$5 million. IT-related investment decisions are made on the recommendation of the CIO.

Four governance mechanisms have the greatest impact

The mechanisms used to implement governance vary in their effectiveness. Not surprisingly, the most effective are the four we have found that most foster business involvement. These mechanisms are business–IT relationship managers, IT councils composed of business and IT executives, executive committees, and IT leadership groups, which bring together corporate and business unit IT executives across the enterprise. If you don't already have these mechanisms in place, you should work on assembling them as you strive to improve IT governance.

The IT leadership team is critical for infrastructure and architecture decisions

Once IT maxims and investment guidelines are well established, they provide the guidelines for IT infrastructure strategy decisions, which are generally made by IT leadership groups with input from business colleagues. However, the IT leadership must pay attention to business maxims when making infrastructure decisions. Too often, these decisions end up being swayed by IT's desire for simplification and rationalization, rather than the needs of the business. The same holds true for IT architecture decisions. While the decision rights for IT architecture generally rest with IT leadership groups, the decisions need to be constantly evaluated against the business maxims so that architecture decisions are not being overly influenced by existing skills and knowledge in IS.

Once you've mapped out your current governance, compared it to your business and IT maxims for consistency, and made the necessary changes, then you can be confident in moving toward an IT strategy. The governance system you have created provides a firm foundation for ensuring that your IT strategy is perpetually synchronized with business strategy, no matter how business strategy changes, or how frequently. Now we're ready to build ongoing IT strategies that support business goals and implement your vision.

6

Weave Business and
IT Strategies Together

Many CIOs have an IT strategy. New CIO leaders will have strategies that clearly and effectively weave together business strategies and IT decisions. The difference is that new CIO leaders' IT strategies are built on knowledge of their enterprises, vision, business maxims, and IT governance. In this chapter, we'll explore exactly how to develop an IT strategy on these foundations.[1]

Create and Implement an IT Strategy on Governance Foundations

---

Your IT strategy will take your business-driven IT maxims to the next level of specificity: a targeted set of objectives, initiatives, and investments for a specific period. You can't create a good IT strategy without good governance.

Let's consider the context. We've gone from understanding your enterprise's strategic goals, the context and the persistent business needs of your business or agency, to developing IT maxims based on that understanding. These maxims, or principles, are guidelines to action because they connect IT to the overall purposes and priorities of the enterprise as a whole.

But maxims are guidelines, not actions. You and your IS organization need a timely IT strategy that tells you where to focus your efforts and resources. Your governance arrangements will enable you to create an appropriate strategy.

Governance is critical here for two reasons: First, because there's always more IT work to do than can be done, choices must be made. Some projects get done, and some do not. Some investments are made, and others are not. Governance provides the means of making these often difficult and contentious trade-off decisions. Second, things change. Objectives and needs that dictated the selection of one strategy over another often shift. Business conditions and goals rarely remain the same over time. Governance provides for the continuing oversight of strategies, so that any changes and adjustments can be made in an expeditious but clear and thoughtful way.

Your governance systems indicate who gets to decide on IT maxims or principles, architecture, infrastructure strategies, business application needs, and IT investment and prioritization. Your IT strategy is about the *content* of the each of those same five domains and their implementation over a defined period. To ensure that your IT strategy clarifies the necessary areas, it should include at least the following:

- A statement of the *content* of the IT maxims, that is, the guidelines that will drive other decisions.

- The key enterprise architecture decisions. These are your technical choices for all forms of media, including data, hardware, software, communications, and possibly processes, and the level to which each choice is mandated. (Is it required, preferred, or optional?)

- How your IT infrastructure capabilities or processes are offered. You need to know which services or processes are to be centralized or delivered as shared services, and which are to be decentralized or provided at individual business levels.

- What business applications are to be retained, which are to be replaced, and which new ones are to be put in place.

These elements determine where financial and other resources should be allocated to maximize business value.

The key to an effective IT strategy for many enterprises is to take a portfolio approach. Good decisions about architectures, infrastructure capability, and applications can create an IT portfolio that achieves in total the highest business value across the enterprise. Think of a financial or an R&D portfolio with different risk and return approaches over a certain time. The portfolio can be, and often needs to be, reconfigured to fit changing conditions; an example might be the need during tough economic times to shift funds into investments with lower risk and short-term returns.

Your IT strategy should develop and sustain a portfolio of services and capability. At the heart of the strategy is prioritization and the investment decisions you and your business colleagues make. Choices *will* have to be made—constantly—in an orderly fashion. Prioritization, in turn, requires disciplined governance based on a good understanding of enterprise goals and the careful balancing of multiple evaluation criteria.

Consider the alternative to this approach, which is to continue the standard IS approach from the 1990s. This approach responds to any service request and measures performance by the ability to manage the request queue, based on available resources and user clout. Project advocates inflate expected benefits, minimize cost estimates, imply that their initiative is mandatory, whisk aside notions of risk, and even force acceptance with their political power.

However, increased financial pressures, business realization of IT's central importance, declining IS credibility, and, most of all, the search for business value from IT all require the replacement of this approach by the one we describe here. Our approach leads to better decisions by halting low-value, conflicting, and redundant work. It forces a discussion of the real business issues and leads to far better integration of IT with the enterprise. It creates an IT strategy based on the good governance approaches outlined in the previous chapter.

The result will be a solid portfolio of IT-related projects and decision processes that enable quick decisions and shift resources as needed.

Making a portfolio management process work requires both strong governance and accountability among participants. Many enterprises we've seen form an investment council (IC), a governance mechanism composed of business and functional heads. The council evaluates, prioritizes, and selects major initiatives; allocates resources; and routinely reviews portfolio performance. Besides these IT decisions, the council might make investment decisions in many areas, as was the case described earlier for DBS's series of project councils. Or, the IC might focus just on information and IT investment decisions.

Investment council membership typically includes the CIO, COO, CFO or financial controller, strategic planner, and the heads of the business units. The CEO may or may not be a member, depending on the enterprise's culture. The council may be a subset of the executive committee or IT council. People setting enterprisewide priorities on the IC must be able to take an enterprisewide view and are usually a level above the project sponsors (except for very large initiatives). The purpose of the IC is to ensure that the following objectives are met:

- Priorities are driven by business strategy and are periodically reviewed

- Business case data is realistic

- Initiatives not meeting requirements are canceled

- The portfolio reflects current and emerging business needs

- Risk is understood and managed to appropriate tolerance levels

Table 6-1 presents one way we have seen enterprises effectively break down accountabilities among those involved in setting IT strategy.

UNICEF, a United Nations agency, offers a unique opportunity to look at how IT strategy was developed and implemented in the context of effective governance. Beginning in the late 1990s, IT

TABLE 6-1

IT Strategy Roles and Accountabilities

Role	Accountabilities
Investment Council (IC)	The decision-making and oversight group that is composed of business and functional heads and that prioritizes and selects initiatives and allocates resources
Business Sponsor	The business executive responsible for requesting approval for an initiative, supporting its implementation, and committing to achieve projected returns
Portfolio Manager	The person responsible for monitoring the portfolio and providing the IC with the information and reports needed for informed decision making
Program Management Office	The competency center responsible for coordinating all programs, projects, and related tools; can provide the staff support and expertise to the IC
Program Manager	The person responsible for managing a program, usually made up of multiple, related business IT projects
Project Manager	The person responsible for the day-to-day management of a single project; communicates status to the portfolio manager, program manager, and business sponsor

moved rapidly from minor to major significance in this worldwide UN agency. With a budget in 2003 exceeding US$1.2 billion, UNICEF operates in over 160 countries, areas, and territories, where it plans and implements programs in cooperation with governments, non-government organizations, other UN agencies, and local communities. It is funded by voluntary contributions, two-thirds from governments and one-third from the private sector.

Until the mid-1990s, there was little IT in UNICEF offices and IT was far from a CEO-level concern. The IS organization primarily supported the UNICEF headquarters staff; the field offices were essentially on their own with what local IT support they could muster. Agency management launched a broad and ambitious initiative in 1995–1996 to improve efficiency and effectiveness, streamline operations, and decentralize decision making and accountability to regions and countries. With these changes, management recentralized responsibilities for IT decisions and resources so that the IS organization was then responsible for supporting all UNICEF staff, not just headquarters staff IT. Moreover, under the leadership of CIO Andre Spatz, the IS organization became an integral and enabling part of organizational transformation.

In that process of transformation, Spatz guided IT and the IS organization through three stages. In the first stage, what had been ad hoc management of IT evolved into individual project governance. For example, four division directors took on accountability for implementing on time and within budget the headquarters financial and logistics portions of an enterprise resource planning (ERP) suite, which replaced more than a hundred legacy systems. The management process for this project became the prototype for subsequent projects.

In the second stage, Spatz focused on building UNICEF's IT infrastructure. Today everyone in the agency has a standard desktop or laptop, office automation tools, Internet and intranet access, and applications on his or her PC. There is a global Internet protocol (IP) network in 80 percent of UNICEF's countries, with guaranteed bandwidth services, quality of service, and caching. Field staff now can leverage real-time information about projects, finances, and other resources, and feel connected to the organization as a whole. Enterprise management systems provide common tools, systems, and user support processes like the Global Services Desk. These systems, along with the disciplined collection of data, allow resources to be targeted to specific program areas quickly and effectively.

The third and current stage of IS evolution began when demand for IT services grew to four times the IS budget. Spatz helped UNICEF management install a process for reviewing and selecting the IT programs and strategies of most benefit to the organization as a whole. Under this approach, division and business heads, rather than IS alone, present and justify IT investment requests. This process provides a clear framework for choosing investments and priorities. There is one overall IT strategy encompassing headquarters, regional, and local levels.

Without an increasingly sophisticated system of governance, creating effective IT strategy that weaves together business strategy and IT, UNICEF would not now enjoy the obvious benefits of information and IT. Governance has been Spatz's secret weapon in becoming a new CIO leader.

Develop Your IT Portfolio as the Centerpiece of IT Strategy

The process by which an enterprise effectively selects and then manages its portfolio of IT strategies includes five steps:

1. Define initiatives using a comprehensive, uniform format.

2. Evaluate initiatives using an objective framework.

3. Prioritize initiatives and balance the portfolio.

4. Match prioritized initiatives to resources.

5. Manage the portfolio actively.

The process is not strictly sequential. There are feedback loops at each step. Furthermore, this is not a onetime activity, but a periodic review process that continues throughout the life of initiatives.

Step 1: Define initiatives

Prioritization decisions are only as good as the data supporting them. Gathering consistent, reliable information about each initiative is a key challenge, as is presenting it in a uniform format, so that competing initiatives can be compared.

Enterprises take either a one-stage or a two-stage approach at this point. In the one-stage approach, a team prepares a full business case or cost-benefit analysis, with sufficient information to determine the initiative's worth to the business.

In the two-stage approach, a team prepares a preliminary project proposal with less information, perhaps only a two-page summary outlining the project concept. The decision makers need just enough information to judge the viability of the concept and to

TABLE 6-2

Two Stages of Developing an Initiative

Preliminary Proposal	Business Case
1. Project name, description, or both	1. Project name, description, or both
2. Business need or objectives	2. Business need or objectives
3. Project sponsor	3. Project sponsor
4. Rough cost estimates	4. Alternatives
5. Rough benefits estimates	5. Assumptions
6. Fit with business and IT strategies	6. Cost estimates
	7. Benefits estimates
	8. Fit with business and IT strategies
	9. Implementation strategy
	10. Infrastructure requirements
	11. Risk factors
	12. Project schedule

decide whether to fund the development of a full business case. Larger initiatives usually go through a two-stage process (table 6-2).

Step 2: Evaluate initiatives

To achieve a balanced portfolio, you must create a prioritization framework of investment categories and evaluation criteria.[2] Logical investment categories, in which initiatives with similar characteristics are grouped, can help you allocate resources intelligently. For instance, smaller projects, such as maintenance and enhancement projects, might be grouped in one category with its own budget. You can use objective evaluation criteria, which would be based on business maxims, familiar financial measures, and risk, to rank initiatives within each category.

A portfolio of strategic initiatives and investments contains different types or categories of investments, and the proper mix will depend on the enterprise's objectives. The simplest categorization is the classification of *mandatory versus nonmandatory*. Mandatory projects should be treated as a separate category, but it's important to verify that they are truly mandatory. Some executives argue that these projects should be excluded from any selection process precisely because they are mandatory. Our view is that, because they use resources, mandatory initiatives should be part of the portfolio and should be tracked like any other project.

You also must choose the criteria for evaluating strategic initiatives. There are many possible criteria. They, and the way they're weighted, often differ from category to category. For example, how you evaluate a strategic investment may differ from how you evaluate a transactional investment. The relative importance of the criteria should be determined by business context. For instance, risk may be more highly weighted in a fighting-for-survival enterprise than in a breaking-away one.

Most criteria we've seen contain five basic elements: business impact, financial impact, risk, architectural fit, and benefits-delivery responsibility. Whichever combination you choose, financial measures should be only one criterion. Otherwise, your portfolio of strategic initiatives will be too heavily tilted toward cost-reduction programs.

Business impact

This criterion is generally the most important test, at least for the critical business-performance investments. It measures the degree to which the IT investment directly contributes to achieving the enterprise strategy. The impact may be economic, such as lower cost of business operations or a reduced need for working capital. The business impact can be noneconomic as well, such as faster time to market, shorter production cycle times, fewer errors, better quality, new services, greater convenience, or more personalization. Eliminating a threat also has inherent value.

Financial impact

There are a variety of funding options, much more than just the corporate budget, that need to be part of your portfolio—we'll look at them a little later. Regardless of which funding option you use, financial impact is fundamental, whether you have all the relevant data or not. The goal is to obtain the most complete picture possible, using information that the CFO would be willing to support; this information will be vital to choosing the best funding option. Costs should include ongoing support costs projected into the reasonable future. In general, try to use the same financial measures the business uses, because they're familiar, credible, and already part of the enterprise culture. Work with finance staff to adapt the enterprise's capital expenditure methodology to suit the evaluation of proposed initiatives.

If the benefits are all qualitative and cannot be expressed in financial terms, this is not unusual. Such a result, however, needs other strong pluses to provide justification. Some firms take an extra step of estimating the potential economic impact of hard-to-measure benefits, such as higher customer retention. Use these abstract benefits with great caution.

Risk

No investment can be evaluated without you or your team considering the likelihood of success or failure. Low-risk projects can be expected to meet their projections, but high-risk projects will often fail and must therefore offer a much higher return to compensate. There are at least four types of risk to consider. *Business risk* considers the possibility that the initiative will not realize business benefits. For instance, IS might build a portal that, it turns out, no one is interested in seeing (while the IS organization should have little say here, the risk itself must be recognized). *Organizational risk* considers the planned users of the new system; if they strongly resist, the system may be doomed to failure. Assessment of this risk must be included. *Technical risk* is the usual uncertainty regarding a vendor's viability in a volatile industry, or the short life of some standards. *Execution risk* relates to the degree of uncertainty of the costs, benefits, and timing. If a project has never been undertaken before, or if experience is lacking, then the execution risk of a project can be a showstopper.

Architectural fit

The question of architectural fit or compliance is not a common criterion when enterprises are considering the merits of other classes of capital investments or projects. However, compliance, or at least a lack of interference with established IT architecture, can have a major impact on costs and benefits. If, for example, a proposed project includes a brand-new database, the challenges can include (1) a big learning curve for operations, data management, and support, as well as developers; (2) major difficulties in exchanging data to and from existing databases; and (3) reduced ability to leverage the expertise of purchasing, maintenance, and diagnostic personnel. The difficulties can occur in costs, timing, and the ability to implement desired tasks.

Responsibility for the delivery of benefits

Having a benefits-management or value-realization process in place is one of the big differences between those who do and those who don't realize value from their initiatives.[3] Make sure this criterion is part of the initial evaluation and business case. Who will make sure the benefits from this initiative are delivered? Is it part of his or her accountabilities? Will the person's bonus be tied to the successful delivery of benefits? The sponsor should be a businessperson whose business is dependent on this initiative—unless it is purely an infrastructure investment, in which case the sponsor could be the CIO. If there is no one willing to be named as the benefits-delivery sponsor, then we believe the initiative should be rejected. No one will have enough "skin in the game" to ensure a successful outcome.

Step 3: Prioritize initiatives and balance the portfolio

This step is typically done by the investment council (IC) or some similar body, depending on your governance approach in the domain of IT investment and prioritization. Each strategy investment is scored around the kind of criteria just discussed. In some enterprises, scoring is done as a group effort by the IC. In others, the scored proposals are circulated to council members before they meet so that they have time to become familiar with each initiative and to prepare questions for the sponsors.

In scoring, use weights to reflect the relative importance of each evaluation criterion in each investment category. For example, risk level might be much more important in the infrastructure category than in the strategic category, where a higher risk level is acceptable. Some enterprises use *knockout factors,* or thresholds, rather than weights. If, for example, the strategic value of an initiative is zero, that project would not be approved, whatever its other merits.

In this step, project sponsors present short summaries of why their proposals deserve funding. Using the insights the council members gained by discussing projects with the sponsors, the IC determines whether the business cases and scorings are realistic. For each proposal, the council can then decide to approve it, cancel it, put it on hold, or send it back for rework.

Surviving projects are then ranked within each category based on scores. The IC should balance portfolios by choosing projects that support all major enterprise goals and are diverse in size and category.

This is an appropriate time to give the list a sanity check. In taking such a step, you simply review what business processes and departments benefit from the proposed projects, the comparative risk level, the relative spending, and so on, to make sure your portfolio isn't already out of balance. Some companies find that the criteria and weights used in steps 1 and 2 create an out-of-balance portfolio. If this happens to you, you need to revisit your criteria and determine how to prevent your process from skewing approvals too far in one direction or another.

Step 4: Match initiatives to resources

In this step you match projects against available resources. This step can also incorporate any necessary requirements for sequencing or building order, or other types of dependencies among projects.

As the projects are laid out in sequence, you must assess their use of available resources. Make this assessment on a coarse level of detail regarding staff skills, among other things. You then manipulate the projects in terms of start and completion times, total time span, and so on, to achieve maximum utilization of available skills and the least demand for supplemental resources. Trade-offs of completion dates and the addition of resources are made where necessary. Deferred initiatives go into the opportunity portfolio, which will be revisited at subsequent portfolio reviews.

Step 5: Manage the portfolio actively

While project sponsors will always be tempted to "game" the process to get their projects approved, the IC (or whatever the decision-making body is) must follow up on actual costs and benefits versus the business case estimates. This step is necessary so that underperforming projects can be corrected or killed. Some enterprises link actual project performance to bonuses in order to deter "cheating."

Improving portfolio performance requires active management. Enterprises good at this typically conduct complete portfolio reviews at least every year as part of their annual planning and budgeting cycle. Many CIOs conduct a review quarterly if they have many short-term initiatives in the pipeline.

Tracking of in-progress projects should be complemented in two ways: first, by full reviews, at least quarterly, of recently completed projects; and, second, by publication of weekly or monthly progress reports from project leaders. These reports should be based on performance indicators from the project proposal or specified during the approval process. We tend to favor frequent reviews, because they're needed to

- cancel seriously underperforming initiatives early in their life cycle;

- delay or accelerate initiatives to respond to internal and external changes, such as a merger or an acquisition;

Enterprise IT Strategy Review
in Decentralized Enterprises

IMPLEMENTING an enterprise-level IT strategy review process like this is especially challenging in decentralized enterprises because the business units are used to controlling their own priorities. Initially, they may have a difficult time collaborating in unbiased ways. When it comes to divvying up money, enterprisewide objectivity doesn't come naturally.

It's important to establish this process at the enterprise level, because it identifies overlapping and redundant projects across business units. That's why it's critical that the participants understand their roles and are held accountable for carrying them out. Here are some tips for overcoming these challenges.

First, you should assign a process owner. One person needs to own the process of overseeing a strategy review and setting stakeholder expectations. The most appropriate owners are experienced, respected executives with excellent interpersonal skills. They need to be comfortable working with high-level executives. Historically, owners have been in IS, because the process was originally created for prioritizing IT projects. But process owners today can also come from product development, finance, or strategic planning.

Second, create a qualified support team. The strategy review process needs to be staffed with the right level of people. The team that designs and implements the new process must be respected throughout the enterprise and understand its political environment. The team also creates the templates and scoring models and tests them to ensure that they provide the information the IC needs to make informed decisions. Finally, the team needs to know how to engage sponsors when completing the business cases. It's likely the team will have to help draft the initial cases until the business units understand what's needed.

- redefine the scope to reduce risk and cost, or increase benefits and strategic fit; or

- combine or split initiatives to eliminate overlap or make them more manageable.

Build a Portfolio of Funding Options

To get the most from an IT strategy portfolio, new CIO leaders also need to create a portfolio of funding options. By using a variety of financing options instead of just the corporate budget, you can succeed on more initiatives. What's more, you can manage risk better and make sure that the IT work is clearly connected to cost and value. (Both cost and value are on the new CIO leader's agenda and are discussed in later chapters.)

Traditionally, most IT-enabled business initiatives have been funded in two ways—corporate funding through IS's budget and business unit funding—but there are six additional funding models. In corporate and business unit funding, the enterprise has to fund the whole initiative. But this method is bound to annual budget cycles, so it limits how many IT-enabled initiatives can be started. Financial risk is focused in the enterprise. Unforeseen IT initiatives between budgets are difficult to fund.

Because annual budgets are linked to departmental planning, they are more suited to funding large, low-risk initiatives. But many innovative or opportunistic initiatives are high risk, with the potential for high return. Using different funding models can lower the up-front expense of an initiative, allow for more initiatives, and spread financial risk.

More sources of funds can bring benefits. Given the economic turmoil of recent years, managers and investors have refocused on such basic financial measures as return on assets (ROA). For many initiatives, though, it's difficult to make a clear link with ROA, so the trend is to fund initiatives from operating, rather than capital, budgets. But operating budgets (expenses) are always being squeezed, while IS groups are being asked to do more by business units. External funding can free you from this trap and allow you to do more with less.

In addition, new CIO leaders need to be agile, reacting quickly to market conditions. That means being able to fund initiatives quickly outside the annual budget. You can think of alternative funding mechanisms as risk management for your ability to deliver.

Let's look at all eight funding models, including a fresh look at internal funding.

Internal funding options

Of the four internal funding models, *corporate funding* and *business unit funding* are widely used. Two other models, *IS funding* and *venture pool funding,* have also been used with great success by new CIO leaders.

Corporate funding

Corporate funding is by far the most commonly used source of funds for IS. The enterprise allocates funds to the IS budget, which are then used to pay for planned initiatives. Getting corporate funding takes time and is bound to the annual budgeting cycle. In a weak economy, the investment council or capital approval committee, which allocates the funds, usually demands great detail, often asks for several iterations, and is rarely generous. Because of this reluctance, corporate funding is best used for long-term, strategic IT initiatives, like large infrastructure upgrades, whose benefits are spread across the enterprise.

Business unit funding

The second most common funding model is business unit funding, where benefiting business units fund initiatives from their budget. Business unit funding directly matches the beneficiary with the costs and is simple to run.

This funding model needs strong IT governance to ensure that the selection of initiatives is part of the enterprisewide IT governance process. Otherwise, pet initiatives that don't align with strategy can tie up resources and add little value.

Business unit funding is best suited to planned, lower-risk initiatives, where there is a clear beneficiary willing to put up the money. An example is the implementation of a personnel system for human resources.

IS funding with chargeback

The third internal model is for IS to fund an initiative from its own funds on hand and then recover the costs from the beneficiaries through chargeback. This form of funding gives IS and business units the ability to respond quickly to opportunities.

For example, suppose a business unit wants to add a computer-aided design (CAD) package in the first quarter to its engineering department's desktops. IS could buy the package with funds earmarked for an IT initiative in the fourth quarter and recover costs through chargeback. Getting the timing of funding and chargeback right in IS funding will be vital. Otherwise, IS can find itself with a serious budget problem.

Venture pool funding

Venture capital has been a popular way to fund risky start-ups. Some enterprises have taken the venture capital model and applied it internally. They set up a venture pool and use it to fund initiatives with high potential benefit and also high risk. Think of it as a way to strike at opportunities (such as the IT-enabled opportunities, discussed in chapter 4).

In venture pool funding, the finance organization usually lends funds to IS, but requires a high return on investment. On completion of the initiative, IS uses chargeback to recover the funds (and the promised return) from the benefiting business units.

Each initiative must have a business sponsor who can vouch for the benefit, and whose business unit is willing to pay the chargeback. A panel composed of the CIO and cross-business representatives should also review the initiative. If you're considering venture pool funding, keep in mind the high credibility price of failure. Before starting such a project, make sure that your IT project portfolio is well balanced and that you have effective risk management in place.

External funding options

Although there's no such thing as a free lunch, external funding sources provide real benefits. Up-front cost savings can be used to fund other initiatives and to spread risk across several parties.

External service provider funding

In external service provider (ESP) funding, the external provider makes the investment in return for supplying IT services, provided IS commits to regular payments. The two most common examples of ESP funding are outsourcing and vendor financing.

Outsourcing is by far the biggest chunk of ESP funding. This funding model is likely to become more widespread as the range of IT services on offer expands and as enterprises seek to reduce the up-front cost of their IT initiatives. In this scenario, the ESP makes the required capital investments to provide a service in return for a long-term services contract.

ESP funding is useful when no other funding is available for the vendor's offering. The enterprise needs to be comfortable with the contractual terms and conditions and with being locked into regular payments over a long term. Vendor financing has fallen somewhat out of favor because of the abuse of this mechanism by many vendors during the Internet boom.

Grant and incentive funding

Most government agencies offer grants or incentives to encourage enterprises to invest locally. The European Union offers grants to enterprises to relocate in areas of high unemployment. Every year, some thirty EU bodies give several hundred million euros in grants to companies and local authorities. Many U.S. states offer similar grants and incentives. Government funds may also be earmarked for public-sector and higher-education initiatives.

Grants and incentives are normally used to fund large initiatives, such as building a call center, which will increase local employment. Although much money is available, grants and incentives can be difficult to find, have lengthy processing times, and offer all the frustrations of dealing with governmental bureaucracies. These funding options are best suited to long-term, strategic initiatives with a demonstrable benefit to a local economy.

Consortium funding

Enterprises are becoming increasingly interconnected. From airline alliances to integrated supply chains, consortia of interest groups are springing up. In these arrangements, several enterprises pool their funds and resources to develop a common solution—spreading risk across the parties involved. A good example is health care providers and related insurers. The use of common systems not only spreads the cost of investment but also improves the level of service delivery and the provision of health care.

Consortia benefit from *platforms,* by creating the *network effect* of Metcalfe's Law, discussed in chapter 4 (as the number of enterprises involved increases, the power and attractiveness of the platform grows). Open standards are one such platform.

But the setup of consortia is difficult and time-consuming. The participants need to agree on the working arrangements and how much funding each will contribute. Controlling and protecting intellectual property can be a challenge, too.

Funding through sale of IT services

In this approach, the IS organization generates revenue by selling an IT service on the outside market. Selling IT services works best where the service is a commodity that's similar across enterprises and doesn't confer competitive advantage; economies of scale dominate. Examples are data center capacity, Web hosting, and banking back-office systems.

Selling IT services externally requires sales and marketing know-how that most IS groups lack. External customers need to be treated as well as internal customers. Managing these relationships takes time, effort, and specific expertise, because you are then becoming an external service provider. We urge great caution in external sales, as many IS groups have failed to deliver on expectations in this area.

Deciding which funding model suits your IT initiatives

Work with your finance group to evaluate which models are most suitable for each initiative, and balance your portfolio of funding options. This involves five steps:

1. Identify the characteristics of an initiative that drives funding requirements by asking these questions:

   - Where will the benefit of the initiative be felt, locally in a business unit or across the enterprise?

   - Is the scale of the initiative small or large?

   - What is the time frame—when will the benefits be realized, in the short or long term?

   - What is the risk of promised benefits not being delivered?

2. Review alternative funding sources, considering the benefits, scale, timing, and risk, as discussed in this section.

3. Before talking to the CFO, CEO, and board, develop a list of concerns that require answers.

4. Inject reality into the equation. Consider the fit between the funding model and financial strategies. Adjust the initiative to find the best fit.

5. Get CFO and business unit agreement on the funding model (in the case of external funding models).

Consider one example. A sales director wants to give the sales force a handheld wireless device to get real-time data from the enterprise. The sales force then can give accurate quotes on the spot—something competitors can't do. It's a cutting-edge solution, but it's high risk, and the sales director wants it now. What are the best funding options? Consider the characteristics of the initiative:

1. The benefit is local—only for the sales department.

2. The scale is small—the application is limited to the sales force.

3. The timing is short—the sales director wants to beat competitors to wireless use.

4. The risk is high—the application will use cutting-edge technology.

With the preceding characteristics, business unit and venture pool funding are the best options for this initiative. The sales director can either fund the initiative directly from his or her business unit, or IS can obtain funding from the Finance Department and charge back the cost to the sales function.

The choice depends on how the enterprise funds sales force applications. If IS supplies the service and it's charged back, then the venture pool is the preferred option. If that's not the norm, though, then it's up to the business unit to fund the application.

A different example involves upgrading the security of the IT infrastructure. The enterprise needs this improvement to meet its legal and regulatory obligations. What are the best funding options? Here are the project's characteristics:

1. The benefit is enterprisewide—the aim is to tighten security for all business units.

2. The scale is large—the whole enterprise.

3. The timing is long term—upgrading and integrating the security solution, architecture, and other procedures will take time.

4. The risk is relatively low—the enterprise can buy a package from a vendor specializing in infrastructure security.

The two best options in this example are corporate funding and ESP funding. ESP funding is a realistic option if a suitable trusted ESP can be found and if the enterprise is willing to commit to the contract and payments.

Using a wider range of funding sources can be a challenge. For example, IS needs skills in financial modeling, financial risk management, financial control, and financial data collection. Few IS organizations have these skills readily available in house. More funding models means dealing with more stakeholders and potentially additional controls. Managing stakeholders is difficult enough when they're inside the enterprise. It's even more complex when they're outside. Do move slowly toward using external funding, and work to build the vital skills and experience in this area. But there are many benefits to be gained from these nontraditional alternatives.

Creating and Maintaining an IT Strategy at AXA

AXA Group's experiences creating and maintaining an IT strategy may help show how this process works in the real world. AXA ranks among the world's leading insurance and financial service providers. Headquartered in France, with offices in sixty countries and 140,000 employees and agents worldwide, the company brought in gross revenues of 71.6 billion euros in 2003. It operates a two-level governance scheme for selecting IT strategies and programs. The process is used for all major company initiatives, not just IT projects, though 70 to 80 percent of all business initiatives have a significant IT component.

At the corporate level, the governance council is called the IS Strategic Committee (ISSC). It meets quarterly and is chaired by the company's group executive responsible for IT, procurement, and operations. All major IT stakeholders are members. Though the ISSC does not become involved in the actual management of projects, it operates as a transparent decision-making body where differences and priorities can be discussed and settled. The corporate-level body becomes involved in all proposals that either (1) exceed a defined investment level or (2) are strategically significant. All other proposals remain at the business or divisional level, where management has the right to approve them. All proposals at both levels generally follow the same presentation and analytic format. AXA maintains transparency and access by placing all the project outlines and documentation in an online repository.

The ISSC operates on an annual cycle, with major planning done once a year and frequent meetings—at least quarterly—throughout the year. The once-yearly process takes place through a series of workshops with business unit executives. The purpose of the first workshops is to agree on seven to ten *strategic imperatives* (the term AXA uses for what we have referred to as maxims), such as increasing customer retention or reducing costs. These become part of the criteria for evaluating projects. Then a description of potential projects is collected from project business owners. The final workshop focuses on selecting the best projects. After that, during the year, some projects may need further assessment of costs, benefits, and risks. In addition, projects initially passed over may be selected, because of a change in circumstances.

The benefits of this approach to IT strategizing became clear immediately after September 11, 2001. Literally overnight, several AXA companies were able to reprioritize their projects to focus on expense reduction in light of increased insurance exposure and the global economic slowdown.

Critical Success Factors for Investment Prioritization

From our research in many enterprises, we know that some factors influence disproportionately the success or failure of the process for selecting and implementing IT-enabled initiatives. The critical success factors range from the basic criteria used to select which initiatives to choose to how you communicate the process to key stakeholders.

Allocate sufficient resources to support the process

The prioritization of investments is such a major undertaking that it needs to be treated as a project itself if it is to succeed. The start-up effort is likely to be larger than expected, depending on what's already in place. The CIOs we interviewed spent from six to eighteen months gaining support, designing and setting up the framework and process, and educating the participants.

Ensure the process is disciplined and sustained

A disciplined process means all proposals go through the same screening; there's no way to circumvent the process to get a pet project funded. Every initiative should receive the same rigorous review and be stacked up against all other investment opportunities in its category. The process also should encompass a project's entire life cycle, from initial proposal to benefits realization and retirement, with major reviews at key points along the way.

Make sure the process is objective

The investment categories and evaluation criteria need to be well defined, understood, and considered fair by all the stakeholders. The perception that decisions might be influenced by factors other than the merits never completely goes away, but unbiased evaluation criteria and categories can reduce it. To minimize the perception of unfairness or favoritism, keep everything simple and straightforward. Three or four categories are usually enough to capture the meaningful distinctions and enable the IC to make its resource allocation decisions. Use categories and criteria that fit your enterprise and how it operates.

Maintain communication and education programs

Communication and education programs help the stakeholders accept the portfolio management process. In fact, until key stakeholders understand there is a problem in the way the enterprise allocates resources, they won't willingly adopt a new process to fix it. You should provide for education and workshops, to explain not only the benefit of the process, but also how to use the process (e.g., as templates for project proposals, frequently asked questions, primers on criteria, maps of the various stages of the process, as well as a contact for questions and assistance). Make sure your IS group takes responsibility for documenting the lessons learned from each IC meeting. Then use those lessons to refine the process. Don't fall into the trap of believing that any process, no matter how refined, will not need adjustment over time. For example, as their enterprises gain experience, many of the CIOs we spoke to are lifting the size limit that determines which initiatives must go through the formal portfolio management.

Support decision making with tools

To facilitate the use of portfolio management, new CIO leaders need to provide tools that make compliance easier. These tools both ensure consistency and support group decision making. Commonly used tools include standard business case templates, techniques to improve cost-estimating accuracy, financial models or spreadsheet templates to calculate financial measures, an online repository of data for all projects, and scoring or decision models to analyze and evaluate proposals. Again, tap your business colleagues for help. Make sure the tools you provide match their needs, and include those tools they're accustomed to using. Certainly, you and your staff don't need to waste time creating tools that are difficult to use or that don't meet the needs of the enterprise.

The Value of the Governance Process for Selecting Initiatives

At the end of the review process, when the IC has produced a list of accepted initiatives, you may find that the list contains no surprises or breakthroughs. The outcome may seem almost obvious and logical, even anticlimactic. That may lead you to wonder if the process was worth the time and work that went into it.

The answer is a clear yes.

Before the prioritization process, participants may have had their favorites, as well as a good idea of what was right, but they could only speak from their own perspectives. As a result of going through the process, even if some participants disagreed on certain items or scores, the group as a whole reached conclusions based on an explicit set of criteria and on the information and opinions presented. Any single participant would be able to explain where funds will be spent and why they were chosen.

Most important, you emerge from the process with a set of IT initiatives that key business managers support and understand, because they participated in selecting them and making sure they support the overall objectives and needs of the enterprise. This support and understanding will be critical to you as you deliver on these projects. Because of their participation, these key business managers will much more readily see and acknowledge the benefits of your efforts—a vital part of building your credibility and becoming a new CIO leader. All because of a process—governance—that they trust.

Seizing IT-Based Opportunities

As we mentioned, good governance and proper strategy setting will often yield a portfolio with few surprises. In fact, one largely positive outcome is a reduced rate of IT "mutation" and heterogeneity. However, this more stable IT environment also has a downside. It can limit the opportunity for truly innovative, pathbreaking applications of technology to business needs. These applications are more than strategic; they're often disruptive to the business. But they are also where the greatest leaps forward are made.

You may also be wondering where your vision, crafted from a deep knowledge of your enterprise and technology, fits in with the IT portfolio and strategy process we've been discussing. Your vision should have influenced your business and IT maxims considerably and therefore be reflected in the strategy you've developed, but your vision should also include some of these pathbreaking applications of technology.

Enterprises more and more will rely on new CIO leaders to introduce innovation in business processes. These extraordinary innovations and opportunities (called ITOs, for IT-related opportunities) need to be a vital part of your IT strategy on an ongoing basis. Therefore, you need a way of introducing the more radical parts of your vision, as well as finding ITOs you haven't anticipated. You can't rely solely on the deliberative process of the IT strategy, which may kill the truly out-of-the-box thinking and opportunities. However, ITOs are also too important to be approached willynilly, with no process or discipline.

As often happens with big opportunities, ITOs bring problems, too. It's difficult to predict the course of ITOs. In the beginning, since they hold the potential for significant change, you can't know how they're going to turn out. They're inherently risky and can even require something of a leap of faith, because by definition, no one's tried these opportunities before. Because ITOs threaten "the way things are done," they can generate resistance. They often break rules and make new ones.

A further complication of ITOs concerns the role of the IS organization. To be effective, ITOs should be seen as business initiatives, and so they should be led and managed by business leaders. But ITOs are more than merely IT-enabled opportunities; they owe their existence to IT, and often to a risky, emerging technology. This suggests that the role of the IS organization should go beyond providing support systems and infrastructure for these opportunities. In fact, because IT is at the heart of these opportunities, ITOs often provide real opportunities for new CIO leaders to play a strong leadership role as an enterprise executive. After all, if you're not identifying and bringing ITOs forward, who will?

Most ITOs we've encountered end up making only an incremental difference—but enough do deliver on their original promise, to cause a real transformation. For this reason, every business

FIGURE 6-1

Integrating Governance and ITOs in IT Strategy

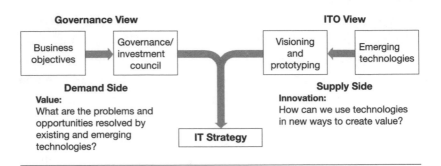

needs a disciplined, systematic way to explore ITOs and integrate them with IT strategy (figure 6-1). In some ways, it's appropriate to compare the creation and pursuit of ITOs to the strategy pharmaceutical companies use to find new drugs. Many ideas are tested, but few finally make it to market. High failure rates, however, don't stop these companies from pursing blockbuster drugs.

The ITO process in practice

How can you nurture the right ITOs and stop the wrong ones with a minimum of effort? Just like the pharmaceutical companies, your enterprise needs an ITO process, and you need to work constantly at making it better. Several major enterprises were good at generating and developing ITOs. Here are two of those companies.

International Airways

In the late 1990s, International Airways (a pseudonym) established a new unit called eAirways, whose purpose was to develop bright ideas related to every aspect of IT-enabling the business. An in-house incubator and development factory, eAirways has a staff drawn from IS, sales, marketing, and distribution. The new unit dreams up ITOs, assesses their commercial viability, and develops them to the point that they can be handed back to mainstream managers. eAirways takes on forty to fifty separate projects a year. These projects have passed through an "ideas" panel into at least the initial testing stage. eAirways strives to push each project from inception to pilot (no pun intended) delivery in less than three months.

To carry that kind of project load, eAirways has developed a rigorous approach. Step one is the development of a three- or four-page customer proposition identifying such essentials as target customers, competitive advantage, project life span, and an outline of the business case. If a proposal survives scrutiny by the project prioritization board, which meets biweekly, it will move on to a product development team of four persons with specializations in IT, business analysis, marketing, and project management. This team has two or three weeks to make a more robust business case for the idea, which (if the idea still survives) will then move to a development phase. At that point, the proposed initiative may be launched internally, for example, as an interim mini-project to test the end-to-end technology. Once the project has met all the requirements, including a demonstration of cost savings, revenue generation, and customer acquisition for the enterprise, it will be handed over to an exploitation group. The job of this group is to launch the service to customers and determine the rollout plan and communications plan for internal and external use.

DHL Worldwide

The international courier firm DHL Worldwide also has an organizational unit, the Business Development Group, which is responsible for moving innovations from conception to implementation. It looks for ideas in three areas—from the core business, from a focus on customers, and from innovation, that is, from radically new ways of doing some part of the business. Each focus area offers strengths and weaknesses, DHL believes, so the development group tries to balance the three areas by creating a portfolio of opportunities across all three.

The Business Development Group has found that, with the portfolio approach, the group must be capable of managing the three kinds of opportunities in different ways. Innovation has turned out to be the most difficult to manage because it requires creative processes that can clash with the culture of the organization as a whole. Indeed, all three areas require the company to organize itself differently and to have multiple cultures all working together, which can be difficult.

Not every enterprise needs such substantive and sophisticated organizational units as International Airways and DHL have. But what you do need is a process for managing ITOs. The numbers almost demand it. To achieve one ITO success requires placing numerous small bets, since many won't pay off.

The sheer number of ideas being evaluated at any given time means the process cannot be managed by some informal, ad hoc system. This effort must be properly and formally managed. When we looked around the world at enterprises like International Airways and DHL, which seemed adept at bringing ITOs to commercial success, we focused on how they managed that pipeline of opportunities. We emphasize three stages in the process: (1) *generating* an ITO idea in the first place, (2) *developing* the idea once it's approved, and (3) *transferring* the management of the ITO to operating managers. At every step, we paid specific attention to the role of new CIO leaders.

Generate ITOs as part of a deliberate process

Think of the ITO process as a funnel. At one end, where projects enter, it's relatively broad, intended to find or generate lots of ideas.

Companies that are particularly good at this generation stage tend to develop their ideas, we found, in three phases:

1. They initially *find or create a lot of ideas.* They uncover ideas conceived by people throughout the company.

2. Then they work quickly to *reduce the number of ideas* to a much smaller quantity worth considering. Here the funnel becomes noticeably narrower. Maybe one in fifty initial

ITOs and Fighting-for-Survival Enterprises

IT MAY SEEM that ITOs are the exclusive province of CIOs in the breaking-away mode. While ITOs should not be the prime area of focus for CIOs of fighting-for-survival enterprises, this is not an area that they or CIOs of maintaining-competitiveness enterprises can ignore. New CIO leaders are needed in every organization—and generating ITOs is part of being a new CIO leader.

Fighting-for-survival CIOs do need to approach ITOs differently than breaking-away CIOs, however. Breaking-away CIOs will approach ITOs looking for innovations and opportunities to create new revenue streams and investments with longer-term payoffs. CIOs whose enterprises are fighting for survival need to implement filters in their ITO process that look specifically for opportunities to cut the cost of existing business processes and deliver IT services more efficiently, especially opportunities that may offer smaller but quicker payoffs. This selective approach to ITOs is all a part of understanding your business context and reacting appropriately.

Keep in mind, too, that radical IT-led innovation in the form of ITOs can be the instrument that leads your enterprise out of fighting-for-survival mode. Don't pin all your hopes on making one of these breakthroughs, but don't create a situation in which they're impossible, either.

---

ideas survives. Several techniques—consolidation, ranking and weighting, and so on—can be effective here.

3. Finally, the companies *ratify a short list of ideas* to pursue further. This involves writing a short outline—a brief, well-written description and rationale—of each ITO and presenting it for formal review.

Since emerging technologies stimulate a high proportion of ITOs, IS staff has an important role to play at this stage. You should create an environment conducive to creative thinking, perhaps by instituting an ongoing process within IS to generate ideas for how emerging technology might answer some of your enterprise's persistent business needs. The process is similar to the one we recommended for developing your vision.

Develop ITOs with sense-and-respond processes and discipline

The development stage shapes, refines, and demonstrates ITOs in a series of steps, each one capped with an evaluation. Think of it as exploration and experimentation taking place within a disciplined framework.

The inherent uncertainty of an ITO almost requires you to pursue it as a series of steps that allow you to feel your way into the future. We call this approach *sense and respond.* The sense step requires taking some action—an experiment, a small trial or demonstration. Then, the respond step is a pause for assessment, followed by a correction before you take a new sense step.

Many managers find this part of the process discomforting. There's no plan or precision, because there can't be any precision about a future that's unknown. The purpose here is to explore the possibilities. Success requires unhindered exploration within the sense-and-respond framework and its frequent evaluations. Long-term business comfort with this exploration process depends on (1) doing a good job at the generation stage of focusing quickly on the most promising ideas and (2) setting appropriate expectations among all stakeholders about the very low success rate of ITOs.

Transfer ITOs with a real sense of ownership

This stage takes ITOs to sign-off and commercial rollout. Whatever good work has been done on the ITO prior to this point, ultimate success depends on the business staff who must live with and use the innovation. So it's critical to link with operational staff before the actual handoff.

Linking can take several forms. Ideally, the ITO champion and the manager responsible for the operating team will be the same person.

To ensure a smooth handoff, keep the operations staff in the picture during development. Make sure they attend the demo. Solicit and use their advice. Identify and seek the active support of those staff who favor change. Most important, try to instill pride of ownership among the operating staff; allow and help them to embrace the change as their own. During the handover itself, the development team should work hand in hand with operating staff to make final adjustments and ensure that everyone is fully familiar with the implications of the ITO. Handoff should end with a formal sign-off and transfer of responsibility.

Be sensitive to the highly disruptive nature of some ITOs. Disruptive opportunities require painful change and adjustment in the organization and even in the way people think and feel about their work. These ITOs usually present problems at the handoff stage. Disruptive ITOs might require a spin-off or some other organizational device that allows the ITO to develop on its own, outside the existing organization whose values and processes it threatens. Your relationship and stakeholder management skills will be most tested at this stage. Truly disruptive ITOs may be your biggest successes and credibility builders, moving you far down the path you have chosen to pursue. But if you don't create, manage, and sustain executive support, these ITOs could also be your biggest failures and credibility eroders.

The new CIO leader's role in ITOs is pivotal

ITOs will be one of the primary places your vision of an IT-enabled enterprise begins to become reality. Therefore, your role in developing and progressing ITOs is critical. The Rexam story provides some insight into how a new CIO leader can be directly involved in creating significant new business opportunities.

Rexam is the world's leading beverage-can maker and ranks among the top five consumer packaging companies. Globally, Rexam has sales of US$4.5 billion and twenty thousand employees; Rexam Beverage Can Americas has sales of US$1.6 billion. The beverage can business is over a century old, with business processes that have changed little in all that time. Many processes remain manual, such as order-to-cash, which on industry average is 50 percent handled manually.

In 1999, Paul Martin joined American National Can as CIO. In 2000 the company was acquired by Rexam and became Rexam Beverage Can Americas. At the beginning of his tenure, Martin discovered that most orders were taken by phone or fax, keyed in to a spreadsheet, held for days in anticipation of changes, and then faxed to a plant near the customer, where the orders were rekeyed into back office systems. Martin perceived an opportunity to use technology to provide significant business benefits—reduce errors and costs in the ordering process, and more tightly integrate customers into Rexam systems, thereby making it harder for them to change to another vendor.

When he told his commercial and sales colleagues, "There's a way to leverage the Internet here," they told him Rexam customers would never enter an order online. He argued that consumers would do so, "if we can demonstrate the value to them."

Rather than invest in a large customer-relationship management (CRM) system, Martin's IS staff and some consultants first built what they called "CRM made simple"—a platform and some applications based on feedback from Rexam's commercial group and some customers. Martin tested the system on one customer and one location. The customer liked the system and suggested a number of improvements. Under the new system, order errors dropped to essentially zero. The customer rolled out the system to all locations and standardized its U.S. operations on Rexam's system. Martin's vision of using technology to bind customers to Rexam was being fulfilled.

The system benefited both Rexam and its customers. Rexam improved its cash flow by millions of dollars. The customers enjoy convenience, a range of reports, and the useful ability to slice and dice their data in many ways. They can inquire about order status online, and changes are handled automatically. The system allows more interaction but hides the complexity of the interactions, making work simpler for both sides.

The beverage can business normally grows a mere 1 to 2 percent a year. Generally, the only way to improve margins is to cut costs. In late 2001, there was a price increase for the first time in twenty-five years. In renegotiating contracts, Rexam's vice president of commercial sales added a new clause that said, in essence, "If Rexam delivers exceptional value to you . . . we will come back to you for another price increase."

Obviously, customers wanted to know what this new clause meant. In response, Martin visited these customers and gave them presentations about what Rexam was doing and the potential benefits for them. "The CEO sees me as a business person," Martin explains. "These are not IT projects. These are company projects. But it's my job to translate our systems solutions to their business problems." Martin now spends as much time giving presentations to these stakeholders as he does to Rexam employees.

Clearly, Martin's vision for his enterprise and his role in creating, developing, and implementing this ITO was a huge credibility boost for him. In fact, Martin says his CEO has directed him to focus on "strategy and getting our external relationships under control." That is a new CIO leader. As a result of his success, he was named CIO of Rexam Worldwide in January 2004.

How the entire ITO development process is managed will depend on the enterprise as a whole and how it's managed. Many organizations, like International Airways and DHL, centralize ITO development. Whatever the approach in your firm, you as CIO leader should play an important role, since the purpose of ITO development is to discover extraordinary opportunities based on technology.

By using both the governance process for evaluating and implementing IT-related initiatives, yet having an exception process to deal with highly innovative ways of using new technologies, you can ensure that you are providing for the persistent business needs of the enterprise without shutting out opportunities to look behind, around, and through these persistent needs. Ultimately, these two areas provide the output of your leadership on the demand side. On the one hand, you are implementing IT-related initiatives based on your knowledge of, and engagement with, your business colleagues— you are leading them to uses of IT that create business value. On the other hand, you are leading your colleagues by showing them the exciting new potential of technology in your enterprise. Mastering both sides is required to fulfill the role of the new CIO leader.

From here we turn to the other side of the leadership equation— the supply side. That is where new CIO leaders guide the IS organization to deliver on the promises made in IT governance and ITOs.

PART TWO

Supply-Side Leadership

As we've noted, new CIO leaders must deliver results that are valued by enterprise leaders. Demand-side leadership covered the "valued by enterprise leaders" part of that statement, but it's supply-side leadership that takes care of the "deliver." Both are critical for success.

In this section, we'll cover the points of focus within the IS group, the traditional domain of CIOs, that distinguish a new CIO leader. You will need to follow up on these points of focus if you are to meet the expectations you've set on the demand side. Of course, failing to meet those expectations, no matter how well you've led on the demand side, will destroy your credibility and prevent you from being seen as a new CIO leader.

These are the four points of focus in this section:

- Build a new IS organization. *You need to have an organization that is as focused on delivering business results as you are.*

- Develop a high-performing IS team. *Organizing your IS group to deliver business results won't work if you don't have the right leadership and competencies.*

- Manage enterprise and IT risks. *New CIO leaders have to take the point on enterprise risk management related to IT.*

- Communicate your performance. *No matter how well you've done in any other area, if you can't quantify and communicate your success you won't be recognized as a new CIO leader.*

7

Build a New IS Organization

So far we've talked about how to lead your business colleagues, and thereby the enterprise demand for IT, as a new CIO leader. The demand side of leadership focuses on the needs of the enterprise and the ways IT can enable the enterprise to achieve its strategic goals and fill its persistent business needs.

As a demand-side leader, you should now have a clear idea of the work the IS organization needs to do. This is the *what*, the agenda for leading your business with technology. It's the promise of technology's enabling the business. This is, of course, not the only area of priorities and focus that needs to change for you to become a new CIO leader. There are also changes in focus and priorities on the supply side—the IS organization and its ability to deliver on the promises you've made on the demand side. As we discussed earlier, credibility underpins everything a new CIO leader does. If you are to take the path to becoming a new CIO leader, you must also maintain and improve your credibility by delivering on all you have implicitly and explicitly promised with your vision, IT maxims, governance, and IT strategy. If you can't deliver, you'll have no credibility; if you have no credibility, you won't be able to lead your business colleagues and you'll suddenly find yourself well down the path to being chief technology mechanic.

So, to be a new CIO leader, you have to build and lead a new IS organization that is dramatically different in its makeup, what it does, and how it measures and communicates its progress. Keep in mind that these changes, like those discussed on the demand side, are not, and cannot be, immediate. We're laying out the direction you need to take your IS group—not where it has to be tomorrow.

In this chapter, we address the need to lead IS toward a leaner structure that focuses on processes (business processes, not just IS processes), that sources IT services strategically, and manages its finances like any other business unit.[1] In the remaining chapters in this book, we'll discuss the new and broader risks that IS must now manage for the enterprise, building your IS team, and how to communicate your success back to the business.

Before proceeding here, however, we need to look at how IS organizations have come to be what they are. For the truth is, traditional IS structures no longer offer the best means of delivering the promise of technology to the enterprise. Some history will help explain.

A History of IS Organizations

In the 1960s and much of the 1970s, IS was a centralized data-processing department for the parent business. Governance and organization were straightforward. As time went by and technology became more focused on the individual, IS became more costly and less able to cope with growing demand, just as it was providing ever greater benefits to the enterprise. For example, IT enabled greater innovation and agility, leveraged intellectual capital, lowered costs, supported interoperability between shifting alliances and partnerships, and helped maximize productivity and collaboration. Ironically, IS organizations struggled with the very success of IT, with the higher expectations and growing demand that success fostered.

Consequently, by the 1980s, when large corporations tended to break themselves up into profit-centered business units to improve management control, IS was often broken up as well. Decentralizing IS helped make it more responsive to users in the business. The downside, however, was duplicated effort, lost economies of scale, and—worst of all—incompatible technologies across the organization as a whole.

Enterprises tried to correct this problem by adopting a compromise—a federal IS organization—with some activities centralized and some decentralized among the business units. Today, federal IS structures are widespread. But for most businesses, the federal model falls far short of perfection. Deciding which activities to centralize and which to decentralize is a perennial problem. The optimal solution changes over time as a result of both business and technological changes. (The maxims process helps establish the guidelines for synergy and shared services, but these guidelines need to be regularly reviewed.)

The way most IS groups were internally organized only exacerbated the problem. Traditional management more or less drove service organizations into functional silos. That approach in IS was easy to manage and understand (at least for IS people), but it made service delivery unreliable because it required multiple handoffs, generally across IS units. For example, for a long time, IS organizations were organized to support hardware systems—to the point, for example, that one team supported IBM mainframe systems, another handled Digital Equipment Corporation's midsize systems, and yet another managed PCs when they came along. Only a rare few IS staff understood how information was stored, maintained, updated, and supported across the enterprise. IS organizations responded by creating additional processes to deal with the handoffs. The result was a bureaucracy of process tracking that added even more complexity and internal focus, without adding much value.

It didn't help that all this complexity made the IS organization structure completely opaque to business users in the enterprise, since these users had no understanding of technical functions. To these "outsiders," traditional IS organization charts read like a book written in a foreign language. The IS organizations themselves, like the technology they operated and applied, became a black box.

This outcome has produced a bitter irony. While IS staff feel overworked and stressed out (for good reason), business leaders often perceive IS (and other internal service organizations) as noncompetitive in cost or value with external service providers (ESPs). These executives consider internal support groups inflexible and nonresponsive almost by definition. Treated as overhead and often lacking even the most rudimentary chargeback systems, IT appears to be free and therefore without much value. Lacking a price point to encourage responsible decision making, business leaders demand more service than they fund, creating a perpetual backlog of demand and placing IS in the position of continually saying no.

IS organizations respond by restructuring from time to time to try to correct misalignments and deficiencies. This effort typically occurs in an ad hoc way, in response to immediate pressures. But the restructuring usually means tinkering and tweaking and does little more than create further complexity and confusion. Some IS organizations that did not restructure in a timely way found that IT services were outsourced at the initiative of the CEO or CFO. ESPs were able to take out costs, but the result often did not deliver better business value, much less improved service, to the ultimate customer.

As a result of the history we've briefly outlined, many IS organizations find themselves in a position that can't be sustained. They must move somewhere, somehow. At Gartner, we've been studying this challenge for several years to learn where IS organizations need to head in response to these organizational challenges.

A number of trends are unfolding. We have observed a sharpening demarcation between IT services performed or coordinated centrally and those performed or managed in an enterprise's business units. There has also been a move to specialist units (they may be corporate or located in business units), often called centers of excellence, where specific IS and IT skills can be pooled and nurtured. Most significantly, we see trends toward process-based work in IS organizations and the strategic sourcing of IT services.

IS Lite: The Convergence of IS Organizational Trends

Of all the trends now developing, process-based work and strategic sourcing are more prevalent than the others. Process-based work is a way of organizing the IS group around the processes it supports, whether they are IS processes (as opposed to IS functions) or business processes in the broader enterprise. Process-based work means organizing people, operations, and technology around end-to-end work flows—in the business or IS—rather than around functions, platforms, or skill sets. For example, the traditional approach to order fulfillment might have separate functions for order entry, inventory control, shipping, billing, customer service, and claims processing. In process-based work, on the other hand, a single team with the requisite expertise manages the entire end-to-end process—from taking the initial order to resolving warranty and billing issues. As a result, the entire process appears seamless to the customer. This trend is rated by CIOs we've surveyed as the strongest new contributor to customer satisfaction.

The second trend that stands out is the strategic sourcing of IT services. For many—wrongly—strategic sourcing means solely outsourcing part or all of IT to an ESP. The commonly held assumption is that the reason for outsourcing is cost savings, but many organizations that have outsourced solely for cost advantage have been and continue to be disappointed by the meager savings they actually realize. Leading organizations who source in a truly strategic way know that sourcing is more than just outsourcing. They also see that the primary benefit of outsourcing, when invoked, is to offload operations work and free up IS staff to focus on more strategic issues. Outsourcing IT activities that support infrastructure (e.g., data center operations and network management) is particularly popular, as is outsourcing the development, maintenance, and integration of applications and systems.

These two developments—process-based work and strategic sourcing—are part of the maturation of the business uses of IT. Think about the evolution of manufacturing. Products can now be created through a series of processes—parts of which are completed in different parts of the world. This same evolution is now occurring with IT.

Rather than being swept along by the changes, you need to look at where the trends are all heading if you are to lead effectively. This future point of convergence between process-based work, IT strategic sourcing, sharply delineated central services, and specialist units is a simplified IS structure we've dubbed "IS Lite"—a leaner, more agile IS, more aligned with and responsive to the enterprise.

Compared with conventional IS organizations, IS Lite will be smaller and more sharply focused, but more effective as well. Much conventional IS work will be either outsourced or embedded in the business units, with IS serving as an intermediary between internal and external suppliers on the one hand and users on the other. Most of all, however, the IS Lite group will concentrate on driving business innovation (figure 7-1).

The full implementation of IS Lite is years away for many IS groups, but we already see leading-edge organizations moving that way. Getting there will not be easy. But even if the road ahead is rocky and twisting, we think it's better to envision a destination than to have no idea what lies ahead.

JDS Uniphase provides an example of how and why one IS organization moved to a leaner yet more strategic IS organization. A worldwide leader in optical technology, JDS Uniphase designs and manufactures fiber-optic products for communications equipment. The company operates from joint headquarters in San Jose, California, and Ottawa, Ontario, and manufactures in over twenty locations in the United States, Canada, Europe, and China.

Recent annual revenues were US$834 million, which represented a sobering drop of 80 percent from a high of US$3.2 billion

FIGURE 7-1

The Shape of IS Lite

An IS Lite organization will move portions of its traditional work to business units and external service providers.

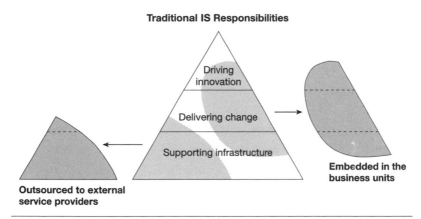

at the peak of the telecommunications boom. When the telecom industry imploded, the company undertook a rapid global restructuring, with the goal of not only surviving but positioning itself to quickly capitalize on the eventual upturn in technology markets.

JDS Uniphase managed to bring its costs down in line with reduced business revenues, while still providing the IT support crucial to the business. As a percentage of revenues, IT costs dropped from 10 to 5 percent. Total employees dropped from 28,000 to 7,000, as IS employees dropped from 200 to 150.

The company's IS organization was well positioned to respond quickly to this sea change in the business environment. It had already outsourced much of its applications development and infrastructure to ten service providers. The organization was accustomed to relying on outsourcers to meet most of its IS needs. Business processes had been standardized worldwide, making application support easier.

With the downturn in business, the company's IS strategy changed from using several ESPs to forming a strategic partnership with a single service provider. The goal was to reduce costs, create a single point of contact for problem resolution, and maintain the potential for quick scalability once business volumes recovered. A software vendor that also provided hosting was selected as the partner, and all JDS Uniphase applications were migrated to run on a single instance of the vendor's application suite that was hosted, maintained, and supported by the vendor's staff.

Desktop support, site-specific systems support, and network management were the major IS functions not outsourced. This decision was based on the geographic diversity of JDS Uniphase's facilities, which included three plants in China. The mission-critical nature of the network for plant operations and the lack of a credible service provider with the reach to perform these functions better and cheaper justified keeping these functions in-house.

The move to a smaller, more focused IS organization at JDS Uniphase was completed in an intense six-month effort. It required consolidating three data centers, redesigning the wide area network, migrating to the latest release of business applications, terminating or renegotiating existing outsourcing contracts, developing the hosting contract and service-level agreements, and staff reductions.

The results have been very positive. Costs declined while service levels improved. Since the business application vendor was hosting its own application suite, there were no middlemen to deal with and no finger pointing over who owned a problem. The reduction in complexity, both in the number of vendors needing managing and in a simplified infrastructure, allowed IS to reduce its staffing level without affecting service. The financial result was impressive, with US$40 million in savings passed to the bottom line.

Process-Based Work: A Step Toward IS Lite

Leading toward IS Lite means embracing the trends we mentioned earlier. To create a smaller but more strategic IS organization (rather than just a smaller IS organization over which a chief technology mechanic might preside), process-based work is a necessity. The traditional IS organization has been organized around functions (e.g., programming or help desk). Specialists in a function do their job, then hand the work over to other specialists in a different function. By contrast, processes are complete entities staffed by specialists working in teams that cut across functions, delivering a final "product" of value to the customer. It's analogous to the distinction between a manufacturing assembly line, where each worker does a small piece of the overall task, and manufacturing teams, where the team takes a product all the way through completion and delivery. Process-based IS most often supports complete business processes (as opposed to partial business processes or IS processes). Organizing and working this way typically delivers faster results, reduces errors, and improves customer satisfaction.

Servicing customer inquiries through a customer contact center is an example. A well-designed center presents a consistent interface to customers, and the standard of service is independent of which business unit provides the follow-up or which communication mode the customer uses—phone, fax, e-mail, or Web site.

Organizing around processes often requires that process teams be overlaid on top of the existing IS structure (figure 7-2). Process-based work depends for success on skilled resource management and the ability of IS staff to work in teams toward a common purpose with other IT specialists and with staff from the business. The competencies required to work this way may not be common in your organization, but they can be developed, a topic we'll look at in chapter 8.

Process-based work in IS may be organized around providing support for a business process. Increasingly, businesses are supplementing their existing structures by adding to their organization an additional dimension that focuses on one or more key processes.

Focusing on business processes inevitably leads to process reengineering. IT is a major factor in reengineering: It enables work to be done more efficiently. So it makes sense for IS to get involved with supporting businesses and for this support to be an extension of the processes themselves.

Some enterprises have created IS structures featuring so-called centers of excellence—such as programming, project management, or application integration—from which IS staff were drawn to support

FIGURE 7-2

Process-Based Work at Anglo Platinum

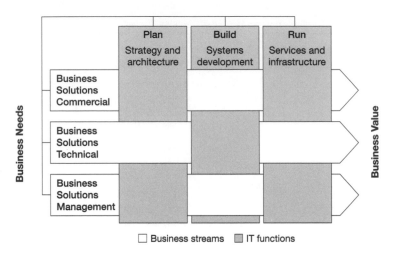

Source: Used courtesy of Anglo Platinum.

such business processes as raw materials to warehousing. One difficulty with this approach is managing conflicts of interest between
the process and the business units. Priority conflicts of this kind can
be resolved by a steering committee, but it's often simpler to dedi-
cate a complete IS unit to the business process. Of course, there are
downsides to this approach as well, the primary disadvantage being
duplication of effort.

Deciding how best to support a business process—either by teams
drawn from centers of excellence or by a dedicated IS unit—means
trading off the cost of coordination on one hand and the cost of
duplicated efforts on the other.

Relationship managers are key to process-based work

Successfully creating an organization based on process-based
work requires more than merely changing the organization chart.
The relationship between IS and the business is central to process-
based work and to enterprisewide sharing of business process

expertise. The relationship is often best handled by high-level relationship managers in IS.

Relationship managers are the (internal) customer-facing section of the IS organization and are charged with understanding customer demand and communicating that demand to IS. They must earn a high degree of personal credibility with their customers and are responsible for driving IS credibility to an acceptable level. They understand how technology can be used for business advantage, and they're adept at working through IS delivery managers for fulfillment. CIOs support their relationship managers by coaching and mentoring them about corporate decision-making processes, prioritization, and IS–business alignment.

Relationship managers typically engage in the following tasks:

- Manage the relationship between IS and one or more business units or business process owners

- Negotiate IT services and prices

- Negotiate service-level agreements (SLAs)

- Resolve disputes between service recipients and service providers

- Ensure that IT standards are established and observed

- Recommend new uses of IT to enhance business performance

- Act as a broker of IT services, negotiating for both internal and external resources

- Remain abreast of, and communicate, competitors' use of IT

- Manage expectations and demand for IT services

Process-based work in practice: Anglo Platinum

Anglo Platinum, the platinum mining and processing subsidiary of Anglo American Platinum Corporation Limited, is a leader in converting IS to process-based work. The world's largest platinum extractor, the company employs some forty-four thousand people, mainly in South Africa, and generates revenues of some 20 billion rand (US$2.5 billion).

Several years ago, the company decentralized its IT systems to eleven business units, most of which were mines in the North West province. The result was system duplication: eleven ERP instances, eleven e-mail systems, and so on.

Then the company began a strong drive to exploit the inherent synergies across today's thirteen business units, by standardizing business processes and centralizing decision making. Anglo Platinum's IS organization supported this effort by rapidly adopting a process-based work paradigm, as well as expertise in sharing and outsourcing.

Demand from the business units for IT services was stated in terms strongly process oriented and standardized. With some inevitable differences among the business units, the key enterprise-wide processes were safety, health, and environment; metallurgy; research and development; finance; human resources; supply chain; physical asset management; corporate services; and IT. Process champions at the corporate center encouraged standardization and coordinated governance across the group.

Each business unit identified and prioritized IT requirements at monthly enterprisewide user group meetings, which were chaired by the appropriate corporate process champions. Business unit IT requirements were coordinated by an IS manager (ISM), then were submitted to an ISM meeting, which also included representatives from a central IS department called Group IT. ISM meetings also focused on business unit services and infrastructure matters.

This strong process orientation was mirrored within Group IT, where a process coordinator headed each business process. Process coordinators were divided into three streams: business solutions commercial, business solutions technical, and business information management.

The process coordinators in IS interfaced with the business's process champions. They strove to share process-change requirements across business units and hence to benefit from standardization, economies of scale, and expertise sharing. The process coordinators

The New IS and the Three Types of CIOs

IN THE INTRODUCTION, we pointed out that the building of a new IS organization needs to be the top priority of the CIO in fighting-for-survival enterprises. Without the right IS organization, these CIOs will be caught in a downward spiral of cost cutting and indifferent delivery that ultimately undermines all credibility and is completely incompatible with their role as a new CIO leader. But as we also explained, your current business stance is not a predictor of your success in becoming a new CIO leader.

Each of the three modes in which CIOs operate will dictate a different focus in building their new IS organization. In fighting-for-survival enterprises, CIOs will want to aggressively explore strategic sourcing, looking for ways to use outsourcing in particular to improve service delivery at the same or lower costs. If you are in this situation, make sure, however, to carefully follow the advice in this chapter about strategic sourcing. Otherwise, you may find most of your efforts to cut costs an embarrassing failure. CIOs of maintaining-competitiveness enterprises will want to focus on introducing process-based work as a way of raising the effectiveness of IT service delivery and positioning the organization for growth when it shifts to a more expansionary mode. CIOs in breaking-away enterprises, on the other hand, should fully realize the power of strategic sourcing, especially in looking for ways to augment IS capability (and transfer knowledge into the organization) with business change and business strategy services from ESPs.

One final caveat—all the changes we note here and in chapter 8 regarding the new IS group need to be on the new CIO leader's agenda. Though the approach and ordering of change may be different, the need to effect these changes is not conditional on your current business context.

from IS and the process champions from business units agreed on requirements and prioritization; their decisions were reviewed by a Business Technology Council.

The demand side of IT was managed by the process coordinators within Group IT. Managing the supply side of IT was done by the professional IT staff in Group IT, which was organized in three groups: *Plan*, with responsibility for strategy and planning, architecture, R&D and governance; *Build*, which looked after largely outsourced system development; and *Run*, with responsibility for service delivery management, security, and application support. (This organization is illustrated in figure 7-2.)

Strategically Sourcing IT Services

IT outsourcing, the second major trend now reshaping IS organizations, began in the early 1970s, with some companies' transfer of data center equipment and people to large outsourcers such as EDS and IBM. The offshore outsourcing rush since 2000 is just the latest in a historical trend. The initial goals of the first outsourced data centers were to shift costs from multiyear investments to predictable yearly expenses and to offload operational work to infrastructure specialists. The phenomenon spread to other supply-side areas—the management of desktop machines, the staffing of help desks, the running of networks, and the maintenance of legacy systems.[2]

Outsourcing was often a reaction to an unacceptable state—costs too high, service indifferent, or the need for expensive expertise to keep technology current. According to years of in-depth Gartner research, however, 80 percent of IT outsourcing deals, especially those that focus solely on cost, fail to meet the initial objectives. At leading organizations, the rationale has changed—these organizations view outsourcing in a broader context, what Gartner calls strategic sourcing.

Strategic sourcing asks, "What's the best source for every IT service? This broader context for sourcing looks dispassionately at the variety of sourcing alternatives for every IT service to capitalize on opportunities. It's very important not to make the common mistake of equating strategic sourcing with outsourcing. Strategic sourcing certainly evaluates external providers as a possible source for IT services—but it also equally considers internal providers. First, embracing strategic sourcing means that no options for obtaining

IT services are taken off the table; you consider every alternative and always select the one that meets business needs most effectively. Second, strategic sourcing decisions look beyond short-term constraints on resources or currently high costs. Strategic sourcing considers the long-term goals of the enterprise to decide what services, skills, competencies, funding arrangements, and so forth, are needed within the enterprise over the long term. A sourcing strategy is a continuous journey into the best balance between internal and external activities, services, and know-how. It is a continuous alignment between business strategy, business processes, and IT services on behalf of the organization's strategic intent. It is an instrument for flexibility, not a rigid decision or a static outsourcing contract based on a service provider's brand.

Strategic sourcing is a process, not a onetime decision.

One of the reasons strategic sourcing is wrongly equated with outsourcing is that, when all options—internal and external—are considered, most CIOs find that outsourced services are a very viable alternative for many of their IT services needs (especially when they are considering more than just cost). As you probably have experienced, however, strategic sourcing decisions are not as easy as the media hype would lead your business colleagues to believe. There are plenty of pitfalls. We queried many CIOs around the world about the steps they used to ensure their strategic sourcing decisions were sound. Their input is presented below.

Know what you cannot outsource: Five critical roles that every IS organization must retain

In the initial rush to outsource, some enterprises did not appreciate just what capabilities they needed to retain and grow. Drawing on our research, we believe that IS groups must retain a key set of roles and skills within the enterprise (figure 7-3):

1. *IT leadership:* The leadership role is crucial to the implementation of the vision you have created.

Additionally, IT leadership is needed in the conversion of the IS organization to IS Lite—the shift from functional silos to processes, and innovation for business value, as well as the other nascent but not-well-established trends, such as the creation of centers of excellence. In our research, CIOs currently rate IT leadership as the most important role for internal staff, and they expect leadership to retain its prominence in the future. IT leadership received nearly the highest rating possible.

2. *Architecture development:* This capability plays a major role in the new IS organization because of the need to ensure system links with outsourcers, establish process-based work (often supported by Web-based processes), and control standards used in competency centers. Architecture development can only become more prominent, for one simple reason: the growing importance of security management. Developing and implementing security standards are part of this role. This does not mean that the architecture itself is not outsourced, but that architecture planning and decision-making capability must be retained.

3. *Business enhancement:* The business-enhancement role deals mainly with IS–business integration, which is important in shifting to process-based work and in moving IT work to business units. This role is key to shifting from a technical to a business orientation and from a cost-centric to a value-centric focus.

4. *Technology advancement:* This technological capability concerns mostly the introduction of emerging technologies that will directly support business goals. Increasing focus on innovation guarantees the growing prominence of this role.

5. *Vendor management:* Because it's associated with contract management and performance monitoring, vendor

FIGURE 7-3

Five Key Roles to Retain in IS

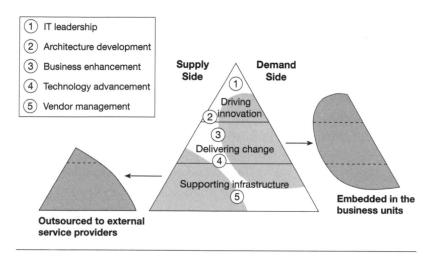

management plays an important role in outsourcing and capability management. It's key to extracting maximum value from ESPs. As those outside suppliers play more important roles for the enterprise, the importance of vendor management can only rise as well.

Diagnose sourcing needs

For sourcing needs, it helps to think of IT services as falling into three categories (which link back to the portfolio approach in chapter 6):

Managing infrastructure services: This category supplies and supports infrastructure, such as data center operations, network management, desktop systems support, Web site hosting, and storage management. Many of these services are now commodity services, and cost efficiency and ready capability are paramount. Once the business needs are established, the expertise needed is more technical than business. These are the services that have traditionally been most commonly outsourced.

Business change services: Services in this category develop and roll out applications and integrate systems. Expertise should be balanced between business and technology.

Business strategy services: These drive the innovative use of IT in the business and weave together business and IS strategies. What counts in these IT services is vision and creativity, more than cost efficiency. The expertise of your service provider (internal or external) needs to be more business than technical for this kind of work.

Once you've categorized the services you need to provide to meet business goals (based on your maxims and IT strategy), you can begin the evaluation of what source will be most effective in delivering the required services.

Evaluate and select the best sources

IT professionals who can weave together business and IT are a valued resource and scarcer than we would wish. It makes sense that scarce internal resources be available to work on the areas that need deep business knowledge, like IT leadership and architecture. Therefore, the best source for many discrete IT services will increasingly be outside the IS group. This source might be a business unit's IT-literate staff who are able to manage a range of IT services, from intranet management to IT strategy formulation. In most cases, though, ESPs far overshadow business unit staff as a source of IT services. These organizations can realize economies of scale and utilization to meet service levels with the minimum-cost approach needed for infrastructure services. These service providers are evolving from their traditional base of strength in infrastructure management to a growing expertise in enabling business change and, in some cases, business strategy development.

To truly develop a strategic sourcing outlook, you must be willing to compare these increasingly capable service providers with your own IS group. Making comparisons can be tricky—the process is fraught with political pitfalls and can create high anxiety among your staff. So how should you go about your evaluation of sourcing alternatives? What is the best place to begin comparing internal and external capabilities?

By now you won't be surprised to hear that you should start with your business context and the strategic intent of your enterprise. However, in this case, these issues must be tempered by your experience in managing ESPs. If your organization is focused on innovation and you see gaps in your IS group's ability to provide business strategy services, these services might seem an ideal place to start outsourcing. You should be very careful, though, about outsourcing any function that requires deep business knowledge. Also, keep in mind that managing the provision of business strategy services is far more difficult than managing infrastructure services. Therefore, you need to balance your needs with your ability and skills to manage service providers when deciding what classes of services to consider outsourcing.

Once you've decided which services you will evaluate, create a level playing field for evaluating all resources, internal and external. Treat your existing IS capability as if it were another competitor for your contract dollars. For instance, if you're using a request for a proposal (an RFP), have your internal group respond to the request (see the box about low-cost bids and RFPs on page 189). In that spirit, from this point on we will use the term *service provider* to mean both external and internal service providers. Don't forget, however, to include the value of maintaining expertise in-house as part of your internal group's response.

Selecting the best available service provider greatly decreases the risk associated with each IT investment. By applying a standardized, flexible evaluation process, you ensure efficiency without imposing structure that does not create value.

Before you get started, make sure you've done your homework. First, involve the end users or business users that will need to work with the service provider. Second, align the requirements and evaluation criteria with the business objectives: Let the business objectives be the beacon in the process. Third, define requirements precisely and carefully: This will enable the service provider to shape its offering and put forth a responsive, credible proposal. Fourth, make sure the service provider actually responds to the requirements: Attention to this detail will make an enormous difference when you compare one service provider with another, as well as save you considerable time.

Now set your evaluation and selection criteria. Our work and that of our colleagues at Gartner suggest that these criteria can be separated into five broad categories:

Process, technical, and industry knowledge: What are the service provider's core competencies? Does it have specific methodologies? Does it have experience working in your industry?

Track record: Has the provider done similar projects? Can it provide good reference accounts? Has it worked for you or other members of your staff in prior jobs?

Contracting flexibility: Is the service provider willing to modify or accommodate its standard practices to fit your business and financial requirements? Is your relationship manager empowered to adjust the contract over time, or does it require multiple layers of approval?

Experience and availability of key personnel: Is the service provider willing to include key personnel clauses? Do you have the right to select from a pool of candidates? Can the provider guarantee specific personnel as part of the agreement?

Cultural fit between the service provider and the enterprise: How has the service provider portrayed itself during the RFP or negotiation process? Does it take the time to figure out your culture? Does it recognize that this is an important part of your decision?

The weight given to each broad category must vary based on the attributes of each service. For example, cultural fit would be a primary criterion if you're considering the provision of long-term, complex business strategy services, but not so important if you're evaluating services for a short-term technology implementation project. Similarly, a service provider's track record would be important for mature services, but a record may be nonexistent if you are entering a transformational relationship that will explore uncharted territory, such as creating a new business line. Using a process that assigns weights to a standard set of evaluation criteria will enable you to be consistent while tailoring your evaluation to each specific project. Don't forget to go beyond these criteria and seek the opinions of outside experts.[3]

Remember, there is no single best provider. Selecting a service provider to execute a particular project or provide a specific service must be done according to the specific type of work being considered and who is available at that time. Again, we need to stress that sourcing strategically means considering the long-term impact of certain skills and knowledge residing inside or outside the organization.

If your evaluation concludes that an ESP is the best source, your next step is to create a contract that fosters success. (If the best source is internal, you should consider following the steps below to create a positive SLA. For simplicity's sake, however, we will assume you are contracting with an ESP.)

Create and manage flexible contracts for the delivery of IT services

Unfortunately, too many CIOs spend far too much time and effort attempting to write outsourcing contracts that will "last." The difficulty in managing outsourced services is not lasting contracts but in the preparing, documenting, and managing of contracts that, by necessity, accommodate change. In a world that changes rapidly, why would you want agreements that cannot change?

To create flexible contracts, it's helpful to think of three different classes of contract arrangements: utility, enhancement, and frontier. These classes roughly parallel the three IT services categories of infrastructure, business change, and business strategy.

Utility contracts focus on cost efficiency. Clients want services equivalent to what they have now, but better and cheaper.

Enhancement contracts provide a significant performance improvement, though not a radical change of direction. The reengineering of an existing process is an example.

Frontier contracts harness IT to add significant value to existing business activities or take the business into new fields (or out of existing ones). A retailer might move into consumer financial services, for instance.

The challenge with all three types of contracts is to strike the right balance between motivating the ESP and retaining control. This is a particular need with frontier contracts, which take the enterprise into new areas, such as new markets or customers. To achieve a proper balance, you must take two additional steps in developing the contract and relationship with the ESP.

First, add supplements to a basic, built-to-last contract with provisions designed to handle change. The basic part of a contract sets out the general terms and conditions, such as confidentiality, copyright, change control, transition, and termination. The contract also defines the scope of the work as well as locations, reporting, standards, security, pricing, and staff and asset transfer. Items like these aren't likely to change much over the life of the contract.

To these basic provisions, add supplements in five major areas: strategy and policy, resourcing, integration, compensation, and audit and feedback. The purpose of the supplements is to form a foundation for comanagement, that is, the sharing of the management burden. You want your service provider to work as hard as you are to find increasingly better solutions to drive down costs, find better solutions to business problems, and adjust to change in the business environment. The degree of supplementation and comanagement will vary, depending on the kind of service being provided. Utility arrangements may not require much comanagement, while frontier services will probably require a high level of it.

The Low-Ball Bid and RFPs

WHEN YOU'RE LOOKING at ESPs and their contracted prices, keep in mind that service providers very often lowball their bid, essentially undercharging on the front end of a long-term contract and expecting to make up the loss in later years. We have seen a great many organizations wowed by seemingly huge cost savings, only to see these savings evaporate as change fees and unanticipated add-ons bring the price up, often to the point at which there are no long-term savings at all. The message: Don't take pricing at face value. Ask how it is being determined and how it will change over the life of the contract. You need to understand your ESP's business model and how the provider makes a profit. (You also must respect that the ESP does indeed need to make a profit to continue in business and serve your organization.)

The use of very long and detailed RFPs distributed to many potential candidates contributes to this problem. Gartner experts recommend using a fast-track process to select the best two, and only two, providers. (We know that this approach unfortunately will not work for many government organizations, which are required to have a public bidding process.) Then, you can get into the details of work statements and contracts while maintaining a competitive environment. Based on work with many clients, our findings show that this approach has consistently yielded the best long-term results—a contract that both you and the outsourcer can live with.

Second, shift the basis of the relationship with the service provider from arm's length and formal to close and trust-based. Successfully managing flexible contracts that accommodate change also requires changes in the relationship between IS and the ESP, from arm's length to tight. Tight relationships are necessary to improve the amount of cooperation and to engender a level of trust sufficient to safeguard shared confidentialities. Yet again, your ability to manage relationships and build trust is crucial to your success. A downside of relationship tightening is the problem of conflicts and how to resolve them. It's wise to agree on a step-by-step procedure for conflict resolution in advance.

Contract comanagement and relationship nurturing are extremely challenging, especially in an environment that blends internally sourced services with services from several ESPs. You need a set of staff competencies to comanage a relationship and monitor a contract. Providing these competencies is the next step.

Provide sourcing management competencies

The IS competencies needed to manage ESPs will vary with the type of service. Although business and behavioral competencies do matter in comanaging utility contracts, the emphasis is on technical competencies. Comanaging frontier contracts is the reverse, emphasizing behavioral and business competencies. Acquiring these competencies is comparatively difficult and a major challenge for most IS organizations. These competencies rarely reside within a traditional IS group. They usually have to be acquired through extensive training or retraining or pulled from other parts of the enterprise or from external recruitment. We'll discuss how to identify and obtain the needed competencies much more in chapter 8.

Strategic sourcing is an emerging approach to delivering IT services. It starts from the premise "What's best for the enterprise?" rather than simply "How do we fix our problem?" But since external sourcing brings its own set of challenges, it's best to be well prepared by understanding your different sourcing needs, your sourcing options, the real nature of contracts, and the competencies that underpin a successful—and less painful—sourcing experience.

Moving from sourcing to strategic sourcing: Pari-Mutuel Urbain

Pari-Mutuel Urbain (PMU) of France learned the downside of outsourcing the hard way before taking a more strategic view. The company is the largest off-site pari-mutuel betting organization in Europe and the third largest in the world, with annual revenues of over US$6.5 billion. Its large online network allows the placing of

Acting Like an ESP

SOME IS ORGANIZATIONS are taking an even bigger step and trying to model themselves after an ESP. They're moving to what Gartner calls the internal services company, or ISCo, model. This model has many characteristics of an IS Lite organization and, according to our research, is particularly suited to enterprises that have more decentralized business units or agencies. In this model, IS essentially manages itself like a for-profit business. It markets its competencies, charging for all services rendered. The ISCo uses flexible funding, pricing, and charge-back mechanisms to reconcile service demand with service supply, particularly market-based pricing, which ultimately aims to charge for services in a way that makes a profit for IS.

Obviously, the competitive elements of the ISCo approach raise many questions. How, for example, does an ISCo adopt a competitive stance while partnering with business units inside the enterprise? Issues like internal competition are why the model seems most applicable when IS operates as a separate business within a decentralized enterprise.

---

bets from eight thousand points of sale right up to the start of a race. Payment of winners occurs just ten minutes after a race.

In 1996, PMU decided to reengineer its core information systems and outsourced its application and systems development to access IT skills not available in-house. A large backlog of development requests built up because the new core system took five years to be developed. In an effort to attack and resolve the backlog quickly, PMU engaged over fifty mostly small ESPs. Most of the work was contracted on a time-and-materials basis, which left PMU exposed to potential cost overruns and gave the ESPs little incentive to minimize costs.

When a new CIO arrived in 2001, he focused initially on bringing the large number of projects under control, reducing the number of ESPs, and changing the roles and competencies of PMU's IS organization. PMU's culture had been one of trying to do everything in-house, and the company was not accustomed to managing

ESPs. The internal staff needed training on developing requirements and writing specifications with more rigor and precision. Otherwise, the ESPs couldn't provide realistic, fixed-price estimates or minimize the need for change orders. The in-house staff also had to be trained in higher skill levels of acceptance testing to ensure that ESPs delivered what was contracted and that the results met specifications. The company put in place various training programs to develop these key skills. It hired four experienced senior project managers to bring the projects and ESPs under control. The ESPs were reduced from over fifty to fewer than ten. Contracts were rewritten as fixed-price rather than time-and-materials. Finally, rates were re-negotiated downward. This way, PMU could take advantage of the competition created by offering larger contracts to a much smaller pool of ESPs in a slowing economy. All these steps allowed IS to reduce its 2002 budget by 10 percent, without loss of service.

Put IS on a Sound Financial Basis

Finally, we come to the third task for the new CIO leader in building a new IS organization: putting the new IS on a firm financial footing. Many CIOs we know consider the whole issue of IT costs a lose-lose proposition.

If the IS organization carries all IT costs in its own budget and they're never allocated or charged directly back to the business users in the enterprise, those users will consider IT free. And *free* in this case means the users feel free not only of any cost burden but also of any responsibility to use IT intelligently.

On the other hand, if the enterprise charges out all or many IT costs to the business units, there are other problems. In particular, the IS organization may have to endure endless, frustrating arguments about the way costs are calculated and spread, about the level of cost, and ultimately about "I can get it cheaper on the outside."

Like the issues companies have with salaries, the issues around IT costs are often not really about money per se but about the perceived worth, value, and contribution. The goal of getting IT costs right, then, is not to zero out the IS budget but to build credibility and foster the intelligent use of IT in alignment with enterprise purposes. As you can see, the proper handling of costs is a vital part of building a new IS organization.

If you and your IS organization are to do your work effectively, you need to confront the issue of cost and value. There are no easy ways to clear up these questions (chapter 10 addresses linking IS performance to business value), but your new IS organization needs a clear understanding of its costs and how and why it incurs them.

Identifying your IT service costs

The first step in addressing costs is getting a firm grasp on what your IT service costs actually are. You can't move effectively toward IS Lite and strategic sourcing without this knowledge. As you probably already know, identifying costs is not easy, particularly for shared IT services, such as infrastructure. Costs are affected by total usage and service levels. Different approaches to cost identification lead to different results, opening the door to accusations of unfairness and inaccuracy.

As a new CIO leader, you'll need to use your relationships to effectively engage your enterprise's finance department for the cost identification and allocation process. We recommend a three-phase process in conjunction with your finance peers: Create a standardized chart of accounts, decide which accounting treatment to use, and draw up an accounting policy to be used consistently.

Creating a chart of accounts begins with an IT services directory that shows what IT services are provided, who uses them, and what cost treatments apply to each. Costs can be accounted for in different ways, taking into account fixed and variable components.

The best approach is to engage a partner from the finance organization, either the CFO or one of his or her top executives. (If within your IS organization, you have a CFO who directly reports to you, then that person should be part of the process.) This way, your methods for costing will be congruent with the rest of the business, which ultimately ensures that the approach makes sense to your business colleagues. With the finance group, you'll need to sort through all the issues such as the use of marginal costing, the capitalization of assets, and approaches like activity-based costing, which, though more complex than traditional approaches, offer greater accuracy.

Allocating costs for better decisions

To make appropriate decisions for IS Lite and strategic sourcing, you'll also need to allocate costs across services, business units, and users. You may decide not to share this information broadly, but you do need it as one of your inputs as you plan your strategy.

Many methods of cost allocation are now widely used. When IT service costs are small compared to other business costs, you can use a simple, high-level allocation that is based on a single business parameter, such as business unit revenue or number of employees. This approach also works best for shared services (like infrastructure), where the lack of a clear relationship between usage and cost doesn't matter.

But when IT costs represent a large proportion of total costs, something more will be needed. A low-level allocation uses an IT-related parameter, such as number of PCs or network IDs, and works best for services like desktop support and IT architectural activities, where a suitable parameter can be readily agreed upon and where everyone has similar levels of use. However, this approach can penalize some users and favor others unfairly if the parameter fails to reflect the real use of IT accurately.

The direct-cost approach, in which all the costs of an IT service are allocated to the service's single "owner," works best for clearly attributable services, such as application development and dedicated projects. Direct cost is obviously unsuited for shared services.

Two other methods, measured resource usage and tiered flat rate, attempt to allocate costs based on actual usage. Measured resource usage applies where actual usage can be accurately and objectively measured, as, for example, in data storage and telecommunications. The tiered flat-rate method places users into service tiers or bands, with each level charged at a fixed rate. This method is best suited to stable environments where service levels are predefinable, like help desks, application maintenance, and data centers. Actual usage cannot be accurately measured, but all concerned can agree on a predefined level or tier of service used.

Getting to the New, Leaner IS Organization Will Be Challenging

The road to this leaner, more focused IS organization won't be smooth and therefore will require you to be a leader and not just a manager. All the leadership skills you need to lead your business colleagues will be essential here as well.

First, the competencies needed to make the new IS organization effective will differ from those of traditional IS. In process-based work and outsourcing higher-level IS work, business competencies and behavioral competencies like collaboration, team building, and conflict resolution will be much more important than traditional technical skills.

It's not surprising that many current IS staff lack the competencies to play the new roles required in the new, leaner organization. To make matters worse, developing those competencies will present a significant challenge. While technical competencies can be acquired through straightforward training, business and behavioral competencies are relatively difficult to acquire. Overcoming this challenge requires a combination of approaches—internal training, the use of external recruiters, and a careful look at other parts of your enterprise, especially among business professionals who have been heavily involved in IT-related projects.

You must expect IS resistance. Process-based work and outsourcing, as well as many of the other, lesser trends we've identified, require major change for IS groups; change is generally resisted, particularly when it involves, as it does here, movement to an unknown and therefore risky future. IS resistance typically springs from staff concerns about changing work practices and outsourcing, especially when your outsourcing decisions lead to transferring some of your IS staff to an ESP.

In spite of the difficulties, the forces pushing IS organizations toward the leaner, more focused model we've described will be hard to deny. What's clear is this: Traditional IS organizations, jealous of providing all the IS services needed by the enterprise and organized around IS functions that no one outside IS understands, won't last much longer. They're already beginning to move through the current confusion and complexity to the simpler IS Lite model we've described, and some are going beyond.

This evolution of IS is not a challenge you can avoid if you want to be a new CIO leader. Building a new IS organization is a crucial step in delivering the promise of technology to your enterprise.

8

Develop a High-Performing
IS Team

In part 2 of this book, we have been looking at the changed priorities of the new CIO leader for leading the IS organization. In part 1, we discussed the new skills you'll need to lead your business colleagues. Now we will take a look at the new skills your staff within the IS organization needs to deliver on your promises. As you probably have already learned from years of experience, no matter how well you organize your staff, if you don't have the right skills in place you won't succeed.

The role of the IS organization is changing along with the role of the new CIO leader, and therefore the skills your team requires are different. In fact, the new skills are similar to the skills *you* need to lead on the *business* side. In other words, your team must also take a leadership role with the business, as we discussed in chapter 7. Most members of your IS group now work in teams—with one another, with their business colleagues, and with external service providers. Increasingly, your team members work directly with your enterprise's customers. The members' skills at working with others and ability to contribute in teams are now crucial to getting work done. These human issues of leadership are no less critical for being a little "softer" than most of the issues we've covered so far.

In this chapter, we focus first on the leadership skills required by your senior IS staff.[1] Later in the chapter we talk about the various IS competencies essential to the new, leaner IS organization. Again, they're different from those needed by traditional IS organizations. We start with the human side of IS and building its leadership capability.

Apply Your Own Leadership Skills and Strengthen Those of Your IS Team

As we discussed at the outset of the book, there is a clear distinction between leadership and management. Leaders influence people to change, to undergo the kind of difficult transformation they're unlikely to see through by themselves. Managers, on the other hand, worry most about execution, about making the trains run on time, improving performance and control. One common distinction is that management is about doing things right, while leadership is about doing the right things.

As you've realized by now, being a new CIO leader means spending far more time outside the IS organization—and therefore you'll need greater staff strength back in the IS group to manage the delivery of services. You need reservoirs of talent there that can provide the full range of essential skills and experience. Each of your direct reports must have a good grasp of both business and technology issues, as everyday business becomes more technology-dependent.

First, the bad news. In IS organizations, promotion often comes through technical expertise and experience. Consequently, senior staff members get promoted into leadership positions that require people skills, even though they lack strength in those skills. It's not just people with technology backgrounds. Staff who come to IS from the business side of the organization may have been promoted because of their financial or analytic skills, and they're likely to suffer the same shortage of people skills.

Now, two pieces of good news. The required people skills can be learned, and the payoff from developing them can be huge. Although flawed leadership begets low motivation and morale, effective leadership encourages strong group coherence and high productivity. Leadership skills are not easy to develop, but it's possible to acquire them.

As you think about these skills, ask yourself how well you practice them. Don't neglect to consider as well how others might assess you. Researchers have found, unfortunately, that the higher they looked in organizations, the wider the gap between leaders' self-assessments and others' opinions of them.

Human skills are at the core of leadership

As we discussed in chapter 1, leaders with higher levels of emotional intelligence possess the capacity to deal with their own feelings, as well as the feelings of others. Daniel Goleman explains how emotional intelligence affects IS staff: "There's a direct link between the performance of a team and the emotional intelligence of its members. Productivity is one measure. Take software development. Teams with the highest EI score routinely outstrip the productivity of other teams, despite their technical skills' being equally matched. On high-scoring teams, people take time to help the others out, listen to their problems, suggest solutions and pitch in when needed. Another measure is staff retention. High EI correlates with low turnover. Of course, the EI of team leaders is important, too. Leaders set the tone. Leadership EI has a major impact on team performance."[2]

As we also discussed, there are four basic dimensions of emotional intelligence: self-awareness, self-management, social awareness, and social skills. To be effective as a new CIO leader, you have to apply emotional intelligence in dealing with your IS organization as well as with your business colleagues—and your IS leadership team needs to develop those same skills. As CIO, however, you bear a special burden of meeting the needs of your IS leadership team.

Effective leaders meet the needs of those they lead

Group performance—of your IS leadership team, for example—depends on your ability to fulfill three team needs: *task* needs, *group* needs, and *individual* needs.

Task needs

Of the many factors that influence team performance, clarity of direction (challenging but reasonable goals and objectives) is the most important. A survey by the Hay Group (with Richard Hackman and Ruth Wageman) found clarity of direction to be the most significant difference between teams' actual and desired performance.

Task clarity obviously applies to specific projects, but it also applies to the overall work of a group. Clear mission, vision, and IT maxims with meaning for IS employees can guide and drive higher performance in organizations.

As well as needing direction, groups have other task needs. One is appropriate procedures—for instance, to review and prioritize objectives, to set time scales, and to replan when necessary. Another requirement is evidence of progress: milestones passed, results achieved, and targets met. As leader, you must see that these task-driven needs are satisfied.

Group needs

Foremost among several group needs are size, structure, and coherence. Each new member of a team adds capability, of course, but the trade-off is *process loss:* the coordination problems and the myriad inefficiencies, from late starts to personality clashes, that occur when more and more people try to work together. Productivity generally declines beyond about five members. If it's productivity that counts—and that's usually the case—then the message is clear: Keep working groups as small as possible.

A group also needs clear roles for its members. Those roles can emerge and then be recognized as a new group coalesces, or the leader can designate them. If roles aren't clear, then members will probably waste time in duplicated effort and power struggles.

Groups need the right mix of experience, skills, talents, and personalities. Homogeneity may prevent discord, but at the expense of creativity and fresh thinking. You have to find the right mix of all those elements, striking a fine balance between members who are similar and those who are different.

Other group needs include strong communication among the members and between the members and you, the leader. Clear processes matter—for setting agendas, giving input, setting or rethinking priorities, and settling disagreements and conflicts. Norms are needed, too, so that the organization can set out the ground rules for what is acceptable behavior. Essentially, you need to think about governance issues for your group, call it *IS governance,* just as you created governance systems for IT-related decisions.

Individual needs

Each of us needs to feel that we're seen and heard as individuals, that we're able to make a contribution, and that our contribution is recognized. It's the leader's role to make sure these needs are addressed—both in his or her own interaction with group members and in the emotional intelligence skills of the people selected for membership in the group.

Because individuals need to contribute and feel included, group members should be chosen on the basis of empathy—their ability to connect with others—as much as their technical skills. Empathetic group members help their colleagues feel heard and understood, which will boost every member's sense of contribution, inclusion, and recognition.

Another survey by the Hay Group illustrates the importance of empathy.[3] The researchers found that team performance improved dramatically with the proportion of members who identified empathy as important in teams. (The assumption, of course, was that those who believe empathy is important will also practice it.) Team performance was measured by financial results, team climate, customer satisfaction, and growth and development of team members.

Meeting individual needs shows up in two other areas we discussed in chapter 1—leadership styles and personality types. Each topic is worth a brief review.

Understand your staff's personality types

We recommended in chapter 1 that you determine your own personality type and try to evaluate the personality types of your business colleagues. Within your IS group, you should be formal— have your direct reports, at least, take a personality inventory like Myers-Briggs (recall that a short form is in appendix A). It's a matter not only of courtesy but common sense that your leadership of your staff will be much more effective if you try to communicate with your colleagues in the terms they are most comfortable with. This is central to how teams do their work effectively—that each team member understands both how he or she personally gets work done and how others like to interact and work. As a leader, you must build on a knowledge of your own preferences to be intimately aware of the preferences of others so that you will know how to motivate and accommodate them.

Leadership styles in the IS group

Of the six leadership styles discussed in chapter 1 (commanding, pacesetting, visionary, affiliative, coaching, and democratic), we explained that you need to develop your visionary, affiliative, and democratic styles with your business colleagues. To be the most effective new CIO leader within your IS organization, the three other leadership styles will also come into play. Within your base of formal power, you can use the commanding style occasionally to get things moving. However, you will also need to put the coaching and pacesetting styles to use. In fact, for your IS leadership team, pacesetting is what the new CIO leader is all about. Lead your staff to make the necessary changes because you are making these changes as well.

As leaders, you and your senior IS team must understand the range of leadership styles, know when each is appropriate, and be able to use each when it is needed. Leaders who have authentically expanded the range of their styles beyond the dominant one to include at least two others can improve the results they get from their teams.

Building your—and your team's—human leadership skills

Although it isn't easy, the soft skills of leadership can be learned. Good leaders don't have to be born that way—they can grow in the workplace.

As Goleman says, "Emotional intelligence is learnable, but you have to use the right learning model. Compared with technical skills, for instance, emotional intelligence requires a different way of learning. . . . You have to change habits, which you can only do over time. But it takes very little time out of your day. In that sense, learning emotional intelligence takes elapsed time but virtually no dedicated time at all."[4]

Learning emotional intelligence is more difficult than conventional learning, and takes far longer, because it involves different areas of the brain. Consequently, the acquisition of this skill must occur in ways different from conventional learning. "One must first unlearn old habits, then develop new ones," says Goleman.[5] One-day seminars won't do it.

If you want these kinds of skills to spread throughout IS, both you and your senior managers must develop and model them yourselves. It does no good, and probably much harm, if you talk about them but don't live them obviously. If you do walk the talk, the lessons of leadership and team performance will trickle down through IS over time.

But that's a slow process. You can speed it up through a formal training and development program aimed at improving emotional intelligence throughout IS activities, including the careful selection of new employees. A program to improve emotional intelligence in IS should start at the top and extend to the teams below. The program requires regular training and coaching sessions, as well as the implementations of the principles of emotional intelligence at every opportunity, such as recruitment interviews, staff appraisals, team performance reviews, project reviews following implementation, and off-site meetings and management retreats.

"Great companies have taken these EI concepts on board and used them to great effect," says David Lister, CIO at Boots plc, a UK-based retailer in the health and beauty market. In his company, a mix of competencies and grades based on emotional intelligence has been used to define every role in IS, and a growing number of individuals have been evaluated against them.

"It's easy to send someone off to a training course," explains Lister. "The problem is that when they get back they just carry on where they left off. It's far better to train them on the job with a mixture of coaching and mentoring. These coaching and mentoring programs often run for a year and they take a lot of time and effort. But the results are worthwhile."

Changing yourself, growing your team: General Accounting Office

The General Accounting Office (GAO) is a federal agency that works for Congress and the American people. Commonly called the investigative arm of Congress, or the congressional watchdog, the GAO is independent and nonpartisan. Congress often asks the GAO to study how the federal government spends taxpayers' money. The GAO is based in Washington, D.C., and has a staff of 3,500 and an operating budget of over $400 million. The IT department has around 100 government and 175 contract staff—all reporting to Tony Cicco, who was chosen as CIO in 2000.

"When I took over, IS was very individualistic, there was little teamwork, trust in the CIO was rock bottom, and in the GAO's morale survey, IS ranked dead last," says Cicco. To remedy the situation, Cicco embarked on a major change program. "I wanted to create an atmosphere where people would look forward to coming to work. I recognized that required starting with myself."

The first step was to attend an external leadership-training course. The feedback was startling. "It became clear that I had been very task-oriented [and] impatient and didn't give people enough time to express themselves. I had to learn to stand back and give people the space to express themselves."

The next step was to increase the amount of communication within IS, he says. "I meet with all of my seven direct reports in management council meetings once a week, and have a one-on-one with them every two weeks. I meet with them and their staff once a month, and that's only the start."

Once a week, Cicco picked a group within IS at random and visited it to give the members of the group an opportunity to voice their concerns to him directly. He also had an open-door policy. "I've made it very clear to everyone that if my office door is open, they can come in and discuss any issue with me."

Of course, Cicco's policy of giving staff easy mechanisms to communicate with him opened up more opportunities for him to communicate goals, set expectations, and give feedback on performance. "It's part of a leader's job to make sure that people clearly understand what's expected of them and to let them know how they're doing," he says.

Building the bench strength of his seven direct reports was high on Cicco's agenda. "One of the things I had to do early was to stand back and trust them. I had to show my confidence in them and their ability, by letting them run their departments without any interference from me. Of course, they know I'm always there if they need me."

Cicco has also worked hard at raising their skills: "I want them to see themselves as part of the IS senior management team and not just one of my direct reports." In many meetings, one of his direct reports would attend on Cicco's behalf, representing IS. Cicco says he was very careful to avoid any actual favoritism or appearance of it.

The Office of the CIO

A S THE ROLE OF the new CIO leader continues to gain in complexity, we've observed a number of changes in how CIOs organize the IS function. Many CIOs have created a small team of dedicated staff who report to the CIO and to whom have been delegated some of the CIO's responsibilities. Most commonly referred to as the office of the CIO, this team operates much like the office of the president or the office of the CEO. With the aid of this dedicated team, the CIO is better able to drive the IT mission, vision, and strategy through the enterprise. Typically found in larger enterprises (i.e., over US$3 billion in annual revenues), the members of the office of the CIO serve as the voice of the CIO to other parts of the business or IS team.

The trusted few within this inner circle have typically transcended the boundaries of traditional IS roles in the organization. As the right hand of the CIO, those in this inner circle often function as key influencers and decision makers for the IS organization. They're often empowered to run with an issue on behalf the CIO. Sometimes they include CIOs in the making.

Some fairly typical roles within the office of the CIO include chief technology officer and special assistant to the CIO. Large enterprises may also have a designated CFO for the IS organization. Recent roles and functions added to the CIO's team include relationship management, project office management, change management, marketing, communications, strategy, and chief architect. These roles are often filled from other areas of the enterprise with people who possess, instead of deep technical expertise, solid business acumen and real team leadership skills.

Another part of raising the skills of senior IS management was to encourage and require greater involvement with the enterprise. IS worked closely with business managers on initiatives and presented the IS component to them. "This has been very successful, both with my direct reports and with business managers. Recently we received a spontaneous ovation at a senior management meeting. That was a first for IS."

High-performing offices of the CIO teams are composed of members who are

- flexible, high-performing individuals focused on driving organizational excellence;

- recognized for business acumen and communication and collaboration skills, particularly within the team;

- capable of maintaining continuity and stability during any turnover of the members; and

- able to step in or represent the CIO at executive team meetings or otherwise be a major contributor to board meetings and preparation.

Installing an office of the CIO enables the CIO to spend more time with other key business executives. It supports better organizational integration between business units and the IS organization. Because team members are highly visible to the organization, the office fosters succession planning and continuity. Properly implemented, the CIO team can even become a breeding ground for future executives across the enterprise.

While this approach has worked effectively for many enterprises, it too has its risks. First is the issue of cost. Not all IS groups can afford this layer of management infrastructure. You may need to think about adding positions incrementally. Second, if the office of the CIO members don't or can't work collaboratively, they can hinder the team, IS, and ultimately the whole enterprise. Last, you the leader must be comfortable delegating key decisions. The team members need the authority and responsibility to make things happen.

In the beginning, Cicco brought in an outside expert, an organizational psychologist. "Initially, she came in and did a study, which pointed to many of the problems within IS. That was enormously helpful. She still comes in around thirty days a year to help us on specific issues."

To make sure all these changes were making an actual difference, Cicco created an employee relations committee. Through the committee, employees could bring forward issues and concerns and provide Cicco with feedback. Cicco adds, "To make sure that there is a sense of openness and fairness, the IS management council meetings are open to anyone who wants to come in and listen. We regularly get quite a few people attending."

What's the result of all these changes? Morale in IS grew to be among the highest of all groups within the GAO, business-side confidence in IS rose to an all-time high, and general enterprise confidence in the CIO and the IS group has never been better.

The trend toward a focus on teams will continue. That's true in business in general, as more hierarchies give way to teams, and in IS in particular, which is spurred by the evolution to an IS Lite approach and links with external service providers.

Our research is clear: Leadership and team performance are set to become key differentiators of new CIO leaders. Those CIOs who have paid attention to the "soft"—as well as the "hard"—issues and developed those soft skills among their staff will have an edge.

Develop Critical IS Competencies

Developing your team's leadership skills is the foundation for taking the next step in building a high-performing IS team: developing the competencies needed by the new CIO leader in his or her new IS organization. At the beginning of chapter 7, we talked about the forces pushing IS toward a new form and focus. We said the new IS organization, evident already in pioneering enterprises, would be leaner and more business focused. It would most likely be organized around processes (instead of functions), both within IS and across the entire enterprise. It would strategically source IS services, and for many, this would mean outsourcing an increasing amount of traditional IS work. If much traditional IS work is sourced externally and engagement with business colleagues and relationship building are paramount, then there are serious ramifications for those employees remaining in IS in terms of knowledge and skills.

Moving to the new IS competencies: Unitor

Rune Rasmussen, CIO at Unitor, has been at the forefront of adapting his own and his staff's competencies for this new world. A leading supplier of systems, products, and services to the international marine, cruise, and offshore markets, Unitor is based in Oslo, Norway. It has widespread international operations centered in Houston, Rotterdam, Piraeus, and Singapore. The company is divided into four areas of business: marine chemicals, maintenance and repair, fire protection, and refrigeration services. More than half of Unitor's IT budget is outsourced, mainly for wide-area networking, data center hosting, and ERP. And that proportion is expected to grow.

With twenty-seven staff plus CIO Rasmussen at the center, and twelve staff reporting to the business areas, IS has become strongly centralized. The center subdivides into two distinct groups: a demand-side staff of three and a supply-side staff of twenty-four.

The demand-side staff looks after architecture, performance requirements (including SLAs and outsource contracting), and project-portfolio management. "These demand-side roles and activities have to be proactive and kept in house, come what may," says Rasmussen. "Otherwise, how can you have influence when business goals are set?"

The supply side takes a process-oriented approach. It reports on system performance and availability and is responsible for such things as security, continuity, recovery, problem solving, support, and training.

What have been the benefits of these changes? Focus, for one, claims Rasmussen. "You're better able to help the business achieve its goals. It's easier to participate in business decision making. And it allows you to spend money where you can best add value."

This new IS Lite approach has been quite different from that of traditional IS arrangements. "The profile of IS staff changes completely. You need staff who can deal with relationships and create the right network of contacts inside an [external services] provider," says Rasmussen.

This changing profile of IS has required new skills and competencies, explains Rasmussen: "They weren't there traditionally—particularly on the demand side—so we're trying to build them. It means a personal development program for the managers to boost appropriate behavior. My role has changed, too, in the three years that I've been here. It's much more that of managing decisions, together with [the] business, and developing the skills of the IS management team."

The new IS competencies

IS Lite, particularly strategic sourcing, raises questions about the role of IS. As Rasmussen found, the work of IS changes, but it's no less vital to the enterprise. Many CIOs and their staffs resist IS Lite and strategic sourcing, because they worry that the shift will diminish their importance. These same people fear the changes required for the new IS organization. We understand this fear. But the new CIO leader has to lead his or her staff through this negative reaction, because it's based on a fundamental misconception: that the importance of the CIO and IS staff is waning with these changes (this is the perspective that ends at being a chief technology mechanic), that having more staff means you are more important. Increasingly in IS, as in business, what matters is influence and impact, not how many people report to you.

In fact, IS has a golden opportunity here—to become broker, or contract manager, between ESPs and the enterprise. In this way, IS receives more resources to work on the demand side of IT, where the potential for visibility and credibility is much higher. To seize this opportunity, however, you must lead IS to focus fully on IT-enabling the business. And that requires new competencies.

Chapter 7 discussed the basic roles that every IS organization must retain: IT leadership, architecture development, business enhancement, technology advancement, and vendor and relationship management. Failure to retain these key responsibilities is likely to lead to failed sourcing arrangements, frequent re-negotiation, and poor client satisfaction.

These key roles, however, don't require the same competencies within IS as do the traditional roles. Whereas before, IS needed primarily technical and application proficiency, it now needs, in equal if not greater measure, business and behavioral skills. If IS is to fulfill its most important role—envisioning and creating an IT-enabled enterprise—then IS staff at virtually all levels must build relationships and credibility. To do that, IS staff members need competencies that allow them to bridge business and technology.

All the required competencies that we've thus far described for you, the CIO, are also required now of IS staff: solid business and industry knowledge, deep knowledge of how your enterprise competes or provides services, and, far from the least, the behavioral skills needed to gain support for initiatives and maintain momentum in innovation. Technical skills certainly remain important, but they've become a base, a given—necessary but no longer sufficient for the IS work to be done.

When we say someone is competent, we mean that the person possesses three characteristics that enable him or her to do a specific task well. The individual has the necessary knowledge, skills, and attributes. Knowledge, of course, is what you know. Skill is the ability to do something, to apply knowledge, to some specific end. Attributes (some call them attitudes or aptitudes) are slightly trickier. Some are inborn, and some are developed. They might include qualities like coordination, patience, visual acuity, or judgment as applied to a given kind of work. They make knowledge useful and allow someone to acquire the skills in the first place.

Analyze the competencies needed for IS jobs

The basics of competency analysis are simple enough and should remain that way. Don't overanalyze, or you'll only overcomplicate things and slow down your progress toward developing the competencies you need in your staff. Once you identify the basic knowledge, skills, and attributes that make an expert truly good at a given job, and then group those elements into appropriate clusters, you'll have the competencies needed for that job. Increasingly, you can use external organizations to work with you on the mechanics of this analysis.[6]

Once you identify—and measure—the competencies required to carry out a job successfully, you have a blueprint for selecting, training, and developing people to do the work. An example of a valuable IS competency is the ability to think creatively. How to brainstorm is an associated skill. Knowing the benefit of creative thinking and how to engage others in the process is relevant, too. Be sure, for any role, to define the basic competencies needed in three areas: technical, business, and behavioral. Some jobs hinge more on one kind of competence than on other kinds. Lower-level technical jobs, obviously, focus more on the technical competencies. But, as we've said, roles crucial to the new IS focus much more on business and behavioral (e.g., relationship) skills.

Consider the difficulty of developing each competency category. Technical competencies are relatively easy to develop. Behavioral competencies are more intrinsic to the individual and much harder to develop. It's this insight that pinpoints the key benefit of competency analysis in IS. It's far more effective to fill roles with individuals who have the right behavioral and business competencies and to build the technology skills on top than it is to work the other way around. That's why the benefits of competency analysis can be so significant. It helps identify the people who will be the easiest to develop and the most productive.

We must reiterate: Resist the temptation to make things complex. Select just a few broad competencies to define a role, and avoid over-analysis. Don't identify large numbers of competencies; your system will soon be incomprehensible and impossible to maintain. Especially avoid complex schemes for measuring how much of a competency is needed. Use a simple point system or a simple spectrum like "basic, proficient, advanced, or coach" to describe the level of proficiency needed.

For its IS group, U.K.-based Boots plc uses a competency model that is based on emotional intelligence and that sets out eight leadership characteristics. Each characteristic is divided into individual competencies, for which there are only three proficiency grades: threshold, core, and world-class.

The necessary mix of competencies and grades has been determined for every role in IS, and individuals are evaluated against them. "To be a world-class organization, we needed to make sure we had the right people in a role. Of course, some people saw this as just another way to downsize, but the majority saw it as an opportunity for increased training and development," says Boots's CIO, David Lister.

Gartner's twenty-five basic competencies

Gartner Executive Programs (Gartner EXP) has developed a list of twenty-five basic IS competencies, including six technical, nine business-based, and ten behavioral (table 8-1). You can use this list

TABLE 8-1

Gartner's Twenty-five New IS Competencies

Technical (T)	Business (B)	Behavioral (H)
T1 Understanding existing systems and technology	B1 Understanding business practices and approaches	H1 Leading, inspiring, and building trust
T2 Designing and developing applications	B2 Understanding business organization, politics, and culture	H2 Thinking creatively and innovating
T3 Applying procedures, tools, and methods	B3 Behaving commercially	H3 Focusing on results
T4 Integrating systems	B4 Understanding and analyzing the competitive situation	H4 Thinking strategically
T5 Designing technical architecture		H5 Coaching, delegating, and developing
T6 Understanding emerging technologies	B5 Managing projects	H6 Building relationships and teamwork
	B6 Managing change in the business from IT applications	H7 Influencing and persuading
	B7 Planning, prioritizing, and administering work	H8 Principled negotiating
	B8 Communicating/ listening and gathering information	H9 Resolving conflicts and problems
	B9 Focusing on customers	H10 Being adaptable

Career Paths and Competencies

NOT EVERYONE will want to expend the effort to develop competencies he or she doesn't have. Assuming that these people are not valuable to the organization is a mistake. You may want to consider creating career paths based on competencies both to illustrate to your staff what competencies are required for advancement in some areas, but also to show there is a place for high performers in just a few competencies. For instance, Paul Coby at British Airways has developed for the IT staff three career paths based on competencies. The first is for the staff with technical understanding. He has set up a program to recognize the "master practitioners" and reward them for technological excellence, not for managing other people. The second path is for IS management and program and project management delivery. The third path is for general managers, who manage the interface between IS and the business. These managers give IS credibility and insights into the business and keep IS informed on how it's being viewed by the business. Individuals can move between paths by acquiring new competencies, but the paths also give personnel clear development guides and provide Coby with a retention strategy for individuals whom he wants to keep but who do not want to acquire specific competencies.

to carry out the competency analysis just described for jobs in your IS organization.

Although this list is unlikely to fit every organization, it can serve as a useful starting point. Regard it as a guide from which you can develop your own tailored set of competencies.

Once you've identified a short list of the competencies that really make a difference for a given role and described each one at four levels of performance, you've created the *role profile* for that job. A role profile identifies the competencies and corresponding performance levels required to fulfill that role satisfactorily. Don't set unreasonable or unnecessarily high standards. You are better off selecting just the competencies that truly make a difference and set performance levels that are high, but not supremely demanding.

Matching roles, competencies, and performance levels

To show how a role profile can work, we've applied the twenty-five competencies to the five crucial roles that must remain in every IS organization (table 8-2). These profiles are for senior-level executives. At more junior levels, the profiles would be less demanding.

Notice that no role profile includes all twenty-five competencies. Notice too that none, not even IT leadership, requires all the relevant competencies to be carried out at the advanced or coach levels of performance. Although technology advancement and architecture development emphasize technical competencies, both business and behavioral competencies are important for these roles, too. Business enhancement places the most emphasis on business competencies, and IT leadership is oriented strongly toward business and behavioral competencies.

Use the information here as a guide to generate role profiles for your own IS organization. By the way, don't expect the roles to remain static. As circumstances and the organizational environment change, so will roles. Your profiles will need to be reviewed and updated periodically.

Comparing role profiles with individual profiles

Role profiles identify the competencies and corresponding performance levels for each role in your IS group. This profile represents what you need.

By contrast, individual profiles, sometimes called personal profiles, measure the actual individuals in your existing work force. These profiles identify the competencies and performance levels of the staff you already have.

Individual profiles can be determined in several ways. Management assessment is the obvious way. Other methods include assessment by the individuals themselves, by a selection of colleagues both within and beyond IS, and by independent evaluation centers.

When the individual profiles are done, compare them to the appropriate role profiles. This revealing and important step will give

TABLE 8-2

Matching Roles and Competencies

	ROLES				
Competency	Vendor Management	Technology Advancement	Business Enhancement	Architecture Development	IT Leadership
Technical					
T1 Understanding existing systems and technology	◍	●	◍	●	▨
T2 Designing and developing applications	○	◍	▨	▨	▨
T3 Applying procedures, tools, and methods	▨	◍	▨	▨	●
T4 Integrating systems	▨	◍	▨	▨	▨
T5 Designing technical architecture		▨		●	▨
T6 Understanding emerging technologies	▨	●	▨	●	▨
Business					
B1 Understanding business practices and approaches	◍	○	●	◍	◍
B2 Understanding business organization, politics, and culture	◍	○	◍	▨	●
B3 Behaving commercially	●	▨	◍	▨	●
B4 Understanding and analyzing the competitive situation	▨	○	●	◍	●
B5 Managing projects	▨	▨	●		◍
B6 Managing change in the business from IT applications			●	◍	◍

B7 Planning, prioritizing, and administering work				
B8 Communicating/listening and gathering information				
B9 Focusing on customers				

Behavioral

H1 Leading, inspiring, and building trust				
H2 Thinking creatively and innovating				
H3 Focusing on results				
H4 Thinking strategically				
H5 Coaching, delegating, and developing				
H6 Building relationships and teamwork				
H7 Influencing and persuading				
H8 Principled negotiating				
H9 Resolving conflicts and problems				
H10 Being adaptable				

Role profiles are for IS Lite at senior executive level.

Performance levels: ○ basic; ◍ proficient; ◉ advanced; ● coach. A blank entry indicates that the competency is not applicable to the role.

you a good picture, individually and for the group as a whole, of where the IS organization stands versus where it needs to be. The differences, role by role, will help you determine what gaps you need to fill.

You may want to take one more step and create an IS competency inventory, a central record of both role and individual profiles. Such an inventory will enable you to compare the two profiles easily. It's also a convenient place to store and maintain the competency manual, which contains descriptions of the competencies needed for each role, along with corresponding performance levels.[7]

One benefit of a competency inventory is that it highlights your top talent—the one in every four or five of your people whom you must hang on to. It also can be a terrific aid to succession planning, as you promote or inevitably lose some staff. But the main benefit of a competency inventory is that it identifies competency gaps you must fill. Even if you've done a rough-and-ready analysis, you'll still be able to see fairly specifically what competencies are weak.

Close competency gaps with training and recruiting

There are two main strategies to close competency gaps: training existing staff and hiring new staff. Building a strong IS team in a short time frame will require both strategies.

Train existing staff

A wide variety of training methods already exists, and newer, online, self-paced training can be both effective and cost-efficient, particularly for the knowledge components of competencies. Technical competencies are relatively easy to develop through participation in education and training programs. Business and especially behavioral competencies are harder to develop, and unfortunately, the variety of effective training methods for them is far more limited. Probably the best approach for business and behavioral competencies is on-the-job mentoring, which complements job experience with access to a capable coach.

It's often better to start with an individual who already possesses the necessary behavioral competencies. Hire or transfer such individuals into IS, then add the necessary technical (and business) competencies, rather than work the other way around.

Hire newcomers with care

Having done role profiles and a competency inventory, you will have specific goals to meet in hiring new staff. The question is how to assess job candidates in relation to those competency goals. In practice, the competencies of newcomers are unlikely to be known or can be difficult to ascertain.

First, make sure you have full buy-in from your human resources staff or partner. Human resources need to know what competencies are key to your team's success and how those competencies are changing your hiring strategy. The solution is to work with human resources to develop a structured set of questions to assess the candidate against the competencies required by the role profile. For each of those competencies, you've already identified its component knowledge, skills, and attributes. Now, as you interview applicants, ask questions that elicit specific, tangible evidence of how the applicant applied or demonstrated the specific components of each competency called for by the role. Don't accept unsubstantiated claims or broad summaries. Ask for incidents and stories. Press for detail that sufficiently demonstrates the presence of a competency and the knowledge, skill, and attributes that comprise it. Use the same approach in questioning the applicant's references. Seek anecdotal evidence of specific competencies.

Assessing candidates is an inexact science, but the use of a well-structured approach makes it less of a hit-or-miss affair than otherwise. Do it well, and you can bring newcomers into IS with the competencies you need.

New IS competencies in fighting-for-survival enterprises: EBRD

Adding and developing these new competencies may seem impossible if you are the CIO of a fighting-for-survival enterprise today. Although it is certainly more difficult to add new competencies while reducing staff, it is not impossible. You can use required restructuring or cutbacks to your advantage. As we will explain, the CIO of the European Bank for Reconstruction and Development (EBRD), facing a tough situation of budget and personnel cutbacks, emerged with a smaller but much stronger IS team.

The EBRD is a for-profit (but non-profit-maximizing) institution established in 1991 to foster the transition toward open-market-oriented economies and to promote private and entrepreneurial initiative in the countries of central and eastern Europe and the Commonwealth of Independent States (CIS). Today the EBRD is the largest single investor in the region, and it mobilizes significant investment beyond its own financing.

In 2002, the bank's vice president of finance, the head of operations (including IT), and IT director (the EBRD's terminology for CIO) Tim Goldstone discussed an initiative for the IS organization to cut costs without reducing service levels. Goldstone used a combination of approaches to reduce the head count of his centrally managed IS organization and cut the bank's IT capital budget by 40 percent and operational budget 15 percent over two years.

Since its formation in 1991, the EBRD had already outsourced much of its IT infrastructure operations and systems development. Approximately 70 percent of the workload was already outsourced, mostly to large ESPs, and contractors and ESP head count exceeded the number of internal staff. Unfortunately, the value of the EBRD's typical outsourced contract could not compare with the mega-contracts that large ESPs compete for. By moving much of its work to smaller ESPs in 2002 and thereafter, the EBRD reduced costs and gained more attention and greater flexibility as a larger customer of smaller ESPs. "Although we now have more vendors to deal with, they pay attention to us because we represent an important part of their client base," says Goldstone.

Because the EBRD had outsourced heavily from the beginning, vendor and contract management was always an important competency for the internal staff. To keep the IS organization small, the bank made vendor management an integral part of most managers' jobs, rather than a separate function. To be given senior positions within the department, candidates had to have demonstrated effective vendor management skills.

Not only were the number and mix of ESPs and contractors changed, but the internal skills mix changed as well to meet the EBRD's new needs. For example, fewer project leaders were required as a result of the completion of several projects, while more business and technical support staff were brought in. These new staff provided better application and technology support, either directly or through more effective management of ESPs and contractors. Although there was an overall head count reduction, new staff were recruited to provide competencies and fill the gaps. In effect, the EBRD used the need to downsize as a way of changing the competency mix within its IS group.

Reflecting on his experience, Goldstone concluded that once the decision to downsize was made in principle, the enterprise should have moved to a smaller, lighter IT organization more quickly than it did (the layoffs were carried out in two distinct phases). Given the business and cost pressures and the inherent stress and uncertainty of any significant organizational change, implementing all the changes right after the announcement and allowing the remaining staff to focus on their new tasks would have been preferable.

We talk about finding the right people, with the right set of competencies, as only one of the necessary elements of the new IS organization. It is a necessary element, but it's more, too. Good people can compensate for inappropriate goals and bad strategies. If they have enough latitude, they'll figure out the right way. But not even good strategies and the right goals can salvage the dire effects of hiring or keeping the wrong people. The right people will fix a bad situation. The wrong people, even with the best intentions, will sabotage a good plan.

The new CIO leader requires a new IS organization with a new set of knowledge, skills, and attributes—competencies—that are fundamentally different from those required in traditional IS and more difficult to obtain. If you don't get these new competencies on board, you won't be able to deliver. Nothing else you do in the end will work, and you'll quickly find yourself headed down the wrong path.

9

Manage Enterprise and IT Risks

Decades ago, a reporter asked the notorious American bank robber Willie Sutton why he robbed banks. "Because that's where the money is," he said. Criminals today attack computer networks for the same reason: In today's data-driven service economies, that's where the "money" is. Although the new millennium brought new fears of cyber-terrorism, the trend in computer crime—from vandalism to for-profit malfeasance—has actually been rising for years. At the same time, new risks have come on the scene. For all of them, CIOs are on the line more than ever. New CIO leaders will step up to the challenge and manage these new and different IT risks for their enterprises.[1]

It's not hard to identify the reasons for the emergence of these new threats that CIO leaders must take on. First and foremost, the dependence of most business processes on IT means that the consequences of IT failure are growing every day. Beyond that, around the world, legislation has been passed (and more is on the way) to place liability, in some cases personal criminal liability, on businesses for misuse or loss of corporate data, particularly data about customers. This legislation includes the European Union's Data

Protection Directive, the U.S. Health Insurance Portability and Accountability Act (HIPAA), the U.S. Sarbanes-Oxley legislation, and the state of California's Database Security Breach Notification Act. (If you don't know what these pieces of legislation require, it's time to start building a solid relationship with your corporate counsel!)

There's more than legislation. CIOs in a recent Gartner survey identified four new kinds of risks that have elevated the importance of risk management as part of their supply-side job:

Interconnection of businesses: This growing interconnectivity increases dependencies and exposures to theft and misuse of information. The mismanagement of these relationships is a new risk outside the traditional purview of IS.

Executive criminality: This type of crime has produced many spectacular corporate failures and new legislation aimed at reducing abuses and punishing abusers. These laws present new legal risks in handling and safeguarding information.

Consumer demand for privacy protection: The attention to privacy issues is based on the rising incidence of identity theft, large thefts of sensitive personal information, and government anti-terrorist programs aimed at mass surveillance. Failure to protect privacy is a new customer risk; noncompliance with new privacy laws is a new legal risk.

Potential IT failures: In your enterprise, IT failures can now impact your customers' or suppliers' businesses, with the possibility of significant damage to enterprise reputation and civil and criminal penalties as well.

A Brief Introduction to Risk Management

Almost every aspect of business operations in almost every business now depends on IT. Both cash and customers come into companies using online mechanisms, for instance. So, no matter what business risks are under discussion, you should be involved in efforts to manage them.[2] The indictment of US HealthSouth Corporation's CIO on felony charges under the Sarbanes-Oxley Act in April 2003 showed exactly how involved you need to be. You're already involved, whether you acknowledge it or not.

But you can't manage these new risks alone. Too many causes and consequences are outside the control of the IS organization. The business must determine the priorities, with IS a part of the discussions. The business can't manage these risks without the active involvement of the CIO, and CIOs must manage their IT response to new risks within the context of an enterprise's risk management program.

Failure to integrate IT risk management with enterprise risk management presents by itself an increasingly dangerous gamble, because managing the two has enterprise-level consequences. A security or technical incident, for instance, may easily jump over the IT wall and become a corporate problem affecting customer retention, regulatory scrutiny, and corporate image.

Certain risks are so dependent on IT that the new CIO leader is the obvious choice to take responsibility, even when the consequences fall largely outside the IS organization. Information security, privacy, and risks stemming from IT processes and products are clear examples. Even when the CIO is not the obvious choice to lead, IS participation is important to success.

You should be part of an enterprise risk council, which takes its lead from the board of directors, which sets the enterprise's overall risk tolerance. The risk council, or whatever it's called in your organization, must be composed of senior managers, must report directly to the CEO, and must manage risks across business units. When particular business units have unique risks, similar councils should be created within each unit. These business unit councils should also include you or one of your senior IS managers to ensure IS's participation in risk management.

Banque Générale du Luxembourg: Managing Risk in a Basel II Era

FOUNDED IN 1919, Banque Générale du Luxembourg (BGL) is one of the largest banks in the Grand Duchy of Luxembourg, with around 39 billion euros in assets. Active in domestic and international markets, the bank has played a key role in the development of Luxembourg as a financial center.

Michel Dauphin, CIO of BGL, speaks of the latest changes in risk management:

> One of the most important risk management issues in financial services at the moment is the new international directive on capital adequacy known as Basel II. Previously, the only risks assessed for capital adequacy by regulators were credit risk and market risk. Basel II goes much further by including operational risks and by assessing credit risk using more sophisticated methods. This leads banks to reinforce their risk measurement and risk management processes.
>
> IT has to make a big contribution, as all relevant Basel II data needs to be centrally collected to feed a Basel II calculator. At the moment, a lot of IT development work is going on. Developing the systems to support the evaluation of capital consumption for Basel II requires some 60 to 70 IT man-years of effort spread over three years.

Four basic strategies for dealing with risk

There are four classic ways of coping with risk: mitigation, transfer, acceptance, and avoidance.

Mitigation: the reduction of risk itself or its consequences. For mitigation to work, the enterprise must have enough control to reduce or eliminate the likelihood or effect of a risk event.

Transfer: the movement of risk to some risk carrier other than the enterprise. For transfer to work, some agent (like an insurer) must be willing and able to take on the risk.

We use ISO 17799 [International Standards Organization regulation] at the IT level. It helps us identify operational risks related to IT security, personnel security, business continuity and so on. The ISO standard defines a framework to refine our processes to manage risk more effectively. We are using this as a basis for developing a list of the business risks that arise from IT and what we can do to mitigate these risks.

To manage not only the technical risks, but also the business risks resulting from the business's dependency on IT, Dauphin and his staff have identified the following key IT-related risk areas for the business:

- Impact on the efficiency of business staff if systems aren't available or user-friendly
- Lack of agility or the capacity to react quickly to new market opportunities, because of system inflexibility
- Poor data integrity, which could have an important business impact
- Fraud, if user access is not well managed
- Inadequate reporting for regulatory and legal purposes, if IS doesn't provide proper means of reporting
- Staff tension, if IT systems don't work well

"Of course, you always have to find a balance between risk management and other objectives," says Dauphin. "To do that, you have to measure potential impact [and] the cost of mitigation and decide on the resources to allocate to it."

Acceptance: the conscious and willing assumption of a risk by the enterprise (for certain kinds of risks, it's called self-insurance). For acceptance to work, the likelihood of the risk's occurring must be small enough, or the consequences of the risk light enough, for the enterprise to bear.

Avoidance: removing the possibility that the risk event will ever occur. For most enterprises, avoidance means exiting a business or market, or dropping a product. For that to happen, the enterprise must have the freedom to exit and must be willing to forgo the opportunities that go with the risk.

Mitigation is the primary strategy for managing most of the new risks. What follows are various approaches and methods you and your enterprise can use to reduce the possibility or consequences of risk events that most directly affect you.

Identify, examine, categorize, and defend against risks

No enterprise can ever be completely secure against all risks. The first question of risk management is, "What risks is the enterprise willing to tolerate?" Identify the answer (in conjunction with business colleagues) using three steps.

First, analyze the targets and threats. To identify risks, start by sketching out scenarios for your enterprise as a whole. Call on the work you did to develop your knowledge of the business and your business maxims. What strategies are the most important to your business? What are the major impediments to each strategy? How might markets, competitors, regulators, and others react to your business strategies? Are there single points of failure? Where will the strategies concentrate data, money, materials, or any other highly valuable corporate assets? If you're not creating these scenarios as part of an enterprise risk council, make sure you validate your ideas with business colleagues.

Move from these scenarios to business processes that are affected by, or exposed to, risks. Be as specific as possible without getting bogged down. Ask your senior IS managers to identify the most important risks and potential consequences they see in the business processes they're involved in. Be sure your managers understand that they are ultimately responsible for risks within their purview, whether they identify them or not.

All targets are not equal. Identify and value the assets at risk— business processes, markets, and databases—in terms like loss of revenue or market share. Translate intangibles, like loss of reputation, to economic terms by estimating the effect on sales and retention, regulatory penalties, or fines. Another good way to estimate an asset's value is by calculating potential criminal profit—that's the value that will motivate outsiders to attack. For assets whose loss or compromise may injure third parties, you should also estimate potential liabilities for negligence. Use scenarios to develop and estimate the vulnerability for the major assets you identify. Here are a couple of equations for doing so:

Vulnerability = Probable number of successful attacks per year

or

Vulnerability = Total attacks × Percentage of successful attacks

At the end of this phase, you'll have a list of assets with cost consequence and vulnerability for each asset.

Second, calculate the annual risk for each attack scenario. It's easier to do this if you have good data about attacks on your enterprise and your responses, a subject we'll return to later. Calculate the risk or potential annual loss for each scenario by using an equation like this:

Potential annual loss = Cost of occurrence × Vulnerability

Then, prioritize your list based on risk level. The result of this step is a prioritized list of your risks.

Third, identify your potential defenses, and balance them against risks. Once you've created a list of possible defenses, review each against four criteria:

1. Cost

2. Alignment or consistency with enterprise objectives

3. Impact on business processes and the cost of changing them. That is, will processes need to be redesigned?

4. Effect on current and future risk management initiatives. That is, will you need to maintain expensive, hard-to-acquire skills, and knowledge? Will the defense limit flexibility or the ability to mitigate other risks? Will it promote long-term and not just stopgap risk management?"

Once you complete this process of identifying risks, you need to classify them into categories, compare risks within and between categories, and assign responsibilities for risk management to specific individuals. Additionally, you need regular reporting on the status of the identified risks and the risk management actions being taken. At each level of the organization, management should focus on about five to seven major risks within its purview and report regularly (how often depends on the level and severity of the risk) to higher levels of management. Even if this isn't happening in the rest of your enterprise, you should lead your IS group to set the highest standards for risk management. Doing so will be a major credibility boost for you and the new IS organization.

The New CIO Leader's Top Risk Management Priority: Information Security

While the new CIO leader has to be comfortable leading risk management across the enterprise in every situation where IT contributes to risk or may help mitigate it, one specific area belongs at the top of the risk management agenda for CIOs: information security. This area represents one of the biggest IT-related threats. With the largest negative consequences should things go wrong, information security is clearly the responsibility of the CIO and the IS organization. Let's look at how one IS group provided security risk management grounded on enterprise goals.

BT Wholesale: IT risk management protects business reputation

British Telecom (BT) Wholesale has built management of the new IT risks into its strategy and governance processes. The company provides comprehensive network services within the United Kingdom to more than five hundred communication companies, network operators, and service providers—including other BT businesses, such as BT Retail and BT Global Services.

Phil Dance, CIO of the company, explains the importance of the public's trust: "BT is in a position of trust. People expect to be able to make phone calls. When they lift the phone and put in the numbers, they expect to get a connection. Losing control of our network, so that people couldn't make a call, would be a very public event and very embarrassing. We have to take a great deal of care of our reputation."

To protect that reputation, risk management has always been a high-priority item. BT Wholesale has taken an enterprisewide approach to risk. Senior managers across the business are required to look at what they themselves do, identify the risks in their areas, and develop mitigation strategies, says Dance. "To identify risks, we run formal risk management sessions. We use a variety of techniques, including brainstorming, to find top risks and develop action plans to mitigate those risks. Then we document and manage those risks in the usual way. It's all pretty standard risk management and is well embedded in the company culture."

"But risk management has changed for us," he says. "The new source of risk comes from the move to e-business. You open yourself to the very real risk that new forms of cyber-attack can enter your business. And you've no idea when or where that attack will come from, or what form it will take."

BT Wholesale has had to develop sophisticated solutions, because countering the threats has become increasingly difficult. Rather than just following conventional wisdom, the company has evaluated the possible responses for every type of risk. For instance, BT Wholesale has extensively studied the best reactions if its network were exposed to a destructive computer virus. In fact, since one could never know when or from where an attack might come, BT Wholesale decided to assume that its networks had been compromised already and to work to limit the effects.

One approach the company implemented was segmenting its IP (Internet protocol) networks according to the applications running on those networks. Data processing happens on a network separate from the one that manages the hardware systems (routers, switches, etc.) that keep the network running. This has allowed the company to keep the switched network sealed off, dramatically lowering the risk of the network's being compromised. Of course, in the design of an IP network, it made sense to have just one network. But from a risk management viewpoint, that would be dangerous. In some reported cases, providers with poorly managed backbones became infected with a virus and lost control of their core networks. As Dance strove to provide information security risk management at BT, his understanding of the enterprise's risk management stance meant that network and information security trumped network efficiency.

Develop a formal security policy

Your first step in addressing information security risk management is to develop a formal security policy. A security policy is a set of business rules that represent the enterprise's tolerance for risk and the security measures that enforce that stance. A policy provides an institutional approach to hard decisions and trade-offs. It also identifies what must be monitored, reported, and flagged for further action (such as access to internal resources or particular external Web sites). Policies should be based on industry standards, such as COBIT (Control Objectives for IT) or ISO 17799, because they lay out security program criteria and the basis for comprehensive security assessment and administration.

The starting point for a security policy is based on your enterprise's attitude toward risk. For instance, determining when to implement new technologies is part of a risk management discussion. Does your enterprise care about innovation more than potential information security vulnerabilities (which new technologies invariably carry with them)? You can only answer this question if you are thoroughly familiar with the enterprise's risk management stance.

Through clear and appropriate security governance arrangements, you need to identify who is responsible for making key decisions and who carries accountability for information-security-related issues. Just as you have a set of decision domains for IT governance (maxims, architecture, investment and prioritizations, and so on), so too your enterprise needs clear governance systems for a set of security domains. These should at least include risk strategy, security policy, security architecture, and business application security (table 9-1).

Using the risk strategy decisions, determine which behaviors are acceptable, and reflect your decisions in your enterprise's security policy. Policy, of course, will not accomplish much if you do not also assign your staff specific responsibilities for implementing the policy and ensuring that it is followed. Finally, you must choose which technologies and processes will be used to ensure enterprise security, basing the decision on your policy, and manage these technologies on an ongoing basis.

Manage security processes on an ongoing basis

Security management must be fact-based management. As the axiom says, "What gets measured, gets managed." Make sure you are capable of measuring your security in terms of your policy. The best, first step is to centralize IT security incident and status reporting under a chief security officer (which may or may not be a job in itself). Many enterprises don't maintain statistics on attacks, responses to attacks, or the effectiveness of defenses. Almost half of all chief security officers (CSOs) responding to a recent *CSO Magazine* survey didn't track all attacks or report cyber-crimes to police.[3] Without metrics, an enterprise's information security runs blind. Measures should include types of attacks (both successful and unsuccessful), perpetrators (if known), targets of attacks, effectiveness and per-incident cost of defenses, and losses attributed to attacks. (See chapter 10 for more about creating effective dashboards to monitor your progress.)

Consider questions like these to provide a high-level assessment of your security processes:

- Do you review the security architecture of new applications to help ensure that vulnerabilities are not built in from the outset?

TABLE 9-1

Security Governance Arrangements Matrix

DOMAIN

STYLE	Risk Strategy		Security Policy		Security Architecture		Business Application Security	
	Input	*Decision*	*Input*	*Decision*	*Input*	*Decision*	*Input*	*Decision*
Business Monarchy		Mgt Board						
IT Monarchy					IM Leaders Sec Arch Comm	Dir of Info IM Leaders		
Feudal								
Federal	Mgt Board IMSG		IMSG IM Leaders				Sec Arch Comm Biz Liaison Biz Proc Own	
Duopoly				IMSG IM Leaders				Biz Proc Own Sec Arch Comm

GOVERNANCE MECHANISMS:

Mgt Board, management board
Biz Liaison, business liaison officers

IMSG, Information Management Steering Group
Biz Proc Own, business program/project owners

Dir of Info, Director of Information
Sec Arch Comm, Security Architecture Committee

IM Leaders, Information Management
Leadership Group

Source: Security arrangement matrix and mechanisms draw on the "IT Governance Matrix" developed by Peter Weill and Richard Woodham as MIT Sloan CISR working paper 326, "Don't Just Lead, Govern: Implementing Effective IT Governance," April 2002, and is used with permission.

- Do you continuously manage user access and software configurations to prevent vulnerabilities from becoming breaches?

- How close to real time are your incident responses?

- What is the status of your backup, recovery, and business continuity planning?

In your IT security, don't overlook insiders

Many CIOs fall into a trap when they attempt to provide effective risk management for information security: While hardening their enterprises to attacks from the outside, they fail to consider threats from the inside. BT Wholesale, which we mentioned earlier, took an important step beyond preparing for external attacks; the telecom company also developed approaches to control the impact of an internal, purposeful attack. In fact, data show that most damaging attacks are committed by, or with the assistance of, insiders. Though many new risks are indeed external to your enterprise, you must pay more attention than ever to threats from insiders— including highly placed insiders.

Although you can't eradicate such risks, you can reduce them by scrutinizing your staff. There are some simple steps to reduce insider risk. First and foremost is putting in place policies to verify new hires' and promotions' backgrounds. The dangers of failing to do this are obvious. For example, the American Cancer Society of Ohio hired an employee with three misdemeanor and two felony convictions for theft and fraud. By 2000, that employee had risen through the IS department to become chief administrative officer and had stolen almost $7 million.[4]

You also need to train personnel to be aware of security policies and their own personal security responsibilities. Many breaches result from innocent mistakes by corporate personnel. The U.S. Department of Defense reports that by far the most common way outsiders attempt to breach security is simply by calling department personnel and asking for sensitive information.[5] How many of your enterprise's personnel know what information they should and shouldn't provide to outsiders? Of course, any training you put in place needs to be repeated regularly, to refresh staff who generally don't think about security every day, to ensure that new hires are up to speed, and ultimately to create the necessary security culture to support your enterprise's risk management stance.

Evolve your security architecture

Beyond policy and processes, you also need to take a longer-term view of your security architecture. Enterprise security has historically been based on the *fortress model:* static and undifferentiated, difficult to change, location-specific, and reliant on a very few mechanisms (strong walls and a locked gate). The hard, crunchy exterior protects a soft, chewy interior. Anyone outside the gate is suspect; anyone inside is trusted. Once you've passed the gate, you can do what you like.

Emerging today is a new security architecture that is much better attuned to actual risks—remember that information security is all about risk management. This emerging architecture is known as the *airport model.* It is more flexible and situational than the fortress model, with multiple zones of security based on role. "Gates" to zones can employ multiple overlapping technologies for identification, authentication, and access control, depending on the individual's role and the purpose of the zone. The result is a series of fortresses within the fortress.

The airport model works well now, based on current enterprise trends and existing technology. The end game for a highly networked world, however, is the point-to-point *dynamic-trust model.* Dynamic trust requires point-to-point authentication and trust, from any user on the network to any other user. The model uses multiple overlapping or alternative technologies and assumes that all parties to transactions must identify and authenticate themselves and prove their right to participate. The rules-based security of the dynamic-trust model refers to individual and environmental circumstances, history, and current network and environmental status, plus additional application-level modes of protection. This model corresponds most closely to a world heavily populated with intelligent wireless devices.

All three models are responses to specific risks and eras. The fortress model worked in the mainframe era. The airport model works for most enterprises now. The point-to-point model will be required for a world in which data access and transfer is regularly conducted wirelessly, anywhere, anytime.

Make sure you've taken these tactical steps

So far we've focused on information security risk management strategy. We would be remiss if we did not address some specific, immediate tactical actions you should take. Here are a few:

- Ensure that audit trails, including those related to electronic document access and modification, are secure from manipulation and evasion.

- Require that IS personnel follow a code of conduct that recognizes the unusual degree of access and responsibility entrusted to IS.

- Monitor access to systems that contain critical data, and publicize that this monitoring is being conducted. Pay special attention to insiders accessing systems that are outside their normal responsibilities and behavior.

- Tie access rights to defined roles or positions. Set explicit and public limits; monitor and follow up with investigations when limits are exceeded.

- Spend time with corporate counsel to understand thoroughly the requirements of any new or evolving regulations that affect your business. Current regulations include the Sarbanes-Oxley Act and HIPAA (U.S.), the Turnbull legislation (U.K.), and the Basel II requirements (Europe).

- Implement frequent, regularly scheduled testing. Informal surveys with CIOs suggest that most enterprises have a plan in the event of a security breach, but far fewer companies actually test the system regularly.

- Set explicit policies for retaining and managing electronic documentation, including spreadsheets, e-mail, word-processing documents, and anything else that contributes to management decisions and reporting.

You may be wondering at this point exactly where you will get the budget to accomplish all these things. Keep in mind that you have to balance the threats and the defenses. So, first of all, prioritize the aforementioned items as they relate to your enterprise. Second, remember that these risk management issues are not IS issues; they're enterprise issues and need to be treated that way. You need to ensure that your executive colleagues and the board of directors understand the risks and the mitigation efforts required to meet the board's standard for risk management. Then, decisions can be made at the enterprise level about how to allocate dollars and resources and what risk levels are acceptable. Finally, remember the many possible funding options we've just discussed. Many of them are appropriate for acquiring funding for security projects.

Continuously monitor security arrangements and costs

In conclusion, we repeat that security is a process, not a state. Security is not and never will be a goal you can achieve. It's only something you can strive for in a constantly changing environment.

Monitor your security arrangements, first, to make sure they remain effective and, second, to assure yourself and your enterprise of their continuing cost-effectiveness. You also need to loop back to the beginning of the process regularly—risks and mitigation costs change rapidly. You have to make sure you're still defending against the most important risks in the most cost-effective way. Very soon, we believe, most enterprises will be required to provide security status information to multiple government agencies. Enterprises with immature security programs will then need to spend up to 15 percent of their security budget to comply.

Applying an analysis conducted by Gartner, we believe the cost to mitigate damage from a successful attack is at least 50 percent higher than the cost to prevent it. Enterprises that focus on real risks and monitor their program's risk-reduction effectiveness will receive the highest return on their security investments. It's best and cheapest in the long run to develop a capable program before being forced to act by legislation or actual attacks.

Industry norms for security spending and staffing can provide an initial sanity check on total defense costs. Industrywide spending on security has grown from 3.3 percent of IT budgets in 2001 to 5.4 percent in 2003. Moreover, Gartner research predicts it will continue to grow through 2006. As the cost of security continues to rise, many CEOs will ask, "Our spending on security is increasing by over 20 percent per year. Are we better off?" Enterprises that increase their security spending, but don't address changing threats and track key metrics, will come under pressure to restrain or reduce their security spending.

Risk management for the enterprise, not just for IT, will be a daily part of the new CIO leader's job. If you are not thoroughly comfortable with risk management approaches and procedures, start your training today. You are the leader who will most probably have to guide and educate other executives about key risk areas related to technology. At the same time, you need to aggressively attack the biggest area of enterprise risk that is your direct responsibility—information security. Both information security risk management and overall enterprise risk management are crucial to the credibility of the new CIO leader.

10

Communicate Your
Performance

Imagine for a moment (if it requires any imagination) that you're the CIO of a multi-billion-dollar company. You've just finished co-presenting a plan to the board of directors for a major IT-enabled initiative in your company's largest business unit. The board is taking a break, and you were invited to stay and chat.

Just when you thought you were home free, one of the board members, the head of a large state pension fund, a major investor, comes up to you, bagel in hand, and says, "Great presentation."

Before you can say thanks, she forges straight to her real point.

"I get the plan you just presented, no problem. It makes good business sense. But now tell me this. IT expenditures have risen from seven percent to over eleven percent in three years—since you joined the company, in fact. What are we getting for that? I mean, what *business value* are we getting from IT?"

Quick! What do you say?

Many CIOs we know would rather spend two weeks personally installing the CEO's home computer network than find themselves in this position.

Do you have a compelling answer to the shareholder's question, *right at that moment*? A new CIO leader has to have one.

Even if your IT expenditures are dropping, you'll still need a good, pithy answer that speaks directly to the business value of IT in your enterprise. If dropping IT costs are your only answer (a cost-centric rather than a value-centric answer), you're in trouble, for who's to say your IT costs shouldn't have dropped even more?

In fact, the question we're asking you—*Are you ready for a shareholder's inquiry about IT value?*—is twofold:

- Do you actually know the answer to the shareholder's question? Do you know where IS stands—how both IT investment dollars and your IS organization are contributing to business value in your enterprise? Or will you have to go back to your office to formulate a good answer?

- If you do have the information, do you know how to communicate what you know? The way you answer the shareholder's question is different from the way you'd answer the same question from the head of one of your business units, or the same question from a process champion in your enterprise.

This chapter focuses on those twin issues of knowing and communicating, and on the ways they vary with your audience (e.g., shareholders, the CEO, or another colleague) and the type of IT-related investment you're talking about—for example, a new project, an existing system, or a new business process.[1] You cannot stay on the path to being a new CIO leader if you can't effectively communicate your performance to any stakeholder audience in terms they value and understand.

There are three parts to knowing where you stand and communicating it, starting from the macro level and working down:

1. Articulating top-level shareholder value for IT, so that your enterprise board and shareholders are informed (in the case of public sector organizations, your high-level audience might be politicians, prominent citizen groups, and funding authorities)

2. Identifying and reporting on IT value indicators that are clearly and directly linked to business value measures

3. Creating effective IT performance dashboards (sometimes called scorecards) in business-relevant language

These are critical issues because they directly affect the perception of IT and IS, and perceptions directly affect the influence, credibility, freedom, and resources you will be given.

Articulate Shareholder Value

We start with the situation just posed—the question "What's the business value of IT in your enterprise?" as asked by a shareholder.

The question and questioner present a paradox for you and most other CIOs today. Typically, a gulf now exists between the business-case benefits that enterprises expect from IT investments and the measures that shareholders and investment analysts use to value enterprises. It's a gulf, however, that as a new CIO leader you need to close.

Investors don't yet often ask about IT investments, but that day is coming soon. As businesses become more IT-based, the importance of technology's contribution to shareholder value (or lack thereof) will only increase. The challenge this poses for new CIOs is to help educate investors, external board members, and their colleagues about how information and technology assets—including your human capabilities and expertise—create shareholder value. CIOs need to be ready to help their CEOs and CFOs understand and explain these links between IT and value.

Our purpose now is to bridge the gap between the internal analysis of IT investment benefits, which is usually business-unit-based, and an enterprise-level explanation of how IT assets contribute to shareholder value. Many investors, analysts, and commentators find the technical language in IT announcements bewildering. If it's hard for them to understand, or it comes thickly wrapped in what sounds like marketing hype, they'll conclude that the message has no substance. To them, a hard-to-understand message is cause for indifference, or worse, suspicion.

Three challenges in linking IT to shareholder value

No doubt explaining the link between IT investment and shareholder value is difficult. Investors rely on financial numbers, public statements, and industry analysis to assess the current health and future performance of enterprises. They rarely look deeper, because they don't have access to that information or don't want to spend the time and effort to understand it.

Three challenges have made this kind of communication difficult:

1. *The failure challenge:* Even when the expected business benefits of IT investments were successfully communicated, those benefits too often didn't appear in the time frame promised, or didn't appear at all. Depending on which research you're reading (and how a particular study defines success and failure), somewhere between 30 and 50 percent of IT initiatives fail. If you were shooting a basketball, that would be phenomenal success; in business it's failure. Again fault lies both with IS groups and business managers. IS groups have not communicated risks, and business managers have failed to understand or manage to these risks (as they would manage risk in other parts of their business). The result is a set of deeply skeptical shareholders.

2. *The commoditization challenge:* Although the specific value of IT is often hard to determine, every company has invested large sums in technology projects. What major manufacturer hasn't implemented an ERP system? What organization isn't using e-mail to collaborate more effectively? As a result, generating strategic benefit from technology and therefore having shareholders perceive value is becoming more difficult (and one of the major reasons enterprises need new CIO leaders and not just technology mechanics).

3. *The language challenge:* IT investments have traditionally been described in technological terms rather than value terms. The fault for this lies with both IS groups and business managers. Neither side has made the effort necessary to communicate the real business value of IT to shareholders. Consequently, an understanding of value has become a guessing game at best and impossible at worst.

If you've implemented the maxims process and governance processes discussed earlier, you're well on your way to solving, or at least alleviating, the failure challenge. Addressing the commoditization challenge is also dependent on governance, particularly on having a balanced portfolio of IT-enabled business initiatives that include both commodity and innovative investments. But as we have pointed out, today's commodity technologies weren't always commodities, just as today's many new technologies won't be commoditized for years to come. And there is still competitive advantage to be derived from innovative implementation of commodity technology. As we described in chapter 6, beverage can maker Rexam uses off-the-shelf "commodity" software, available to everyone, to produce competitive advantage so significant it gives the company pricing power in a mature, commoditized industry. Technological advantage today comes primarily from how you've integrated technology into your products, services, and processes, and not from the technology itself.

Overcoming the language gap

The third challenge in communicating the value of IT is the language gap. The key to demonstrating the contribution of IT investments to shareholder value is to link the IT business-case benefits to the drivers of shareholder value. Analysts boil down the myriad of shareholder-value drivers to four key ones: top-line growth (revenue), bottom-line growth (earnings), return on invested capital, and reputation.

Top-line growth

To evaluate top-line growth, shareholders want to know the answers to several questions: How fast are revenues growing? What is the enterprise's plan for growing revenues faster? How credible is this plan? How well is the sector doing? What are competitors doing? Do any substitute products threaten the main income earners? Where is the power in the supply chain—is it in your favor, or does it favor suppliers or customers? What are the industry dynamics?

IT affects the top line (revenue) when an enterprise taps new markets and customers, using systems that allow it to adapt to market changes more swiftly than competitors can adapt. IT can improve customer retention, which also affects the top line, with tracking systems to ensure consistent quality of interaction, targeted promotions, cross-selling, and customer life-cycle management.

Bottom-line growth

Other questions shareholders want answered are these: How fast are earnings growing? Are competitive pressures squeezing margins? Are costs under control? Are any big write-offs coming?

IT helps deliver earnings growth when it supports quality and cost-reduction initiatives. An enterprise both increases quality and decreases cost by using IT to reduce product recall rates. IT can also reduce the costs of handling returns and eliminate the need for invoice corrections. Both these improvements save the enterprise money and contribute to profits.

Return on invested capital

Shareholders also have questions about invested capital: How high is the enterprise's return on invested capital? What trend is this return following? Does the return exceed the cost of capital? How strong is the credit rating of the enterprise? Is the cost of capital for the enterprise likely to increase with investment plans or a credit crunch? Is the enterprise balancing good returns with good growth?

IT can help improve return on capital by supporting knowledge sharing and cost-reduction initiatives. By transferring internal best practices on scheduling and optimization to its factories, an enterprise can improve operations, which translates to higher return on invested capital. By creating a network of partners and vendors, a business can remove nonproductive assets from the balance sheet and reduce supply-chain costs—both of which increase asset use.

Reputation

Finally, shareholders want to know about an enterprise's reputation. How good is management's track record? How honest is the enterprise in reporting financial performance? How well can it respond to industry forces inhibiting enterprise performance and growth? Are there any looming environmental, safety, product liability, or operational issues? How well has management handled such issues in the past? How good is management at managing business risks in general? Does it have a record of growing the business profitably?

IT can help track and control business risk factors by providing tracking mechanisms and by supporting well-targeted knowledge asset initiatives. Additionally, IT's support of business continuity, compliance with privacy regulations, and security measures help an enterprise protect its reputation.

Putting it in plain language

As we have outlined, links exist between factors that investors and analysts look at and the benefits articulated in business cases for IT-enabled developments. But unless the story of this link is told clearly and simply, it will have little impact.

Outcomes that interest investors and analysts, like sales and earnings growth, express the highest level of benefit any initiative can provide for an enterprise. You and your business colleagues, on the other hand, probably describe benefits at the business unit level, and probably in operational terms, rather than top- or bottom-line terms.

To overcome the language challenge, you must take those benefits and elevate them to the level of the four drivers we just described. IT investment benefits have most often been expressed in technical terms. For instance, at one company we worked with, we found this benefit statement for upgrading to the latest version of a database program: "Version X will allow 78 percent more simultaneous transactions while cutting unnecessary record locks by more than 50 percent." Frighteningly, this was one of the better benefit statements we found, because it contained at least some quantitative elements. But the real business value was less than obvious, and the value to shareholders completely hidden.

Meeting the language challenge requires connecting the dots across three vocabularies: technical, business benefit, and shareholder value. Technical vocabulary talks about bits, bytes, clock speed, and so on. Business benefit vocabulary consists of statements about such benefits as engaging customers, gaining agility, increasing market share in identified areas, better management of knowledge assets, enhancing quality, and reducing business cost—the types of descriptions your new IT maxims and governance processes should emphasize. The vocabulary of shareholder value, however, is simpler still. It focuses on the four drivers just described: top-line growth, bottom-line growth, return on invested capital, and reputation. To communicate the value of IT to directors and shareholders, you have to connect the dots of each technology investment through these three vocabularies. See, for example, table 10-1, which shows a statement that has been translated from the language of technology benefit, to business benefit, to shareholder benefit.

TABLE 10-1

Communicating the Value of IT to Directors and Shareholders

How a technical benefit would be translated into the language of business benefit and then shareholder benefit.

Technical Benefit	Business Benefit	Shareholder Benefit
Version X will allow 78 percent more simultaneous transactions while cutting unnecessary record locks by 51 percent.	Version X will *reduce costs* by cutting the time required for order entry by an average of 8 percent and *enhance quality* by ensuring that data is updated correctly.	This investment will *improve our bottom line* because of lower costs in our back office and fewer customer returns due to incorrectly entered orders.

Communicate your shareholder value at every opportunity

Investors use messages they hear from CEOs, other corporate officers, and investor-relations people to form their own view of the value of an enterprise—albeit filtered by the press, analysts, and other commentators. Enterprises can communicate with investors in numerous ways: analyst calls, annual shareholder meetings, magazine or newspaper interviews, guest speakers at meetings, and so on. These communications need a clear message structured around the four drivers that interest investors. The contribution of IT investments should be part of that corporate message.

You build your credibility when the IT value message is clearly communicated, but you need to help your CEO and CFO by understanding the corporate story they plan to tell and connecting to it. You must devote time to uncovering the data that links enterprise IT investments to shareholder value and turning that data into market-relevant messages that fit with the CEO's communication strategy.

Drawing on our research and experience working with many CIOs, we have developed some key points about communicating your own message and integrating it with the CEO's.

Be mindful of the risks, including the legal pitfalls

There are, of course, many risks in communicating enterprise strategy to the public. Be aware that they will vary with the type of communicating you do with outsiders about IT and its contribution to the health of the enterprise as a whole.

In general, as the interactivity of the communication goes up, so does the risk. The safest communication for CIOs, even new CIO leaders, is some form of printed document, like the annual report, followed by staged events with relatively few opportunities for give and take. Risk rises dramatically with the introduction of open-ended, unrestricted questions. Most risky is the one-on-one interview with, say, an analyst or a major investor. On the other hand, such direct communications, handled well, can be the most effective at getting your message across.

It's a good idea to talk to your legal experts to make sure you fully understand your legal obligations in public statements. Be very clear about your enterprise's policy in talking with the media (there is no such thing as "off the record"), and make sure that you have good media training. Such training is increasingly part of every executive's tool kit. Consider making it part of yours.

Match what you say to the maturity of your business

As you prepare your messages about how IT-related initiatives drive shareholder value, remember to tie your statements back to the business context and your enterprise's business maturity. Context and maturity will drive the story your executive colleagues are telling. Matching the two does matter, because investors look for different growth drivers on different parts of the enterprise's business life cycle. Does a major part of your revenue come from an emerging business or a mature one?

For example, if your enterprise derives a major part of its shareholder value from an immature market—such as the case for online and biotechnology firms—you may choose to report on how IT is helping improve efficiency of R&D spending and marketing costs because these are important drivers in growing new markets. If innovation is the key, you may choose to emphasize IT's contribution to product development time, number of patents, and new product revenues.

Have a theme and stick to it

There should be a carefully thought-out *enterprise* message—like predictable profitability—that comes through like a drumbeat in every enterprise communication. Your job as head of IS is to echo this theme within the context of IT investments. If predictable profitability is the theme, talk about how IT has both boosted enterprise profits and made them more dependable and easier to track. But if the enterprise theme is rapid growth, highlight those aspects of IT benefits that drive greater market share and higher revenues.

If you can't always keep precisely on theme, then keep focused on the four shareholder value drivers. Translate your internal business-case benefits to these market drivers. Keep your message simple. Investors want the big picture first; they'll dig later.

Advantages to articulating the value of IT

Investment in enterprise information and technology assets does create shareholder value. It's your job to help link the two in the eyes of the shareholder. This requires a focus on those four shareholder value drivers and on the right type of targeted communication to a group of stakeholders—shareholders and investors—that may be new to you. It's not an easy task, but we're finding that more and more CIOs are becoming part of their company's frontline conversations with investment communities and the media. Even if you're not always front and center, your key role as CIO is to prepare specific messages and make sure the CEO and CFO are well briefed on how your enterprise IT investments create shareholder value.

Integrate Business Value Measures and IT Value Indicators

Quick! How would you respond to the following situation?

You're meeting with your CEO in a regular update discussion, and the subject of next year's budget comes up. You've been able to keep IT costs down—a declining percentage of sales, in fact—but another metric is on your boss's mind.

"Ten years ago," she says, "IT investment was fifteen percent of our capital budget. Last year it was over thirty percent, and next year it's going up again. It's bigger than our after-tax profits. I wish I felt more comfortable about the business payoff of all that money."

Would the CEO's statement surprise you? It probably shouldn't, unless you work for a particularly enlightened CEO.

Déjà vu? Yes and no. In the previous section, we focused on the issue of IT payoff from the point of view of a shareholder. We tried to point out how that vantage point focuses on the largest, highest level business issues—revenue growth, return on invested capital, and so on. But now you're inside the enterprise and you probably need to focus on additional material and a different type of answer, one that makes even more explicit the business payoff of IT.

Unfortunately, most business executives continue to find the link between investments in IT and specific business benefits something of a mystery. On the other hand, many IS executives we know assume the link is obvious. We hear them make statements like these:

- "Understanding our total relationship with each customer means we need to have accurate, timely, and pertinent customer data readily available. IT is critical for that."

- "Improving our speed to market requires excellent communication support among developers, planners, and marketers. IT is critical for that."

- "Lowering our costs means streamlining our processes. IT is critical for that."

Unfortunately, those linkages too often remain unstated or—nearly as bad—unspecified and undocumented. Undocumented, these statements simply sound like, at best, unfounded assertions or, at worst, self-serving rationalizations. New CIO leaders must be able to answer questions about business value quickly, succinctly, and with metrics that matter to business executives.

Why is the value question so difficult to answer?

Figure 10-1 shows graphically why the connection between IT investments and business value is typically hard to make. IT investments are necessarily made at the two lowest levels in the diagram: infrastructure and IT applications. However, the business value measures most prized by business managers are those at higher levels. Successful IT investments will improve business value measures at all five levels over time. Less successful investments may show positive impact at the two lower levels, but aren't strong enough to reach the higher levels.

FIGURE 10-1

Hierarchy of BusinessValue Measures

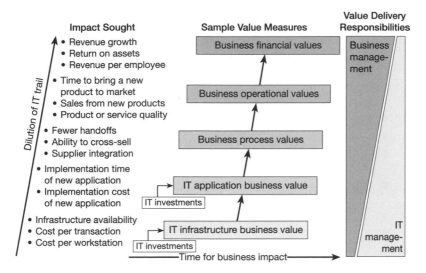

Source: Adapted from Peter Weill and Marianne Broadbent, *Leveraging the New Infrastructure* (Boston: Harvard Business School Press, 1998), 50.

Unfortunately, many IT investments appear to fall into the "less successful" category. Why? Mainly because of time and dilution.

It takes time for the benefits of IT investment to rise to higher levels. The value measures at those levels tend to be lagging measures. By the time benefits from IT-enabled investments are realized, any connection with the original IT investment may seem tenuous.

Dilution does damage as well. As you move up the hierarchy levels, the world becomes increasingly complex. The factors affecting results multiply rapidly—executives might decide to shut down a product line, take a different business direction, cut the training dollars needed for salespeople to learn a new system, or slash incentives needed to kick-start a new IT-enabled customer information reporting process. Sorting out the links between higher-level results and the original IT investments (or any investment at lower levels) can be enormously difficult.

Whether these links are difficult to identify or not, as a new CIO, you need to find them. The purpose of this section is to illustrate how you and your business executive colleagues can identify these connections and thereby make the clearest case possible for IT's contribution to business value. We will focus on developing a trail of evidence between the higher-level business value measures and the lower levels, where IT investments are made.

First, we'll talk about the basic, underlying approach in concept. Then we'll flesh out that conceptual approach by describing how it works using three different starting points.

The fundamental approach

Here's the underlying four-step process for linking IT and business value:

1. *Start with some measure of business value at as high a level in the enterprise as possible.* In figure 10-1, for example, the measure might be revenue growth, or revenue per employee, or new product development time. These measures should flow out of the business maxims and strategic intent statements you've uncovered. The measures you choose must be explicit, with objectively measurable goals and dates associated with those goals. If the value, for example, is profitable growth, there should be a specific revenue goal and a date associated with that goal. If no metric exists for a value, get or negotiate one with your business colleagues.

2. *Look for strategic initiatives in place to improve that value.* Look back now to the strategic initiatives you familiarized yourself with. They're the hook you can use to attach an IT link. Again, be sure to get any metrics (measurable goals and milestones) for those initiatives and programs. For example, let's say business leaders have adopted an initiative to increase revenue per employee as one way to achieve

profitable growth. To pursue that initiative, they adopt a specific program of increasing revenues per salesperson.

3. *Identify how IT can support and add value to those initiatives and programs.* Identifying such links may call on your creativity and ingenuity, but it can be done. To continue with our example: In talking to business leaders, you discover they want to reduce the administrative burden on sales employees so that the employees can devote more time to actual selling. That's a link: IT can provide systems that make administrative processes quicker and easier with templates and the use of mobile technology to simplify and automate sales reports from the field.

4. *Attach metrics to the specific IT investments and IS initiatives contributing to achievement of the business value.* The metrics allow you to track and communicate progress against your IS goal in support of the business goal. For automating the preparation of sales reports, a metric might be percentage completion to date of the software application, the percentage of salespeople able to use the application, or the amount of time saved. Keep in mind when developing these metrics that they will be affected by the approach the sales group uses to reward the original business goal—more revenue per employee.

Following these basic steps will give you a clear trail of evidence between IT and a business value. Table 10-2 summarizes that trail for our example.

As you may have noticed, we constructed this trail by traversing, or linking, all the levels on the business value hierarchy (figure 10-1). It started with a value (or goal) at the top level (call that level five), and then found a link with that goal through the second or operational level (increase revenue per sales employee; reduce the amount of time salespeople spend on nonselling activity). The investment enabled salespeople to use more efficient processes.

TABLE 10-2

Sample Trail of Evidence Between IT and Business Value

Measure of Value	Specific Impact Sought	Metric
Business value	Profitable sales growth	10 percent top-line growth this year while maintaining last year's level of profitability
Business value initiatives/programs	Increase revenue per sales employee	10 percent this year and 20 percent next year
	Free up time of sales employees for more actual selling	Number of sales calls per week
IT value-added	Through easy-to-use templates and tools, reduce amount of time sales employees spend preparing sales reports	Percentage of IT application completed
		Percentage of sales employees using application
		Amount of time saved per sales employee

In this case, the trail of evidence linked with an IT application at the second level. The same approach could also have been used to link with an investment in IT infrastructure, the first level. An improved infrastructure—say, the company intranet—might have been needed to support the templates and tools for salespeople.

Case study: Yorkshire Water

Located in the north of England, Yorkshire Water is the world's ninth largest water utility. In the late 1990s, it found itself rated last in customer service among all of England's water companies. Yorkshire faced rising customer expectations and growing competitive threats. "We were on the edge of a precipice," says Alan Harrison, CIO, who headed an IS group of more than 250 employees.

The company's ambitious survival strategy, to become the best water company in the United Kingdom, led to a major change program and a total investment of US$65 million. Part of the investment was for back-office systems to enhance financial management and supply-chain performance; part was for systems to improve asset management. But most of the investment (US$45 million) was to improve customer service.

That money went into Yorkshire's ICOM (integrated customer and operations management system), which, when completed, fully integrated the customer contact side of the business and work management (including contractors) in the field. For example, a customer who called to report low water pressure could be told immediately the cause of the problem and when approximately it should be resolved, because call center agents could see where the relevant field engineering work was taking place.

The trail of evidence linking the investment in ICOM and the ultimate business benefit was clearly stated at the outset and reinforced often: Poor customer satisfaction—based on poor customer service and inefficient and unresponsive work practices—threatened the utility's survival. To survive, the company had to improve customer relations, which required keeping customers informed (for example), which in turn required IT to provide information to customer service representatives via investments in infrastructure, applications, and systems. The links were clear, step by step, through all four levels of the value hierarchy.

Building the case

While the experience of Yorkshire might appear to have been a case of a relatively easy or straightforward connection of IT investment to business value, success was the result of hard work and regular communication of these links. Certainly, the creation of the trail of evidence was made easier because the business goals were clearly articulated. One of the problems we often see is that the business values (the enterprise or business unit goals) aren't clearly laid out. Or even more likely, the values or goals are clear enough, but the strategies, plans, and programs for attaining them are little more than generalities and platitudes.

What follows are descriptions of three different ways you can identify enterprise goals and plans, so that you can link IT initiatives and investments to them.

Starting with maxims

Clear enterprise or business unit direction—in the form of well-articulated goals, strategies, and programs—offers the best base for creating the trail of evidence between business values and IT initiatives. Sometimes, however, you have to put a considerable amount of effort into working with your business colleagues to clarify their business strategies and programs (and perhaps even their goals, too).

From that effort, as we described in earlier chapters, you can identify business maxims. Most likely, initiatives and programs will be only implicit in the maxims, and you will need to work with business colleagues to identify programs more explicitly.

You can think of maxims in terms of the business value hierarchy diagram in figure 10-1. Maxims are a way of traversing or linking the levels. If your enterprise has only goals at the highest level, maxims are a way of bringing those goals down to the operational or second-highest level.

We've mostly talked here about the enterprise as a whole. But executives in most large enterprises with multiple lines of business soon discover that broad, enterprise-level value measures mask differences between business units. So they often prefer to concentrate on value measures at the business unit level. You have to look at both enterprise value and business unit value—and that is the essence of the "enterprise context" part of the maxims process. Know what you can and should be assessing across the enterprise and what linkages you should be working on for business value at the business unit level. For many infrastructure investments, you will, by definition, need to work at the enterprise level. Still, even for such projects, identifying the benefits of enterprisewide infrastructure services by business unit will help solidify support from business unit leaders.

Starting with a business process

One benefit of starting with maxims is that you're dealing with a business unit's entire set of goals and strategies, because that's the context in which maxims get developed. You're able to take a more comprehensive approach, which will make you and your business colleagues more intelligent in setting priorities and finding synergies.

This strength of maxims is also, unfortunately, a weakness. It's analogous to a long book on some subject important to you. The strength of the book is its length, which means it provides what you need in great breadth and depth. But its length is also its weakness, because it's so long you never have time to read it. (We hope that's not true of this book!)

So can it be with maxims, which take time to develop because, ideally, they emerge from a process of intensive interaction with your business colleagues. Sometimes you don't have the necessary access to their time or you have to do work-arounds, as John Petrey did at Banknorth (see chapter 4). Work must go on, even as you develop maxims or before you do; therefore, you may need some other, more contained starting point for linking IT and business value. Perhaps you need some quick wins to enhance your credibility in the short term.

A business process can be a useful starting point. The virtue of starting with a process is twofold. Everyone in the enterprise recognizes the business value of the process. So, for example, no one will dispute the virtue of helping your sales department sell more, or helping customer service staff retain customers. Second, since processes usually have corresponding organizational units, there will be a business manager—a specific individual, like a vice president of sales—whom you can work with and whose work life focuses on improving the process. (Remember that we identified process-based working as the dominant trend in running a leaner, more focused IS organization. You can now see the benefits of adopting this approach.)

Even in an enterprise or a business unit with fuzzy goals and plans, process managers will probably have specific targets and programs. You can work with those managers to find links in their plans and strategies where IT can deliver value. Once you have those links, you can work backward to identify specific IT investments and IS initiatives, each with its own metric for measuring progress and improvement.

Let's consider a hypothetical case. In working with the operations manager of your company, you discover that one of her goals is to reduce order fulfillment time. Why is that a goal? Because research has shown that quicker order turnaround will reduce the number of returns. That's a promising handle or hook on which you can begin to link IT to business value. The trail of evidence will be clear. IS initiatives (with appropriate metrics) will speed up order processing. The result will be faster order fulfillment, which will reduce returns, which will reduce costs and increase profits.

Starting with a business project

In some ways, a business project is the most difficult starting point for linking IT and business value. Nevertheless, it's probably the most common starting point we see.

Starting with a business project is difficult because such a project (say, the redesign or reworking of a manufacturing process) carries a double burden of proof. The first burden is to demonstrate the business value of the project itself. Why is it a good idea to redesign manufacturing, for example? The second burden is to demonstrate the value of the IT portion of the project.

The logical approach is for the business manager leading the project to make the case for the project, and then for IS to make the case for the IT portion. Even better would be the business manager's making the case for the both the business unit and the IT portion. In both cases (the business manager working with IS or including IT in one justification process), the business link is then clear. If the project makes business sense, then the link between IT and ultimate business value will be relatively easy to make.

Good Metrics Underpin Credibility

CREATING SPECIFIC, quantitative metrics for tracking and ultimately assessing progress at each level of the value hierarchy provides several benefits.

First, it forces greater clarity and concreteness of thinking about results and benefits.

Second, if chosen well, the metrics boost the credibility of the linkage between IT and ultimate business value. The metrics then serve as a basis for developing a scorecard or dashboard that IS can use to communicate the value of multiple activities. We'll discuss this at length in the next section.

Third, business metrics can spark creative thinking about how IS can support the business programs or strategies related to those business metrics. For example, in our original example about improving revenue per sales employee, the strategy, stated in those preceding words, may or may not suggest how IT can provide support. But when the sales manager specified *actual time spent selling* as an interim metric, this immediately suggested ways IT could help.

Fourth, your enterprise is likely to require some form of financial rationale—probably some form of return-on-investment analysis—for an IT investment. The trail of evidence, with appropriate metrics at each level, will provide the pro forma data you need for financial analysis.

Unfortunately, things are seldom so neat. Too often a business project with a significant IT component is treated as an IT project and the burden falls on IT to justify, in effect, the entire effort. This is a trap you want to avoid. In our experience, those enterprises most highly evolved in their use of IT have a corporate mantra: "There are no IT projects, only business projects." IT is a crucial enabler in the enterprise, but it's always a means to an end, never the end.

Consequently, the first task in using a project to begin linking IT and business value is to make sure that the leadership roles for the project are the right ones. The business leader should, at the very least, make the business case for the business project. Then, if the business manager cannot or will not do so, IS should make the case for the IT portion by linking that portion to the business proposition.

Hospitality International Inc. (HII, a pseudonym), a U.S.-based hospitality company with over one thousand hotels and resorts around the world and systemwide sales exceeding US$15 billion, often measures the business value of IT indirectly. What HII directly measures are the business programs that technology supports or enables.

For example, its customer-relationship management system enabled the introduction of a vacation-planning program in seven HII resorts. The system helped hotel employees arrange golf tee times, dinner reservations, and other activities before guests began their vacations. An analysis after the installation of the planning service showed that guests who participated spent on average US$100 more a day at hotel golf courses, at restaurants, and on activities like tours, for which HII earns commissions.

The incremental revenue was compared against the cost of the entire program, not just the IT component. Measures of revenue increase were also supplemented with figures for customer satisfaction and repeat stays. While it was too soon to tell whether more guests were returning to HII resorts, guest satisfaction ratings were up, and that figure should foreshadow repeat visits and increased business value over time.

Create Effective Performance Dashboards

Commerce Bank is the principal subsidiary of Commerce Bancshares Inc., a US$13.4 billion Midwestern bank holding company. In 2003 it invested US$10 million in updating its check imaging system. A project team spent a year justifying and planning the change, which is now in its final implementation phase and is closely tracking the costs and benefits outlined in the original plan.

The plan identified specific links with business goals, among them, increased profitability. For example, instead of citing something vague like "reduced personnel expense," the plan specified the elimination of a named cost center as of a particular date.

The leaders of the affected business units not only participated in development of the plan, but also personally explained to the bank's executive management committee how the imaging project supported their business objectives. Then the business units publicly committed to achieving the benefits numbers.

As the bank put the imaging system in place, it used and continues to use the original plan to track progress. Costs and benefits are tracked monthly, reported to the project steering committee, and summarized for senior management. This tracking has been possible because the original plan identified costs, benefits, and timing so specifically. Such a specific tracking system is desirable because nothing will build IS credibility more quickly than actually demonstrating (rather than merely asserting) the links between IT and business value.

This example raises the important issue of how IS should communicate its work and progress to business colleagues throughout the enterprise. As we said, it is essential that IS claim business benefits in various planning documents and proposals. Equally important, IS must report on its delivery of those benefits. If you do all we outline in this book, yet fail in this final step, the credibility you reap for your work in IS will fall far short of what it could or should be.

To make a solid contribution to business value, you need to do more than just deliver critical support for your enterprise's goals and strategies. Gaining full credit for the quality of your work and that of your team means you must report regularly on your progress, so that the world can see you succeed. Like it or not, others' perception of your success is what truly matters. As happens to all senior executives, failures and near failures quickly become public knowledge. You need to make sure that your successes are well noticed, too.

To do so, you need a set of IS indicators you can put together in various IS performance scorecards, or dashboards. We prefer the term *dashboard* because it connotes a tool for ongoing guidance about IS activities on behalf of the enterprise, rather than merely a summary of past performance.

Once you've sorted out the various basic indicators, you can present them in different dashboards aimed at the many stakeholders in the enterprise. These indicators become the foundation for communicating with the board, enterprise leaders, your business colleagues, business unit managers, and other IS leaders in a wide variety of settings: board meetings, planning sessions, budget reviews, staff meetings, executive retreats, IS annual reports, company newsletters, and wall displays. Your dashboards should literally become the basis of most everything you report inside and outside your IS group.

As you contemplate developing and reporting progress with a dashboard, remember that credibility depends on transparency. If they are to build credibility, your dashboard indicators need to be accessible to anyone who wants to locate them. Why not post your dashboards on your enterprise intranet?

The significant questions are not whether to have dashboards measuring your organization's success, but what to report and how to report it. Too often, IS groups report on issues and metrics that only they understand. We've seen too many business executives roll their eyes when they see such IS metrics as through-put statistics, network uptime, or CPU speeds. The only conclusion the executives can reach is that you don't know how to communicate as a business executive (and you know which path that conclusion puts you on).

What should you report?

Your IS reports need to focus on the services your "customers" want and need, and the business metrics that prove those services are worth paying for. Like any other form of communication, IS reports must be designed to meet the needs of the recipients, not the senders.

Always keep in mind the fundamental reasons for reporting. Behind all you report should be two basic messages:

1. *IS deserves the trust of its enterprise colleagues.* IS does what it says it will do, on time, on budget, and at specified quality levels—and if there are any problems, these are foreshadowed and discussed so that there are no surprises. In short, IS delivers, and in the process, it delivers good value.

2. *IS delivers business value.* IS isn't about technology for its own sake. It's about using technology to enable the business to reach and exceed its goals. Investments in IT clearly contribute business value to the enterprise.

The first message is crucial, but it's not enough. It positions IS as a "good" cost center, but still a cost center. Equally important, it provides credibility for the second message, which can transform IS from a cost center to a source of value. The first message will get IS the respect due competent professionals, and that's good. But the second message will position you as an enterprise executive and your IS team as a fully contributing member of the enterprise team, with all the credibility and trust this implies.

Given those fundamental messages, you need two types of IS dashboards. The first, corresponding to the first message, reports measures of basic IS operational performance. The second dashboard builds on the first by reporting clear indicators that link IT-related investments to agreed-upon business values.

Type 1 dashboard: Report basic IS operational performance

It's important to report basic performance (assuming it's done in a way that makes sense to a nontechnical person), because the work of the IS group can profoundly affect the ability of other enterprise groups to meet their own performance goals. Excessive downtime in a call center, for example, will inhibit the completion of sales orders. Or the failure to complete new IT-enabled business initiatives can stop a business unit from opening new sites, developing an online sales channel, or exploiting other IT-based business opportunities.

We and our colleagues, working with CIOs, have created a metrics framework for reporting on basic IS performance.[2] The framework consists of six basic parameters that define IS performance overall. Each measure is supported by more detailed metrics in tiers at lower levels, which you would use for inside-IS operational monitoring and in-depth analysis. The six measures are what you report outside IS.

The measures are system performance, IT-support performance, partnership ratio, service-level effectiveness, new-projects index, and cost index. All six can be cast at enterprise level or at each business unit. They sum up how productive your IS group really is, as you track and compare the figures over time. For each measure, where you're able to obtain relevant outside numbers, you should also benchmark the performance of your IS group. Just be careful when you benchmark to select enterprises in similar industries or with a comparable economic model.

System performance

System performance is the percentage of time that systems, applications, and infrastructure services are available when needed and are performing at levels required by users. To prepare this metric, you will need to define the key systems, both applications and infrastructure, and prepare two target measures for each—availability and performance level (as well as the operating windows when those target levels apply). Service-level agreement (SLA) metrics of availability and response time can be combined to determine this metric. You can probably extract the target numbers from SLAs; if not, you will need to negotiate them with IT users within the enterprise (and be sure to include them in future SLAs). Then, you must report on the time intervals when both criteria were met and map the exceptions to total time.

IT-support performance

Support performance is the percentage of time that IT support staff and organizations (1) are available to help with problems and new requests and (2) perform at the level necessary to address these requests properly. Call-center/customer-care metrics are combined to determine this metric. Again, you will need to define key customer care measures (e.g., mean time to respond, mean time to fix) and targets for each measure. These measures should roll up to two metrics—availability and performance. Don't forget to define the operating times when specified targets apply.

Partnership ratio

The partnership ratio is an index of the percentage of projects and initiatives in which IS has a partnership or leadership role with the business early in the strategic planning process. Tracking this metric ensures IS's early involvement in business planning. Defining this parameter will depend on the process used in your enterprise to initiate projects. For example, is there a kickoff meeting or funding approval process? What is the earliest appropriate point that IS would become involved, in the best of all worlds? Track if this happens or not.

Service-level effectiveness

Effectiveness is a measure of "customer" satisfaction with IS work. It's often based on customer satisfaction surveys or such measures as complaints coming in to call centers or unresolved issues. Some portion of this measure might be anecdotal, based on interviews or a general sense gathered from asking around the various parts of the enterprise. Alongside the other five metrics—particularly system performance, which describes IS's basic ability to do its work—this metric helps determine whether user needs have changed, SLAs are structured properly, or service is suffering from under- or overinvesting. Measures of service-level effectiveness can be used to gauge user needs and begin to identify cost-cutting opportunities or areas needing more investment.

New-projects index

This index measures IS's ability to deliver new projects on time (in concert with the business) and on budget, which meet the agreed-upon requirements. As we said earlier, most projects are business projects, and most responsibility for achieving full business value falls on your business colleagues. The new-projects index is a high level indicator of the effectiveness of the IS organization in planning and forecasting, anticipating resource requirements, and managing and delivering projects with the necessary quality and timeliness.

IT total cost ratio

This is a measure of the total cost of IT (your IS organization and the IT services provided), directly and indirectly, as a percentage of revenue and expenses. (An alternative is to show total costs as a percentage of earnings before interest and taxes.) This metric is useful as a ballpark indicator of your costs and the trend of those costs over time. Organizations such as Gartner collect and report such costs over many industries, and you can compare yours to those. However, the cost ratio has to be used carefully. For example, if your business really uses technology to compete, you probably have a ratio that's higher than your competitors' or the overall industry average. Business context always matters, even in your metrics and benchmarks.

Taken together, all six metrics inform the business about overall IS operational performance with just enough information and measurement to keep attention on the right areas at the right level. The general difficulty lies not in finding the data for such metrics but in finding a way to combine all the available data and information and reporting something the business cares about. The six metrics were designed to address that problem. Each is an aggregation of a number of analytical and operational metrics used within IS organizations. In combination, they cover all the bases: efficiency of service (doing things right), effectiveness of service (doing the right things), and ability to innovate (doing new things).

FIGURE 10-2

Dashboard for IT Responsiveness

What the Business Watches	Demand management	Market responsiveness	Sales effectiveness	Product development effectiveness
	Supply management	Customer responsiveness	Supplier effectiveness	Operational efficiency
	Support services	Human resources responsiveness	IT responsiveness	Finance and regulatory responsiveness

IT Responsiveness

What You Report to the Business	System performance	IT support performance	Partnership ratio
	Service-level effectiveness	New-projects index	IT total cost ratio

New-Projects Index

How You Monitor New Initiatives	On time	On budget		
		Sales cycle index	Customer care performance	On-time delivery

As we noted earlier, the six metrics can be reported for the enterprise as a whole or for each business unit. What you present, and how, will depend on your organization and its structure and needs. If you do report the measures by business unit, you may find it useful to show how each unit compares with its peers.

Figure 10-2 illustrates how these six metrics fit into an enterprisewide system of tracking performance. IT responsiveness is one component of what the enterprise watches overall. Part of the support services portion of the enterprise, IT responsiveness represents the six metrics we just described. Each of the six in turn is composed of a number of measures, which you monitor within IS. (The figure shows the breakdown of only one metric, the new-projects index.)

Type 2 dashboard: Report indicators linking IT to agreed-upon business values

While you are not solely responsible for delivering the business benefits of IT investments, you do need clear, frequently updated dashboards showing how both the IS organization and IT investments are contributing to business value. The key way to do this is through dashboards covering specific IS activities.

For that purpose, you will need a number of dashboards that link specific IS programs, initiatives, or investments and the creation of business value. These IS/IT business-value dashboards, comprising a number of indicators, can fall wherever they make most sense in an overall IS reporting scheme. For example, they might be grouped under the new-projects index metric in the reporting system just outlined.

The IS/IT business-value dashboards are based on the indicators of IS and IT contribution we described in the previous section on linking IT and business value. These indicators are a highly useful management tool and a vital means of communication, the culmination of the trail of evidence linking business value to IS contribution.

The focus should be on a manageable number of IT value indicators that are meaningful to business leaders. The indicators should be linked to familiar business measures—such as business strategies and goals, business maxims, and business processes—and show both current status and progress to date. Ideally, these indicators might be jointly reported with the appropriate business unit or included in each business unit leader's dashboard. This is most easily achieved if the indicators are developed as part of the project design and approval process and used to assess the success of as many projects as possible in your portfolio.

IS/IT business-value dashboards help support the second basic message of IS reports: *IS delivers business value.* The dashboards illuminate the trail of evidence by showing each of the distinct links (across each of the levels of the value hierarchy) between an IS activity or IT investment and the ultimate contribution to business value.

In our earlier example of IT's contribution to a business unit goal of profitable growth, the linkage across the business value hierarchy might look like this.

Business unit goal: profitable growth

Key business strategy for that goal: increase revenue per sales representative

Key business program for that strategy: increase the time that sales representatives actually spend selling

IS project to support that business program: provide IT templates and tools that save sales representatives time

In this case, IS should develop a set of metrics to measure both its progress and ultimately its impact on time available for selling.

Where the links are as clear as they are here, the dashboard should show each of the metrics, starting with IS progress and including the program metric (sales representatives' time saved and available for actual selling) and perhaps even the strategy metric (revenue per sales employee). Of course, the success of the strategy will depend on many factors beyond the IS project (it's the dilution effect we described in the previous section), so you may or may not want to include the strategy metric. But you certainly should include the business metric—time saved—because there the link is direct.

Reporting on IS readiness

Although the current business value of IT is important, the future readiness of the IS organization is also increasingly crucial. Because IT now underpins enterprise and business processes, and as the pace of business and technological change accelerates, the readiness and agility of the IS organization can become a competitive differentiator.

Consequently, you may want to include IS readiness indicators in your regular reports on IS. You and your colleagues can use the indicators to estimate how well IS is positioned to add value in the future, based on its capacity to anticipate and act quickly.

IS readiness can be measured in four major areas: IT services capability, application characteristics, expertise availability, and process maturity. Frameworks such as reach and range gap analysis, application assessment, expertise gap analysis, and process maturity levels can help quantify the IS organization's state of readiness.

IT services capability: reach and range

The concept of reach and range, first proposed by Peter Keen, describes the business scope of the enterprise's IT infrastructure.[3] Today we would describe *reach* as the locations and people your IT services are capable of connecting in a seamless and reliable way. Reach can extend from a single location to the ultimate level of connecting anyone, anywhere.

Range refers to functionality—what work can be done—in terms of business processes or activities. It answers the question "What business processes or activities can be completed and shared automatically and seamlessly across every level of reach?"

Reach and range can be used to assess IT services readiness by indicating where you are today and where you want to be in twelve months' time. Measuring the status of your IT services capability today and engaging your business partners in a discussion of future requirements can help identify the gaps in reach and range. These discussions can analyze the trade-offs between reaching the goal and justifying expenditures to upgrade the infrastructure in the needed time frame.

Application characteristics: flexible and scalable

You can rate major applications on their flexibility and scalability to provide a picture of the overall portfolio's readiness. The assessment can indicate which applications need replacing because they lock the organization into current ways of working. The flexibility and scalability of applications is an important determinant of readiness. Rate major applications as low, medium, or high (you don't need more granular ratings than these) on each characteristic.

Expertise availability: appropriate competencies

New CIO leaders measure readiness in the staffing area in several ways. One large company we know measures level of achievement in developing staff from all its IS units, while another measures turnover rate for top-performing employees and average training days per employee per year.

In chapter 8, we suggested looking at the various competencies that your team needs to do IS work. We specifically recommended making an inventory of competencies, both needed and currently on staff. You can add to that inventory a set or level of competencies needed in the future (as best you can predict) and keep track of on-staff competencies compared with anticipated future needs.

Process maturity: consistency and reliability

The maturity of key IS management processes is another indicator of IS agility and readiness to support new business initiatives. Maturity levels can be assessed for such operations as e-business, security, procurement, applications development, software acquisition, and project management.

Many models are available for this kind of assessment, from consulting firms and such trade groups as the Software Engineering Institute (with its Capability Maturity Model for software development) and the Society for Information Management. The European Quality Award and the Baldrige Award in the United States also provide ways to assess the maturity of different IS processes.

Dashboards at work

To see how an IS metrics program (similar to though not exactly the program we've just described) actually works in one company, we can look at American Mutual Insurance Company (AMIC, a pseudonym), one of the largest financial institutions in the world. The firm serves more than 13 million individual and institutional customers in more than twenty five foreign countries. Providing value to customers is a primary goal of the company, which is supported by the Corporate Information Technology (CIT) department, whose mission is to "provide world-class IT business solutions and services which will add value to our customers and give our business groups the opportunity to win in the marketplace."

Over the course of several years, the CIT group established a consistent reporting discipline across all IT functions within the enterprise. That reporting process has since evolved into a well-automated, consistent, integrated world-class metrics program.

One result of the program was a set of common dashboards (AMIC calls them scorecards, but we will use *dashboards* here for consistency) for each business unit. The dashboards provided more than a twelve-month history of business partner satisfaction; mainframe, network, and distributed computing performance; plus applications portfolio analyses covering such aspects as delivery performance and business impact and risk, measured against world-class external benchmarks.

The reporting system carefully measured new initiatives along five dimensions: business impact, cost, business risk, benefit, and IS confidence to deliver. Business impact, a parameter added after the program was under way, looked at an initiative's planned ability to decrease cost and maximize efficiency. It also covers other business goals, including revenue growth, customer retention, quality, decision support, and compliance and control.

The program focused as well on the use of innovative technologies. A dashboard showed the number of such initiatives and the amount of investment. AMIC considered the ability to use innovative technology a critical success factor in its highly competitive market.

Once the reporting program was well established, American Mutual's CIT group began to focus more on using the dashboards as communication vehicles and levers to change behavior. The department began using dashboard data for playback sessions, in which CIT staff members played back to the managers of each business unit what their strategy looked like, based on an analysis of their IT plans and discretionary IT investments. New IT investments were categorized according to the primary business strategy each investment supported. This approach proved to be an excellent communication vehicle and helped improve alignment of IT investments with business unit strategy. It also pointed out to business unit heads where their strategy had not been clearly communicated to all stakeholders.

CIT leaders noted three lessons they learned in developing, implementing, and evolving their metrics dashboards: (1) Keep it simple, (2) start small and evolve over time, and (3) involve management in using the data to change behavior.

Overall, reporting on the ability of the IS group to respond to changing enterprise needs can be an important part of delivering the first message, namely, that the IS group can be trusted to play its role in the enterprise well. Indeed, as you decide on how you will report on the contribution of IS to the enterprise, keep in mind both key messages you want to deliver:

IS deserves the trust of its enterprise colleagues.

IS delivers business value.

In a broad sense, this entire book has been about little more than earning the right to proclaim those two messages in your enterprise. If you proclaim them appropriately and often, you will ensure your progress on the path to being a new CIO leader.

Conclusion:
Bring It All Together

We began this book by asserting that CIOs today are at a crossroads and must choose for themselves which path to follow: to become new CIO leaders or chief technology mechanics. We wish there were other options, but the state of the world today doesn't offer any other choices. Simply maintaining the status quo—focusing on managing request queues, keeping as large an IS organization as possible, being wowed by emerging technology, and operating IS divorced from business goals and specific business benefits—is itself a choice to follow the path to enterprise irrelevance.

For those CIOs who aspire to more, to being integral parts of their enterprise leadership team, to having a valued and respected seat at the enterprise strategy table, there is an alternative. This alternative is built on the ten areas of focus we have covered in the ten chapters of this book. How far you are along the path can be determined by completing the assessment in appendix D. We hope you've at least taken a glance at it, perhaps even filled out part of it. The assessment will help you build your own agenda, which will be customized to where you are today and adjusted to your business context, whether it is breaking away or fighting for survival. We have explained that, besides building the foundation of leadership and acquiring knowledge of your enterprise, you have key priorities depending on the nature of your enterprise: for breaking-away enterprises, the priority is vision; for maintaining-competitiveness enterprises, IT governance; and for fighting-for-survival enterprises, a new IS organization. While a new CIO leader cannot ignore any of the ten points we have laid out, these three priorities are the most crucial for CIOs in these types of enterprises.

New CIO leaders exist today; we hope the various stories we've provided throughout the book have given you a flavor of what this role looks like in the real world. Unfortunately, because the demands of a book force a linear structure, the stories and steps we've laid out may occasionally seem disconnected. There is one more task that we have not yet covered—bringing all these points of focus together every day to deliver business results. As we mentioned in the introduction, the new CIO leader's job is not linear. All the items we've discussed interact with each other and influence each other.

To close on this theme of bringing it all together for effective business results, we'd like to share three more stories. We hope these stories, and this book, inspire you to boldly take the path of becoming a new CIO leader.

British Airways Uses IT to Change the Enterprise Cost Structure

British Airways (BA), the world's largest international airline, carries 40 million passengers a year, flies to ninety-four countries, and has forty-six thousand employees. It has fought back after 9/11 by taking US$3 billion out of its cost base and reducing labor by twelve thousand people. "But it's been tough," notes CIO Paul Coby, "because we're competing against no-frills carriers in Europe (whose cost base is lower than ours) and against U.S. carriers in Chapter 11 bankruptcy. It's not a level playing field at the moment."[1]

Since the 1980s, IT has revolutionized the airline industry, beginning with online reservation systems, then departure-conferral systems and frequent-flyer systems. Online selling since the late-1990s has dramatically changed the nature of customer interactions. For example, BA.com receives 250,000 visits every day; four out of five direct flight bookings in the U.K. now come through BA.com.

The business goal is cost-competitive full service

Coby also speaks about the importance of cost-competitive service:

> To maintain our full-service characteristics, we've absolutely got to reduce our cost base and change our business model. We are doing that by redesigning all our processes to be self-service; making them so easy to use and attractive that customers will want to serve themselves. We've branded it customer-enabled British Airways (ceBA). It requires radically simplifying our processes. Customers tell us they want self-service. They like online check-in. They like self-service kiosks. They want to be in control. Our vision . . . is to make self-service completely pervasive, end-to-end.
>
> This new business model also means that employees should use the same systems and processes as customers [do]. For the past thirty years, the airlines have been using employees to translate for customers. The results have been obscure and complex call-center processes. It's much better to build simple systems for customers to use themselves. It will take significant amounts of cost out of operations and gives customers what they say they want.

This shift in BA's business model is dramatic. To achieve it, Coby sponsored the creation of business and IT maxims, which BA calls "golden rules." "The first [maxim] is that we must have a simple and compelling customer proposition," says Coby. "We had twenty-four thousand separate fares. That's ludicrous. The second is to design processes for end-customer use, not for internal departments. The third is to build quality into systems. And the fourth is to have a single BA solution, not different solutions for different departments."

Meeting the business goal requires IT

Coby describes the importance of the IS organization in meeting BA's business goals:

> To simplify our business and improve our cost structure, we've needed to centralize. BA has centralized remarkably in the past two years. IS lies at the heart of the transformation. For instance, I lead the ceBA board and am a member of corporate investment committees. It's my department's role to drive change throughout the business, and its profile has greatly increased.
>
> To simplify our financial processes, I am using the Sarbanes-Oxley regulation as a lever. British Airways is registered on the New York Stock Exchange, so we must comply. We have established an information security and control board with the CFO and head of HR. So Sarbanes-Oxley is a force for process change and simplification here.
>
> We're focusing our investment on commercial systems because that's where the revenue and most of the costs lie. You don't always need advanced technologies to make things more efficient. I am trying to encourage a sort of "anti-IT ideology" that asks, "Can we do that with our existing technologies and processes?"

But because there is merit in looking forward, Coby also has an innovation group. Mobile systems are a key area of investigation. BA is establishing wireless networking in its BA lounges and has piloted Internet access and e-mail on its planes. The airline was the first company to test fee-based wireless service over the Atlantic.

As a CIO leader, Coby's job is to coordinate the transformation

All IT projects are viewed as business projects at BA. Coby's job is to pull all the elements together, maybe using legacy systems, maybe using bits of new technology, and always changing business processes. An example is BA's calendar-led selling on BA.com. Using in-house built systems, BA.com can show fourteen days of flights between any two cities, by price. The Web design presents the options clearly. But this new feature required business change as well. The revenue management department had to adopt new pricing processes, and the marketing department had to create a good ad campaign to tell flyers that BA is a high-quality, but not high-priced, airline. By combining technology with business process changes and advertising, the whole airline worked together to meet the challenges of competitors. "I think it's the CIO's job to pull these elements together," says Coby. "My job is also to lead our IT staff and enable them to go forward on the exciting and important new work in customer enablement and employee enablement."

Through its transformation efforts, BA is developing a high-performing organization, delivering a competitive cost base (to compete with the no-frills airlines), simplifying the business, and strengthening its balance sheet. Paul Coby is an enterprise leader in driving to meet these business goals—in other words, a new CIO leader.

Yallourn Energy: Remaking an IS Organization in One Year

In the mid 1990s, Yallourn Energy, an Australian utility, was privatized and sold to a U.K.-based consortium. In December 2000, China Light and Power (CLP) bought a majority 72 percent stake in the company; the company increased ownership to 100 percent by February 2004. Maintaining an emphasis begun by the U.K. consortium,

CLP has focused on cost reduction and restructuring the business to make it profitable. A large part of the effort involved outsourcing parts of the business and mining operations. Employee numbers were reduced by over 25 percent as a result of the restructuring. IT was not affected, though, pending appointment of a new CIO.

The challenges for the new CIO

Joe Locandro was brought on board as CIO of the utility in November 2002. He found a lot of fear in employees as a result of the downsizing, and much pressure from management to downsize IS as well. But he insisted on taking stock of the situation first.[2]

The environment of mistrust and apprehension persisted after his arrival because employees were not sure of his leadership style. He also had little credibility because he came from the entertainment industry rather than the utility industry.

Locandro viewed the situation as "a renovator's delight" because it held so much potential. The environment was autocratic, with a command and control structure. Locandro also found a disconnect between IT and the business. Corporate management did not fully understand IT or IS people, so it handed off oversight to finance.

The first ninety days: Understand the situation

Locandro knew that management expected him to deliver a strategy and downsizing plans by March 2003. Consequently, from November 2002 through January 2003, he spent his time creating baselines by learning about the people, situation, processes, and technologies. Because he also wanted to know the issues, he spent a lot of time talking with management and staff to cull the issues from the hype.

He found no regular activity reporting, no metrics, and no IS accountabilities. Anyone could buy any IT item. IT was fractured among the businesses. Developers performed duplicate work in different locations. And a July 2002 customer satisfaction survey of IS yielded a poor approval rating overall. The staff worked hard, but because they were not focused, they often were working on the wrong things, at least from a management viewpoint.

Locandro's primary goal for the first ninety days was to get to know the people and be sure they understood him and realized that he was fair. He spent November and December bonding with his IS team, using the Christmas period as a good opportunity for that. His team members expected him to follow the past authoritarian management style and cut staff. But they soon realized he was going to be different; his style was informal, which was foreign to them.

He asked all the IS staff to give a presentation on what they did and the issues they saw. Numerous problems, mostly tactical, came to light. IT roles were not clear. Training was not sufficient. Most of the team's skills were technical, but not on current technology and not on project management. IT literacy was low in the enterprise; users employed only 40 percent of the capabilities of applications. Locandro found a grim situation, but one ripe for transformation by a new CIO leader.

The second ninety days: Assess and validate

From February through April 2003, Locandro had the entire staff's IT capabilities assessed. Being short on time, he engaged an external company to assess the staff's capabilities and careers. He presented the exercise as personal development and career assessment. He told the personnel assessment consultants, "My people may or may not be performing adequately. They could be unhappy or in the wrong job. I need to know their behavioral and technical capabilities, ASAP, so that I can see where they fit into the structure going forward." By March, the consultants had profiled behavior and given feedback to the staff on their career possibilities and productivity.

Locandro also needed to build his vision and then effectively communicate it during these ninety days so that he could move forward quickly. He spent a great deal of time working with business colleagues to develop the IT strategy and vision. By the end of the second ninety days, he had a baseline on all his people, a draft of the IT strategy, and a proposed organization chart.

The third ninety days: Get the strategy approved and move forward

From May through July 2003, Locandro worked further on the new IS organization and IT strategy. He presented these in May, first to executive management in Hong Kong, and then to the staff.

During this period, he achieved a big win: a large boost in capital and an increase in staff size. The executives had expected him to tell them the cuts he would make—instead, like a true CIO leader, he told them the benefits he could provide. He walked out of the meeting with more money and more staff, rather than less. Organizationally, everything was then in place. The staff members were clear on their roles and responsibilities, so they could move forward.

The fourth ninety days: Install a performance management culture

From August through October 2003, Locandro focused on educating his department about how to have a performance management culture. He asked for monthly budgets and reports. He changed the staff to support specific functional lines, which consolidated all the business lines.

He demonstrated for his staff how to manage relationships, creating, as he said, "a wake" for his people to follow by delegating work to them and empowering them. For the first few months, his staff members often asked, "What do I do next?" Gradually, they understood that the next move was their choice. He got them the money, approvals, and resources. But for every project, he also recruited externally (such as from Microsoft and IBM) to increase his staff's knowledge base.

Moving forward: Getting it all together

By October 2003, every measure of Yallourn's IS group had improved significantly. Systems were more robust, a scalable and flexible architecture had been implemented, business executives understood IS service costs and trends, new IS competencies and a performance management system were in place, and reporting was being automated. Locandro has built a new IS organization with the right competencies and effectively communicates his progress in terms his business colleagues understand—a new CIO leader bringing it all together.

Citigroup's Transformed IS Leads Business Units

Tom Sanzone at Citigroup's Global Corporate and Investment Banking Group is another new CIO leader. He is bringing together many of the items we've discussed to have executive-level impact on his enterprise. Sanzone took over as CIO for a group that comprised several companies that Citigroup had acquired (among these companies were Salomon Brothers and Smith Barney). When he took over, Sanzone discovered that the financial discipline required by a new IS organization needed dramatic improvement: "In my first budget discussion, I didn't have good numbers. There were no trends, no comparisons. We didn't really know how much was being spent on what by who."[3] Sanzone knew that this was not a tenable situation. Sandy Weill, CEO of Citigroup, had a consistent message about what he wanted the business to deliver—15 percent annual revenue growth. If Sanzone was to succeed, the CIO knew that he would have to contribute to that goal and communicate his group's performance. "The only way you achieve a goal like that is by continually improving productivity. We had no way to make sure we were doing that."

Measuring and communicating performance

Sanzone describes the challenges he faced as new CIO: "The budget problems I found when I arrived were only a symptom of the larger problem—IS couldn't track its performance and contribution. So I needed to build, quickly, both performance tracking and a performance management culture." While Sanzone took a number of tactical steps to shore up his immediate situation, his primary effort was building a tool that his entire worldwide IS group could use to track performance. "We started out with seven dimensions of performance, but we soon realized that was too many. We narrowed down to three, which helped us measure the major categories that matter in our environment, including productivity, quality, and control." As the performance management system was built out, Sanzone began displaying every member of his group's performance to the entire team. "It was a shock to almost everyone, but behavior change was immediate. My people started to focus on the right things the next day," he says.

The system enabled Sanzone to see where the opportunities were for improvement. Over the course of two years, Sanzone's group cut costs by US$200 million while delivering more and better business results. "One of the key things we track is delivery to business deadlines," explains Sanzone. "Once we started showing everyone's track record on this, our performance against deadlines improved dramatically—from 60 percent on time to 80 percent on time—and the business noticed." His system also enabled him to more effectively bring in the right competencies and move out the wrong ones.

Leading business units

Sanzone's leadership was not limited to the supply side, however. He has used his knowledge of enterprise goals and relationships with business executives to provide demand-side leadership as well. Sanzone has a vision: "The system we've developed for tracking performance isn't an IS-specific system. Every business leader needs to know how their organization is performing. The system can have the same impact for other enterprise leaders as it has had for me." As IS performance improved, Sanzone began working with business colleagues to see how the performance management system he had developed for his own group could be used to similar effect in other lines of business. Today, the system is being rolled out to one major part of the company, with other executives poised to follow, based on results.

In short, Sanzone has built a new IS group that has new competencies and that can deliver and communicate results to the business it supports. What's more, he is helping lead the improvement of other business lines' performance. That's a new CIO leader bringing it all together.

New CIO leaders exist today, delivering on the promise of information and IT to yield real, measurable, and bankable business results. More such leaders are needed—every enterprise, including yours, needs a new CIO leader. You can become that leader. We urge you to start down that path today. Good luck.

A Short Assessment of Personality Type Preferences

Within this appendix, we've included a short assessment of personality type. It can quickly give you some insight into your own personality and that of your colleagues and your team, enabling you to tailor your leadership approach to your audience for maximum effectiveness.[1]

Using Personality Type Preferences in Leading and Managing High-Performance Teams

Knowledge of personality type and preferences can be used strategically by new CIO leaders. There are a number of type indicators, but the best and most proven is the Myers-Briggs Type Indicator (MBTI). Such positive, easily understood instruments measure psychological type preferences along different dimensions. The feedback on each dimension helps you develop critical teamwork areas such as accurate communication, balanced problem solving, and change management.

We recommend the use of the full MBTI, but as an exercise, take the following introductory self-test of psychological type. The results will provide a point of departure for understanding personality preferences from the vantage point of one's particular preferences. To understand what this self-test measures, take a moment to write two sentences on a blank sheet of paper, one with each hand. Note that the sentence by your preferred hand is fast, practiced, recognizable as

authentic, and therefore representative of you. The sentence by your nonpre-
ferred hand is slower, childlike, and usually not representative of your best work.
You grew up right- or left-handed by endowment, and you have a physical preference for one side and often do your best work there. However, you can function on the opposite side as well, even if it is slower and less practiced, and you
may be sensitive to critique of your performance on that side. Psychological type
preferences closely parallel preferences in handedness. Note that the sample test
is an introductory self-test of type, whereas the full Myers-Briggs Type Indicator
(www.mbti.com) is more accurate and has a wealth of validation studies and an
archive of over seven thousand titles applying MBTI type profiles to various
populations and work processes (www.CAPT.org).

Instructions: Answer the items by marking the appropriate circle on the score sheet below.
Then add the marked circles in each column and write the sum in the box below the column. Circle the letter below the higher sum for each pair. The circled letters indicate your
psychological type preferences.

	a	b		a	b		a	b		a	b
1.	O	O	2.	O	O	3.	O	O	4.	O	O
5.	O	O	6.	O	O	7.	O	O	8.	O	O
9.	O	O	10.	O	O	11.	O	O	12.	O	O
13.	O	O	14.	O	O	15.	O	O	16.	O	O
17.	O	O	18.	O	O	19.	O	O	20.	O	O
	□	□		□	□		□	□		□	□
	E	I		S	N		T	F		J	P

Circle the letter below the larger number of each pair. You now have a "type" profile. It
will be one of the following:

ISTJ	ISFJ	INFJ	INTJ
ISTP	ISFP	INFP	INTP
ESTP	ESFP	ENFP	ENTP
ESTJ	ESFJ	ENFJ	ENTJ

1. To solve a work problem, do you first like to:
   (a) talk about it with someone
   (b) think it through by yourself

2. Which is more interesting to you?
   (a) day-to-day production
   (b) theory and design

3. In an important discussion, do you first:
   (a) ask clarifying questions
   (b) make a personal connection

4. Do you like your work day to be:
   (a) scheduled and decided
   (b) open-ended and flexible

5. Do you prefer organization change to be:
   (a) active and fast-paced
   (b) careful and deliberate

6. In solving problems, do you first look for:
   (a) accurate facts
   (b) meaningful patterns

7. It is more important for you to be known as:
   (a) fair and accurate
   (b) concerned and compassionate

8. When beginning a project, do you:
   (a) get organized to get something done
   (b) explore your options

9. To communicate effectively, do you like to use:
   (a) speaking more than writing
   (b) writing more than speaking

10. For quality improvement, do you prefer to:
    (a) see what works and improve it step-by-step
    (b) use innovative ideas to create breakthroughs

11. Beginning a work relationship, do you focus more on:
    (a) competence
    (b) teamwork

12. Do you base your daily work more on:
    (a) goals
    (b) opportunities

13. Which is more stressful to you?
    (a) prolonged isolation
    (b) having your concentration interrupted

14. Which stresses you more?
    (a) impractical brainstorming
    (b) repetitive detail work

15. Which is harder to tolerate?
    (a) sloppy thinking
    (b) opposition and resentment

16. Which is more stressful for you?
    (a) missing a deadline
    (b) losing an option

17. With someone new, are you more likely to:
    (a) initiate contact
    (b) wait for them to initiate

18. Are you more interested in:
    (a) implementing what works
    (b) exploring something new

19. At work do you typically focus:
    (a) more on the task than the people
    (b) more on the people than the task

20. Do you do better work:
    (a) following a timetable
    (b) reacting to what happens

How can personality types help new CIO leaders?

If you know your own personality type preferences and those of your colleagues, you can identify where you differ on specific dimensions and then adjust your approach as necessary in specific areas for best results. Additionally, in your IS organization, you can create teams with members of different types of preferences to produce synergies in specific areas.

The first dichotomous dimension, Extroversion/Introversion (denoted by the first letter of your type, E or I), measures the preference for attending to the inside or the outside of oneself to find natural energy. Extroverts find natural energy by attending to the outside of themselves and by making contact; introverts center and focus on the inside of themselves and do their best work by internal concentration. Thus, extroverts prefer to have a dialogue or to call meetings to develop ideas and to do team problem solving; introverts, however, may withdraw from contact to concentrate internally, then return to present a finished product to the team. Extroverts often prefer speaking more than writing to communicate with team members, while introverts prefer writing more than speaking. Extroverted team members like to pace change quickly and announce it interactively; introverts often take time to plan change thoroughly, then may provide change updates in writing instead of holding team meetings. Extroverts need to give introverts advance warning about critical discussions and to do follow-up after a meeting to get introverts' deeper ideas; introverts need to sustain extroverts' energy by interacting with them, and listen as extroverts generate ideas face-to-face.

Preference on the second dimension, Sensing/Intuition (the second letter, S or N), indicates the kind of information a person prefers. In teamwork, a sensing person wants the facts of experience, such as data that can be nailed down empirically, and the next-step deliverable. An intuitive person (designated "N" because "I" is used for introversion) prefers an explanatory framework and an overview that recognizes connections, context, and implicit models. CIOs who link team members differing on sensing and intuition can facilitate faster and more balanced problem solving. Not only does one preference point out information that the other does not attend to, but each type helps the other get "unstuck" in problem solving. Sensing types sometimes get bogged down trying to apply tried-and-true solutions to out-of-the-box problems; these people get unstuck quickly by intuitives, who generate innovative solutions rapidly and easily. By contrast, intuitives can get stuck trying to put a complex or an original design on the ground when they see many potential start points; this impasse can be quickly solved by sensing types, who know instinctively where the first step occurs.

The third dimension, Thinking/Feeling (T or F), describes individual preference in organizing information and making decisions. Persons with a thinking preference take a logical, impersonal, fact-based approach in coming to objective conclusions, while persons with a feeling preference favor a subjective, values-oriented approach that attends to interpersonal connection as much as to accurate content. CIOs must be accurate and well researched to lead thinking team members, yet they must also keep a "values connection" with feeling team members, remembering that feeling team members cannot learn from or follow a leader unless they first make a positive personal connection. Cultural emphasis on thinking and feeling preferences has much to do with different business courtesies around the world and can make or break working agreements on international teams.

Finally, the Judging/Perceiving (J or P) dimension, the fourth letter of type, describes personal preferences in lifestyle and work style. Persons with a judging preference approach the day with organization and planning, using goals and timelines to regulate behavior throughout the day. Perceiving persons approach the day with adaptability and timing, seeking to maximize present opportunities. Leaders with judging preference use advice and example to inspire teams, drawing on best practices; leaders with perceiving preference allow for real-time challenges to bring out the best in individual team members. Most important, though, is a CIO's linking of judging with perceiving team members to manage change. By himself or herself, each team member has one-half of what is needed for effective change management as a result of a judging or perceiving preference. Judging team members approach change with planning. They preserve the best of the past and supply feedback about progress to goal. Perceiving team members prefer split-second timing, resourceful adaptation, and political relevance to effect change. In quick-paced corporate environments and markets, team members should not confront change individually; instead, they should leverage a specific synergy by joining with team members opposite them in judging or perceiving preference.

Although a certified trainer is required to administer the MBTI and provide feedback, many publications can provide an introduction to psychological type for CIOs and their high-performance teams. These resources include S. Hirsh and J. Kummerow, *Introduction to Type in Organizations* (www.mbti.com), and J. Kummerow, N. Barger, and L. Kirby, *Work Types* (Warner Books).

Identifying Strategies and Synergies to Create Maxims

Creating good business maxims is a prerequisite to creating appropriate and useful IT maxims. For this reason, here we provide the initial questions that you and your business colleagues need to think through and agree on so you can create good business maxims. The questions and the answers they produce fall into two categories, strategic context and corporate synergies.

Strategic Context

To develop business maxims, you should begin by considering what we call the strategic context of the enterprise. Strategic context has three components:

1. Enterprisewide strategic intent
2. The extent and nature of business unit synergies sought in the future
3. Business unit strategic intents and current strategies

Thus, managers begin defining their strategic context by answering such questions as these:

- What is the basis of our enterprise positioning?
- What are the strategies, competitive choices, and value propositions of each of the business units, and how are they similar?

- To what extent do the businesses—or our many products and services— have overlapping customer and supplier bases?

- Are there similarities in products or in the expertise required in different businesses?

- Where are the potential synergies between our businesses?

- How important is it to capture those synergies?

Corporate Synergies

You will also need to understand the synergies between units and the enterprise's experiences with, and beliefs in, the value of leveraging these synergies. Organizations vary in the extent to which they have synergies between their different businesses, customers, products, competitive bases, and suppliers. The extent and nature of potential business unit synergies affect the type of IT that can sensibly be shared across the firm.

A high level of customer overlap between units provides opportunities to cross-sell products and implies a need for common customer profiles and databases. When there is overlap in suppliers, you can derive synergies from a coordinated approach to data interchange and extended enterprise systems and to reduced costs from suppliers. Product similarities indicate that much expertise can be shared among R&D, manufacturing and production, maintenance, and after-sales service. Similar ways of competing across business units often result in similar management approaches and consequent needs for shared information and IS. Many enterprises want to exploit shared services and achieve economies of scale, scope, or expertise in such areas as financial management, human resources management, or information systems.

In some organizations, however, different business units or products have different competitive bases, or the corporate policy is to give units considerable autonomy. Either of these conditions will reduce the efficacy of shared services, leading to lower investments in IT at the enterprisewide level and higher investments at the business unit level.

A process manufacturing firm that we studied is organized around five fairly autonomous business groups.[1] Two of these groups illustrate how different units within the same enterprise can be. These differences have implications for enterprisewide infrastructure investments and therefore need to be recognized in maxims. One group sells mostly commodity products in mature markets and competes on operational excellence. In the face of fierce international competition, this group focuses on reducing costs and improving quality. The second group is composed of smaller, newer companies growing rapidly with strong international sales and focusing on product leadership.

Enterprises often fail to recognize the importance of their specific attitudes about business unit synergies. Hence, synergies are often not sufficiently recognized, articulated, discussed, or exploited within the organization.

Three sets of questions elicit possible synergies and surface your enterprise's attitude toward harvesting their potential benefits.

Extent of Potential Business Unit Synergies

- Do the businesses have an overlapping customer base?
- Is there customer information that you want to share across the enterprise?
- Do the businesses have an overlapping supplier base?
- Is there supplier information that you want to share across the enterprise?
- Do the businesses offer similar or overlapping products?
- Does each part of your enterprise share similar business processes, such as servicing a customer, creating a new product or service, and providing a treasury service?
- Are there areas of expertise, competencies, or capabilities (e.g., product development, financial management, and systems development) that are or could be utilized across your enterprise?

Similarity of Competitive Base: Basic Competitive Strategies

- Which of the value disciplines are represented among the businesses in this organization: operational excellence, customer intimacy, product leadership, or some combination of these?
- To what extent do the business units share the same value discipline?

Exploiting Synergies and Encouraging Autonomy

This third group of questions clarifies the balance between encouraging local autonomy and the extent to which your executive team wants to exploit potential synergies.

- How important is it to maximize independence in local operations in the enterprise?
- How important is it to provide local autonomy with a minimum of mandates?
- How important is it to utilize the potential synergies that reside in each of the businesses?

By answering these questions with your business colleagues, you'll have the basics you need to begin creating business maxims.

IT Services

Once you've developed your business and IT maxims, it's helpful to look at the variety of IT services that may be provided.[1] Doing so ensures that the services provided are appropriate, given the maxims, and that there are no gaps that the maxims dictate closing. Use this questionnaire to compare the necessity and availability of shared infrastructure services, which we have grouped into ten major categories.

1. **Channel Management:** Provide electronic channel to customers or partners to support one or more applications	Available	Necessary
EFT POS/POS (electronic funds transfer point of sale)		
Kiosks		
Web sites		
Call centers		
IVR (interactive voice response)		
Mobile phones		
Mobile computing (e.g., via dial-up)		

2. *Security and Risk Management*	Available	Necessary
Security policies for use of IS (e.g., data protection, access privileges, hacker protection)		
Enforced security policies for IS		
Disaster planning for business applications		
Firewall on secure gateway services		

3. *Communication Management*	Available	Necessary
Communications network services (e.g., full service Transmission Control Protocol/Internet Protocol [TCP/IP] networks linking all points within a business)		
Broadband communication services (e.g., higher-bandwidth activities such as video		
Intranet capabilities (e.g., an intranet to support a variety of applications, including publishing, company policies, directories, message boards)		
Extranet capabilities (e.g., providing information and applications via TCP/IP to a select group of customers and suppliers)		
Workstation networks (e.g., LANs and point-of-sale networks)		
EDI linkages to customers and suppliers		
Electronic support to groups (e.g., Lotus Notes, other groupware)		

4. *Data Management*	Available	Necessary
Key data managed independently of applications (e.g., centralized product data)		
Centralized data warehouse (summaries of key information from decentralized databases)		
Data management advice and consultancy		
Electronic provision of management information (e.g., executive information systems [EIS], management dashboards)		
Storage farms or storage area networks (e.g., major storage separate from LANs and workstations)		
Payment transaction processing (e.g., electronic funds transfer)		
Knowledge management (e.g., contact database, knowledge management architecture, knowledge databases, communities of practice)		

5. *Applications Infrastructure Management*	Available	Necessary
Internet policies (e.g., employee access, URL logging)		
Enforced Internet policies		
E-mail policies (e.g., inappropriate and personal mail, harassment policies, filtering policies)		
Enforced e-mail policies		
Centralized management of e-commerce applications (e.g., centralized e-commerce development, common standards and applications, single point of access, multimedia applications)		
Centralized management of infrastructure capacity (e.g., server traffic)		
Integrated mobile computing applications (e.g., laptop dial-up and Internet service provider access for internal users)		
Enterprise resource planning (ERP) services (Is the service currently available? Which ERP?)		
Middleware linking systems on different platforms (e.g., integrating Web "shop fronts" to ERP systems)		
Wireless applications (e.g., Web applications for wireless devices)		
Application services provision (e.g., applications used by business units and provided centrally)		
Work-flow applications (e.g., Lotus Notes)		

6. *IT Management*	Available	Necessary
IS project management		
Negotiation with suppliers and outsourcers (e.g., centralized and negotiated pricing for software)		
Service-level agreements (e.g., agreements between corporate IT and business units)		
IS planning (e.g., forward plans and strategy—what is the cycle time?)		

7. *IT Architecture and Standards*		**Available**	**Necessary**
Specified architectures (high-level guidelines and blueprint for the way IT will be used and integrated)	Data		
	Technology		
	Communications		
	Applications		
	Work		
Enforced architectures (enforced compliance with high-level architectures)	Data		
	Technology		
	Communications		
	Applications		
	Work		
Standards for IT architectures (standard operating environment to implement architectures)	Data		
	Technology		
	Communications		
	Applications		
	Work		
Enforced standards for at least one component of the IT architecture (e.g., data, technology, communications, applications, work)	Data		
	Technology		
	Communications		
	Applications		
	Work		

8. *IT Facilities Management*	**Available**	**Necessary**
Large-scale data processing facilities (e.g., mainframe)		
Server farms (e.g., mail server, Web servers, printer servers)		
Installation and maintenance of workstations and LANs		
Common systems development environment		
Pilot e-commerce initiatives (e.g., pilot Web "shop fronts" managed in conjunction with business units)		

9. *IT R&D*	Available	Necessary
New technologies identified and tested for business purposes		
Proposals for new IS initiatives evaluated		

10. *IT Education*	Available	Necessary
Training and use of IT		
Management education for generating value from IT use		

The New CIO Leader
Self-Assessment

Throughout the book, we have spotlighted the critical new points of focus for CIOs who want to become new CIO leaders. To help you prioritize these points of focus for your unique situation, we have created this self-assessment. Organized by chapter, it will help you see which of the ten areas of focus are areas of strength for you and which need attention.

For each statement below, score your response (Strongly Disagree to Strongly Agree) according to the guide at the top of each set of statements. Then total your score for the section and compare it to the scoring guide at the end of each section.

If you would like to take the next step and benchmark yourself against other CIOs, visit <www.gartnerpress.com/newcioleader>. There you can take an online version of the self-assessment and see where you rank compared to other CIOs.

Chapter 1: Laying the Foundation: Leadership

Points	Strongly Disagree 0	Disagree 3	Agree 6	Strongly Agree 10	Score
1.1 I have a compelling vision for how we can use IT to enable the enterprise and move to the next level of performance.				✓	10
1.2 I can express my vision in a concise "pitch" that grabs the attention of others and excites them.			✓		6
1.3 I spend more and more of my time building and maintaining relationships with my executive colleagues.				✓	10
1.4 I have developed my emotional intelligence, particularly my social awareness and empathy, so that I can be a good leader.			✓		6
1.5 I know how to "lead from the back" when I don't have formal power and use my skills of persuasion to influence others.			✓		6
1.6 I have fine-tuned my leadership skills so that I am able to modify my style to fit both the situation and the constituency I want to influence.				✓	10

Chapter 1 Total Score: 48

26 or less: Needs attention
27 to 47: Satisfactory performance
48 to 60: Area of strength

Chapter 2: Understand the Fundamentals of Your Environment

Points	Strongly Disagree	Disagree	Agree	Strongly Agree	Score
	0	3	6	10	
2.1 I can articulate the basis on which our enterprise competes in our industry (or provides services if in the public sector).				✓	10
2.2 I understand our business fundamentals and know how to interpret our performance and financial statements (e.g., balance sheets, income statements), as well as other financial, regulatory, or legislative reporting requirements.				✓	10
2.3 I understand the unique operating characteristics of our business units and the need to make trade-offs between synergy and autonomy as part of our enterprise strategy.				✓	10
2.4 I meet with our CEO or senior-most officer regularly and know his or her top priorities and strategic initiatives.		✓			3
2.5 I know and understand the top priorities of the senior executives for each major business or area of the enterprise, and these executives know me.			✓		6
2.6 I know and understand the performance requirements of the senior executives for each major business or area of the enterprise, and they know mine.		✓			3
2.7 I have a strong working knowledge of our industry and am on top of emerging trends and issues.				✓	10
2.8 I have identified the key internal and external stakeholders, and am proactively managing my relationships with them.			✓		6

Chapter 2 Total Score: 58

35 or less: Needs attention
36 to 63: Satisfactory performance
64 to 80: Area of strength

Chapter 3: Create Your Vision	Strongly Disagree	Disagree	Agree	Strongly Agree	Score
Points	0	3	6	10	
3.1 I have a deep understanding of how my enterprise is IT-enabled today.				✓	10
3.2 My business colleagues look to me to understand how our enterprise can be IT-enabled.				✓	10
3.3 My vision is articulated and documented, and my business colleagues can and do understand it.			✓		6
3.4 As CIO, I am proactive in ensuring we have a process for identifying IT-enabled business opportunities.		✓			3
3.5 Members of my IS leadership team are actively involved in identifying IT-enabled business opportunities.			✓		6
3.6 I am constantly examining how we can use our IT resources to extract greater customer value and economic return.				✓	10
3.7 I have integrated network-era thinking (e.g., cheap computing power, bandwidth, ubiquitous communications) into my vision of how my enterprise can meet its business goals.				✓	10
3.8 I have asked all senior executives what real-time information would enable them to better meet their goals and have a plan to deliver that information.		✓			3
3.9 I have successfully secured resources for innovation and investment by linking business demand and persistent business needs to technology opportunities.				✓	10

Chapter 3 Total Score: ___68___

38 or less: Needs attention
39 to 67: Satisfactory performance
68 to 90: Area of strength

Chapter 4: Shape and Inform Expectations for an IT-Enabled Enterprise	Strongly Disagree	Disagree	Agree	Strongly Agree	Score
Points	0	3	6	10	
4.1 I have invested time with my business colleagues so that both they and I understand the extent to which leveraging synergies across business units matters to our enterprise.			✓		6
4.2 I have invested time with my business colleagues in workshops or other processes so that all parties understand the business maxims of our enterprise.				✓	10
4.3 I have invested time with my business colleagues so that they understand the IT implications of any business decision.			✓		6
4.4 Working together, my business colleagues, my team, and I have developed IT maxims that express how we need to design and deploy IT across the enterprise to connect, share, and structure information.				✓	10
4.5 I have communicated our IT maxims appropriately within the enterprise; my staff and my business colleagues know and understand these IT maxims well enough to use them as guidelines for making decisions and taking action.			✓		6
4.6 I have been able to use IT maxims to identify potential infrastructure and shared services strategies that will create synergies (if appropriate) and savings for the enterprise.				✓	10

Chapter 4 Total Score: 48

26 or less: Needs attention
27 to 47: Satisfactory performance
48 to 60: Area of strength

Chapter 5: Create Clear and Appropriate IT Governance

Points	Strongly Disagree 0	Disagree 3	Agree 6	Strongly Agree 10	Score
5.1 I have actively engaged business units, senior executives, and key stakeholders in the creation of our governance process.			✓		6
5.2 Our governance model clearly defines who has input into each IT decision and who owns the final decision rights.			✓		6
5.3 Our IT governance process actively involves both the CEO and the CIO in appropriate decision-making activities.		✓			3
5.4 Our governance model addresses all five IT domains (IT maxims, architecture, infrastructure, business applications, investments).				✓	10
5.5 I have actively communicated our IT governance arrangements so that they are understood by the business units and so that business executives are active participants.			✓		6
5.6 The clarity of our governance models has allowed us to make better investment decisions, with greater speed.			✓		6
5.7 Our governance process has clear and well-understood exception processes.		✓			3
5.8 Our IT governance process is functioning well enough that we will not have to make major revisions within twelve months.		✓			3

Chapter 5 Total Score: 43

35 or less: Needs attention
36 to 63: Satisfactory performance
64 to 80: Area of strength

Chapter 6: Weave Business and IT Strategies Together	Strongly Disagree	Disagree	Agree	Strongly Agree	Score
Points	0	3	6	10	
6.1 My business colleagues understand the challenges of integrating business and IT strategies and plans.				✓	10
6.2 Our IT planning process is flexible enough that it can rapidly reflect changes in our business environment along with incumbent shifts in our technology investments.			✓		6
6.3 Our IT strategy is based on a firm foundation of good IT governance and clarifies both infrastructure and business application objectives and investments.				✓	10
6.4 Our IT strategy ensures that we have properly prioritized our portfolio in light of business needs and our IT maxims.			✓		6
6.5 Our IT strategy makes visible the linkages between IT and customer and shareholder benefits.				✓	10
6.6 Our IT strategy has been built on a sustainable portfolio of services and capabilities that the governance process has identified and that links investment decisions to specific business needs.				✓	10
6.7 We have a process for regularly reviewing the portfolio with business colleagues and the executive committee so that they understand what my team is doing and how it relates to business needs.			✓		6
6.8 My team and I actively manage the portfolio, including prioritization and balancing risk and resources.				✓	10
6.9 The portfolio is expressed in terms that make the IT investment strategy understandable to the board (or political constituents) and is clearly linked to business priorities.				✓	10

(continued)

Chapter 6 *(continued)*		Strongly Disagree	Disagree	Agree	Strongly Agree	Score
	Points	*0*	*3*	*6*	*10*	
6.10 We use a variety of funding mechanisms beyond the annual corporate budget to fund our portfolio.					✓	10
6.11 We manage our IT-enabled opportunities (ITOs) in a fashion that allows us to rapidly assess opportunities, make investment decisions, and track outcomes.			✓			3

Chapter 6 Total Score: ___91___
51 or less: Needs attention
52 to 90: Satisfactory performance
91 to 110: Area of strength

Chapter 7: Build a New IS Organization	Strongly Disagree	Disagree	Agree	Strongly Agree	Score
Points	**0**	**3**	**6**	**10**	
7.1 My "C"-level peer executives (e.g., CFO, COO) believe I run an appropriately lean and business-focused IS organization.				✓	10
7.2 My IS team knows how to work well with external organizations that are part of our enterprise value chain.			✓		6
7.3 I have begun organizing my IS team toward a process-based model whereby people, operations, and technology are structured around end-to-end work flows rather than functions, platforms, or skill sets.			✓		6
7.4 I have adopted, or am moving toward, other forms of IS Lite, such as creating centers of excellence.		✓			3
7.5 I have hired and trained relationship managers who have good communication skills, have credibility with both IS and the business units, and can drive IS delivery to high customer satisfaction.		✓			3
7.6 I have created a dedicated resource inside my IS organization to assess opportunities to strategically source services and partner for external services where appropriate.		✓			3
7.7 Managing the full sourcing life cycle (e.g., the evaluation, selection, and management of external service providers) is viewed as an IS competence by my business peers.			✓		6
7.8 I am considering sourcing opportunities beyond basic utility deals, such as enhancement contracts, which reengineer an existing process, or frontier contracts, which add significant value to existing business activities.			✓		6

(continued)

Chapter 7 (continued)

	Strongly Disagree	Disagree	Agree	Strongly Agree	Score
Points	0	3	6	10	
7.9 My IS organization uses consistent corporate standard accounting mechanisms to account for all IT services costs.				✓	10
7.10 My business colleagues and I understand IT services costs, including trends, at the top line and for individual IT services.				✓	10

Chapter 7 Total Score: _____ 63

44 or less: Needs attention
45 to 79: Satisfactory performance
80 to 100: Area of strength

Chapter 8: Develop a High-Performing IS Team	Strongly Disagree	Disagree	Agree	Strongly Agree	Score
Points	0	3	6	10	
8.1 I have assessed my strengths as a leader, including my emotional intelligence: specifically, the capacity to recognize my own feelings and those of others.				✓	10
8.2 I have put in place training opportunities for my IS leadership team to develop their emotional intelligence.			✓		6
8.3 I have analyzed the task, individual, and group needs of my team members and regularly assess the degree to which I am fulfilling the team's individual and group needs.			✓		6
8.4 I understand my dominant leadership style and that of each member of my leadership team.			✓		6
8.5 I have become more adept at knowing when it is appropriate to employ different leadership styles inside my IS organization; I have implemented training on leadership styles for my IS leadership team.			✓		6
8.6 I know the critical competencies my IS team requires.				✓	10
8.7 I have employed a competency-based model to develop the specific roles required for my team.			✓		6
8.8 I have shared my competency models with the human resources organization and use it as the basis for hiring, recruiting new staff, and training existing staff.				✓	10
8.9 My IS team has a good mix of appropriate competencies to meet our current and future needs.				✓	10

Chapter 8 Total Score: 70

38 or less: Needs attention
39 to 67: Satisfactory performance
68 to 90: Area of strength

Chapter 9: Manage Enterprise and IT Risks	Strongly Disagree	Disagree	Agree	Strongly Agree	Score
Points	0	3	6	10	
9.1 I have examined our risks relative to our key business processes and have translated both tangible and intangible losses into economic terms that my business colleagues can understand.			✓		6
9.2 I have educated my colleagues regarding the variety of IT risks we face, particularly the newer risk factors.			✓		6
9.3 Our IT risk management strategy is fully integrated with enterprise risk management.				✓	10
9.4 I have developed clear and appropriate security governance arrangements that specify who is responsible for making key decisions and who carries accountability for risk-related issues.			✓		6
9.5 We have created a risk council, or something like it, that is composed of senior managers who report directly to the CEO or the CFO and who manage risks across the enterprise.				✓	10
9.6 I have a risk management plan and process in place that is regularly updated and tested.			✓		6
9.7 We have trained both IT and appropriate business personnel to be aware of security policies and their own security responsibilities.				✓	10

Chapter 9 Total Score: 54

32 or less: Needs attention
33 to 57: Satisfactory performance
58 to 70: Area of strength

Chapter 10: Communicate Your Performance	Strongly Disagree	Disagree	Agree	Strongly Agree	Score
Points	0	3	6	10	
10.1 My business colleagues believe that our IT-related investments help create business value.				✓	10
10.2 I can link all IT investments to one or more key drivers: top-line growth (revenue), bottom-line growth (earnings), return on invested capital, and reputation.				✓	10
10.3 My staff and I create a visible trail of evidence between IT investments and business impact for all stakeholders.			✓		6
10.4 I have built my personal credibility by helping my CEO and CFO (or public representative) show how IT investments support the corporate strategy and the story they want to tell to investors and other stakeholders.				✓	10
10.5 My CEO asks me to participate in shareholder and investor meetings (or public forums).	✓				0
10.6 I have clear links between IT performance metrics and business goals or maxims.				✓	10
10.7 For every IT-related project, we develop business value indicators as part of the business case.			✓		6
10.8 For every project, we also create quantitative metrics for tracking and ultimately assessing progress toward specific goals and benefits.			✓		6
10.9 I have a performance dashboard or scorecard that I share with my business colleagues.			✓		6
10.10 My dashboard includes measures of IS readiness for future initiatives.		✓			3

Chapter 10 Total Score: 67
44 or less: Needs attention
45 to 79: Satisfactory performance
80 to 100: Area of strength

Notes

Chapter 1

1. Some material for this chapter was drawn from the following reports published by Gartner exclusively for members of Gartner EXP (Gartner Executive Programs): Andrew Rowsell-Jones and Marianne Broadbent, "Keep Your Balance: The 2002 CIO Agenda," Gartner EXP Premier Report, March 2002; Mark McDonald and Marcus Blosch, "CIO Credibility: Proven Practices from the Public Sector," Gartner EXP Premier Report, November 2003; Andrew Rowsell-Jones, Marianne Broadbent, and Chuck Tucker, "Drive Enterprise Effectiveness: The 2003 CIO Agenda," Gartner EXP Premier Report, March 2003; Marcus Blosch et al., "Preparing for the Upswing: The 2004 CIO Agenda," Gartner EXP Premier Report, March 2004. Unless otherwise noted, direct quotes in this chapter are from interviews conducted for these reports. For more information, please contact Gartner Executive Programs, <www.gartner.com>.

2. As a reminder, throughout the book, we will use *IT* to refer to the technology itself and *IS* to refer to the department or other organizational unit that manages information technology.

3. John Kotter, "Leading Change: Why Transformation Efforts Fail," *Harvard Business Review,* March 1995.

4. Jim Collins, *Good to Great: Why Some Companies Make the Leap . . . and Others Don't* (New York: HarperCollins, 2001).

5. Ronald Heifetz, *Leadership Without Easy Answers* (Cambridge, MA: Belknap, 1998).

6. Paul Coby, interview with authors at Gartner Symposium, Orlando, Florida, October 2003.

7. Daniel Goleman, *Emotional Intelligence* (New York: Bantam, 1995); Daniel Goleman, Annie McKee, and Richard E. Boyatzis, *Primal Leadership* (Boston: Harvard Business School Press, 2002).

8. Heifetz, *Leadership Without Easy Answers.*

9. Continuum adapted from R. Tannenbaum and W. H. Schmidt, "How to Choose a Leadership Pattern," *Harvard Business Review*, 1958 (issue not given); leadership styles adapted from Daniel Goleman, "Leadership That Gets Results," *Harvard Business Review*, March–April 2000, 78–90.

10. The Hay/McBer survey is quoted in Goleman, "Leadership That Gets Results."

Chapter 2

1. Some material for this chapter was drawn from the following reports published by Gartner EXP exclusively for its members: Richard Hunter, Marcus Blosch, and John Henderson, "Making External Relationships Work," Gartner EXP Club Report, February 2003; Andrew Rowsell-Jones, Richard Hunter, and Roger Woolfe, "Managing Your Stakeholders," Gartner EXP Club Report, October 2002; Richard Hunter and David Aron, "The CEO's View of the CIO," Gartner EXP Signature Report, July 2004. Unless otherwise noted, direct quotes in this chapter are from interviews conducted for these reports. For more information, please contact Gartner Executive Programs, <www.gartner.com>.

2. Robert Kaplan and Dave Norton, *The Balanced Scorecard: Translating Strategy into Action* (Boston: Harvard Business School Press, 1996).

3. Gary Hamel and C. K. Prahalad, "Strategic Intent," *Harvard Business Review* 67, no. 3 (1989): 63–76.

4. Michael Treacy and Frederik Wiersma, *The Discipline of Market Leaders: Choose Your Customers, Narrow Your Focus, Dominate Your Market* (Cambridge, MA: Perseus, 1995).

5. See R. K. Mitchell, B. R. Agle, and D. J. Wood, "Toward a Theory of Stakeholder Identification and Salience: Defining the Principle of Who and What Really Counts," *Academy of Management Review* 22, no. 4 (1997): 853–886.

6. Burson-Marsteller, "A Missing Competency: Boardroom IT-Deficit," 2004. Report available by request from Burson-Marsteller, <www.bm.com>.

7. Michael Fleisher, telephone conversation with authors, 4 April 2004.

8. Vince Caracio, telephone conversation with authors, 4 April 2004.

Chapter 3

1. Some material for this chapter was drawn from the following reports published by Gartner EXP exclusively for its members: Roger Woolfe, Andrew Rowsell-Jones, and N. Venkatraman, "Capturing Network Era Opportunities," Gartner EXP Club Report, June 2003; Chuck Tucker and Roger Woolfe, "Building Brilliant Business Cases," Gartner EXP Premier Report, January 2004; Mark McDonald, Richard Hunter, and Jackie Fenn, "Linking Needs, Technology and Innovation," Gartner EXP Club Report, February 2004. Unless otherwise noted, direct quotes in this chapter are from interviews conducted for these reports. For more information, please contact Gartner Executive Programs, <www.gartner.com>.

2. Material for this section is drawn from Kenneth McGee, *Heads Up: How to Anticipate Business Surprises and Seize Opportunities First* (Boston: Harvard Business School Press, 2004).

3. McGee, *Heads Up*, 26.

Chapter 4

1. Some material for this chapter was drawn from the following reports published by Gartner EXP exclusively for its members: Marianne Broadbent, Peter Weill, and Mani Subramani, "Reality Bites: Matching IT Infrastructure with Business Initiatives," Gartner EXP Club Report, November 2001; Marcus Blosch and Roger Woolfe, "Leading High Performance IS Teams," Gartner EXP Premier Report, November 2002; Marianne Broadbent and Peter Weill, "Effective IT Governance, by Design," Gartner EXP Premier Report, January 2003; Marianne Broadbent and Peter Weill, "Tailor IT Governance to Your Enterprise," Gartner EXP Club Report, October 2003. Unless otherwise noted, direct quotes in this chapter are from interviews conducted for these reports. For more information, please contact Gartner Executive Programs, <www.gartner.com>.

2. The management by maxims process was first researched and described in Marianne Broadbent and Peter Weill, "Management by Maxims: How Business and IT Managers Can Create IT Infrastructures," *Sloan Management Review* 38, no. 3 (spring 1997): 77–92; and Peter Weill and Marianne Broadbent, *Leveraging the New Infrastructure: How Market Leaders Capitalize on Information Technology* (Boston: Harvard Business School Press, 1998). This chapter summarizes, updates, and extends the original work.

3. Broadbent and Weill, "Management by Maxims."

4. Ibid.

5. Weill and Broadbent, *Leveraging the New Infrastructure*.

6. Quantitative findings are from Weill and Broadbent, *Leveraging the New Infrastructure*.

7. Peter Weill, Mani Subramani, and Marianne Broadbent, "Building IT Infrastructure for Strategic Ability," *Sloan Management Review* 44, no. 1 (fall 2002): 57–66.

8. The list of services is adapted from Peter Weill and Michael Vitale, "Information Technology Infrastructure for E-Business," working paper 313, Center for Information Systems Research, MIT Sloan School of Management, Cambridge, February 2001. The initial set of services was developed by Weill and Broadbent, *Leveraging the New Infrastructure*.

9. Banknorth has US$26 billion in assets and provides retail banking, mortgage, insurance, investment planning, and investment management services through 360 branches, 400 ATMs, and 7,000 employees. In the 1990s, it had grown tenfold, with a corporate culture that emphasized teamwork, agility, and local decision making.

Chapter 5

1. Some material for this chapter was drawn from the following reports published by Gartner EXP exclusively for its members: Marianne Broadbent and Peter Weill, "Tailor IT Governance to Your Enterprise," Gartner EXP Club Report, October 2003; Marianne Broadbent and Peter Weill, "Effective IT Governance, by Design," Gartner EXP Premier Report, January 2003. Unless otherwise noted, direct quotes in this chapter are from interviews conducted for these reports. For more information, please contact Gartner Executive Programs, <www.gartner.com>.

Also see Peter Weill and Jeanne Ross, *IT Governance: How Top Performers Manage IT Decision Rights for Superior Results* (Boston: Harvard Business School Press, 2004); Peter Weill and Richard Woodham, "Don't Just Lead, Govern: Implementing Effective IT Governance," working paper 326, Center for Information Systems Research, MIT Sloan School of Management, Cambridge, April 2002.

2. Marianne Broadbent and Peter Weill, "Leading Governance, Business and IT Processes: The Organizational Fabric of Business and IT Partnership," Gartner ITEP Findings, December 1998; Weill and Woodham, "Don't Just Lead, Govern."

3. Effectiveness was determined by combining the responses to two survey questions. One had respondents rank four outcomes of IT governance, and the other had respondents rank the influence of IT on these outcomes. The outcomes were cost effective use of IT, use of IT for growth, use of IT for asset utilization, and use of IT for business flexibility.

4. Peter Weill, presentation to Gartner EXP CIO Global Summit, San Diego, May 2003.

Chapter 6

1. Some material for this chapter was drawn from the following reports published by Gartner EXP exclusively for its members: Roger Woolfe and Marcus Blosch, "Turning on Opportunities," Gartner EXP Club Report, March 2001; Marcus Blosch et al., "Expanding Your Funding Options," Gartner EXP Club Report, August 2003; Marianne Broadbent and Peter Weill, "Effective IT Governance, by Design," Gartner EXP Premier Report, January 2003; Mark McDonald, Richard Hunter, and Jackie Fenn, "Linking Needs, Technology and Innovation," Gartner EXP Club Report, February 2004; Chuck Tucker and Andrew Rowsell-Jones, "Getting Priorities Straight," Gartner EXP Premier Report, September 2002; Chuck Tucker and Roger Woolfe, "Building Brilliant Business Cases," Gartner EXP Premier Report, January 2004. Unless otherwise noted, direct quotes in this chapter are from interviews conducted for these reports. For more information, please contact Gartner Executive Programs, <www.gartner.com>.

2. The distinction between evaluating initiatives and a governance mechanism is that the initiative-evaluating process defines how a particular mechanism, in this case the investment council, actually makes decisions.

3. For more on this topic, see Tony Murphy, *Achieving Business Value from Technology: A Practical Guide for Today's Executive* (New York: Wiley, 2002).

Chapter 7

1. Some material for this chapter was drawn from the following reports published by Gartner EXP exclusively for its members: Roger Woolfe, Barbara McNurlin, and Chuck Tucker, "Sourcing: From Remedy to Strategy," December 2001; Marcus Blosch and Roger Woolfe, "Leading High Performance IS Teams," Gartner EXP Premier Report, November 2002; Marcus Blosch, Roger Woolfe, and Jeremy Grigg, "Chargeback: How Far Should You Go?" Gartner EXP Premier Report, May 2003; Marcus Blosch et al., "Expanding Your Funding Options," Gartner EXP Club Report, August 2003; Chuck Tucker and Roger Woolfe, "The Reality of IS Lite," Gartner EXP Premier Report, September 2003; Andrew Rowsell-Jones and Chuck Tucker, "Geosourcing IS: Is It Right for You?" Gartner EXP Premier Report, November 2003. Unless otherwise noted, direct quotes in this chapter are from interviews conducted for these reports. For more information, please contact Gartner Executive Programs, <www.gartner.com>.

2. This material was based on many years of work by Gartner's strategic sourcing team, led by Linda Cohen.

3. For example, Gartner has conducted research that generates Magic Quadrants for competitors offering similar services. Enterprises can use these criteria as a baseline when evaluating ESPs for a specific project. Magic Quadrants categorize ESPs as leaders, visionaries, challengers, and niche players by positioning them on two axes. One axis reflects an ESP's vision of where a specific market is headed, how the provider plans to execute against that vision, and how well the ESP's client base feels that the vision has brought value to the client–ESP relationships. The second axis considers an ESP's ability to execute. The position of a specific ESP on this axis is largely determined by direct client feedback that is gathered during the Magic Quadrant analysis. You can also receive a free booklet from Gartner on strategic sourcing by visiting <www.gartnerpress.com/newCIOleader>.

Chapter 8

1. Some material for this chapter was drawn from the following reports published by Gartner EXP exclusively for its members: Roger Woolfe and Barbara McNurlin, "Evolving Competencies for IS Lite," Gartner EXP Club Report, September 2000; Roger Woolfe, Barbara McNurlin, and Chuck Tucker, "Sourcing: From Remedy to Strategy," December 2001; Marcus Blosch and Roger Woolfe, "Leading High Performance IS Teams," Gartner EXP Premier Report, November 2002; Chuck Tucker and Roger Woolfe, "The Reality of IS Lite," Gartner EXP Premier Report, September 2003; Andrew Rowsell-Jones and Chuck Tucker, "Geosourcing IS: Is It Right for You?" Gartner EXP Premier Report, November 2003. Unless otherwise noted, direct quotes in this chapter are from

interviews conducted for these reports. For more information, please contact Gartner Executive Programs, <www.gartner.com>.

2. The EXP Research Team interviewed Daniel Goleman in November 2002 for the report, "Leading High Performing IS Teams."

3. The Hay Group, "Top Teams: Why Some Work and Some Do Not," 2001, available at <www.haygroup.com> (accessed November 2002).

4. Goleman, interview with EXP Research Team.

5. For more information on emotional intelligence, see Goleman, *Emotional Intelligence* (New York: Bantam, 1995) and Daniel Goleman, Annie McKee, and Richard E. Boyatzis, *Primal Leadership* (Boston: Harvard Business School Press, 2002). Both are filled with references to other works, surveys, and studies that show how important emotional intelligence is to success in the workplace.

6. Some of the ideas here are based on work done by Ron Zemke and Susan Zemke, "Putting Competencies to Work," *Training*, January 1999.

7. For five roles and up to fifty individuals, a spreadsheet is adequate for a competency inventory. If you have more components than that, it's probably worth using specialized software.

Chapter 9

1. Some material for this chapter was drawn from the following reports published by Gartner EXP exclusively for its members: Richard Hunter et al., "Information Security: How Much Is Enough?" Gartner EXP Club Report, April 2003; Richard Hunter and Marcus Blosch, "Managing the New IT Risks," Gartner EXP Premier Report, July 2003; Richard Hunter and Andrew Rowsell-Jones, "Thriving in the Fishbowl Society," Gartner EXP Premier Report, December 2003. Unless otherwise noted, direct quotes in this chapter are from interviews conducted for these reports. For more information, please contact Gartner Executive Programs, <www.gartner.com>.

2. Risk management is a very complex subject. Unfortunately, we can only provide the briefest overview here. We highly recommend that new CIO leaders who do not have a significant risk management background seek training in this area.

3. "CSO Magazine Poll Reveals Top Security Concerns for Businesses and Nation," *CSO Magazine* press release, 19 December 2002.

4. Ted Wendling, "Exec's Criminal Past Stuns Cancer Society," *Cleveland Plain Dealer*, 8 June 2000.

5. See, for instance, Defense Security Service, "Unsolicited Requests," available at <http://www.dss.mil/search-dir/training/csg/security/T3method/Unsolici.htm#1>. Defense Security Service has numerous security-related documents and guides available at <http://www.dss.mil>.

Chapter 10

1. Some material for this chapter was drawn from the following reports published by Gartner EXP exclusively for its members: Marianne Broadbent et al., "Business Value . . . IT Value: The Missing Link," Gartner EXP Club Report, November 2000; Andrew Rowsell-Jones and Marcus Blosch, "Getting Share-

holder Credit for IT," Gartner EXP Premier Report, July 2002; Andrew Rowsell-Jones, Richard Hunter, and Roger Woolfe, "Managing Your Stakeholders"Gartner EXP Club Report, October 2002; Chuck Tucker and Roger Woolfe, "Building Brilliant Business Cases," Gartner EXP Premier Report, January 2004. Unless otherwise noted, direct quotes in this chapter are from interviews conducted for these reports. For more information, please contact Gartner Executive Programs, <www.gartner.com>.

2. The material discussed here is based on the work of Gartner's Applied Research practice, led by Audrey Apfel.

3. Peter Keen, *Shaping the Future: Business Design Through Information Technology* (Boston: Harvard Business School Press, 1991).

Conclusion

1. Paul Coby, series of interviews and telephone conversations with authors, September and October 2003.

2. Joe Locandro, series of interviews and telephone conversations with authors, November and December 2003.

3. Tom Sanzone, interview with authors, New York, 12 April 2004.

Appendix A

1. This appendix was written by Richard D. Grant, Jr. (rdgrant@swbell.net), a consulting psychologist who has trained organizations and corporations with the Myers-Briggs Type Indicator since 1986. The text is reprinted here by permission.

Appendix B

1. This appendix is adapted from Marianne Broadbent and Peter Weill's proprietary executive workshop materials that are part of the methodology for implementing the Management by Maxims process. The workshop process engages executive teams to link their enterprise endeavors with the necessary IT capabilities.

Appendix C

1. This appendix appeared in Marianne Broadbent, Peter Weill, and Mani Subramani, "Reality Bites: Matching IT Infrastructure with Business Initiatives," Gartner EXP Club Report, November 2001. The list of services featured in the report is adapted from Peter Weill and Michael Vitale, "Information Technology Infrastructure for E-Business," working paper 313, Center for Information Systems Research, MIT Sloan School of Management, Cambridge, February 2001. The initial set of services was developed by Peter Weill and Marianne Broadbent and published in Weill and Broadbent, *Leveraging the New Infrastructure: How Market Leaders Capitalize on Information Technology* (Boston: Harvard Business School Press, 1998). For a full discussion of these services, see also Peter Weill, Mani Subramani, and Marianne Broadbent, "Building IT Infrastructure for Strategic Ability," *Sloan Management Review* 44, no. 1 (fall 2002): 57–66.

Index

About the Authors

MARIANNE BROADBENT is associate dean at Melbourne Business School (MBS) and a Gartner Fellow with Gartner, Inc., a research and advisory firm specializing in information technology and business growth. In her current role at MBS, Dr. Broadbent works with senior corporate executives on talent management and succession planning and with senior managers as part of Melbourne's international executive MBA program. From 1998 to 2003, Dr. Broadbent was part of the global leadership team of Gartner CIO Executive Programs (EXP), initially leading the service in AsiaPacific and then as group vice president and global leader of EXP's research and knowledge assets. Dr. Broadbent is an adviser and advice broker with business and IT executive teams and boards of directors. Her particular focus is on how corporate, business, and IT governance link together and the fusion of business and technology strategies and execution. She is coauthor of the book *Leveraging the New Infrastructure: How Market Leaders Capitalize on Information Technology* (Harvard Business School Press, 1998). Prior to joining Gartner, Dr. Broadbent was a professor in information systems management at Melbourne Business School, a visiting researcher at Boston University, and head of an academic department at Melbourne's RMIT University.

ELLEN S. KITZIS is a group vice president at Gartner, Inc. Since 2000, Dr. Kitzis has been part of the global leadership team of Gartner's CIO Executive Programs, which serves over two thousand CIO members. She currently leads the EXP Americas team. Working daily to support CIOs and other IT leaders, Dr. Kitzis regularly engages members in the daily issues of leading and managing IS organizations and specializes in organizational strategy, leadership, and IT and business synergy. Traveling throughout the fifty states and Latin America, Dr. Kitzis frequently speaks with groups of CIOs on topical themes and issues. She is a spokesperson for Gartner for various CIO publications and has appeared a number of times on CNBC. Prior to returning to Gartner, Dr. Kitzis held the position of vice president of strategy and business development for Compaq Services and was the worldwide head of Gartner's Dataquest IT Services Group. She has held previous positions at The Ledgeway Group and Consulting Statistician Inc., a Crowntek company. She holds an undergraduate degree from Boston University and a doctorate in organizational change from Tufts University.